Outside Archaeology

Material culture and poetic imagination

Edited by

Christine Finn
Martin Henig

BAR International Series 999
2001

Published in 2016 by
BAR Publishing, Oxford

BAR International Series 999

Outside Archaeology

© The editors and contributors severally and the Publisher 2001

ISBN 9781841712802 paperback
ISBN 9781407353524 e-format
DOI https://doi.org/10.30861/9781841712802
A catalogue record for this book is available from the British Library

BAR Publishing is the trading name of British Archaeological Reports (Oxford) Ltd.
British Archaeological Reports was first incorporated in 1974 to publish the BAR
Series, International and British. In 1992 Hadrian Books Ltd became part of the BAR
group. This volume was originally published by Archaeopress in conjunction with
British Archaeological Reports (Oxford) Ltd / Hadrian Books Ltd, the Series principal
publisher, in 2001. This present volume is published by BAR Publishing, 2016.

BAR
PUBLISHING

BAR titles are available from:

BAR Publishing
122 Banbury Rd, Oxford, OX2 7BP, UK
EMAIL   info@barpublishing.com
PHONE   +44 (0)1865 310431
FAX   +44 (0)1865 316916
www.barpublishing.com

Contents

Contributors

Tessa Farmer graduated in June 2000 from The Ruskin School of Drawing and Fine Art, Oxford University. she has exhibited in Oxford and Edinburgh and in the autumn of this year will begin a residency in Kings Wood, Challock, Kent, commissioned by Stour Valley Arts. This will be followed by an exhibition in Rochester in January 2002. e-mail: tessafarmer@hotmail.com

Dr Christine Finn read Archaeology and Anthropology at Oxford after a career as a print and TV journalist. Her D.Phil considered archaeology and poetry. She is a Research Associate at the Instititute of Archaeology, Oxford, and a Contributing Editor at *Archaeology* magazine. The author of *Artifacts: an archaeologist's year in Silicon Valley* (2001), she writes and lectures on how non-archaeologists respond to the past. e-mail: christine.finn@arch.ox.ac.uk

Dr Giles Gasper is Junior Research Fellow in Humanities at Wolfson College, Univeristy of Oxford. He is also Teaching Lecturer at Christ Church, Oxford. He has just completed his doctorate on the thought of St Anselm of Canterbury, on whom he has published articles as well. Currently, he is working on a broader project on Light in the Twelfth Century Renaissance. e-mail: gilesgasper@hotmail.com

Lauren Golden has recently completed her PhD at the University of East Anglia. She has taught both at UEA and the Norwich School of Art & Design. She was the editor for *Raising the Eyebrow*: *World Art Studies* and *John Onians. An Album Amicorum in His Honour*, 2001. She is currently writing a book entitled *Darwin and Art History* e-mail: laurengolden2@yahoo.com

Nigel Henbest researched in Radio Astronomy at the Cavendish Laboratory, Cambridge. His palaeoastronomical studies ranged from observing the remnants of historical supernovae to participating in surveys of putative "Megalithic observatories" in Scotland. He is now a leading science writer and television producer; his books include "Mars" (with Heather Couper) and his TV credits include the award-winning international series "Universe". e-mail nigel@hencoup.demon.co.uk

Dr Martin Henig is Visiting Lecturer in Roman Art at the University of Oxford and Supernumerary Fellow of Wolfson College. He is Honorary Editor of the British Archaeological Association and the author of a number of books including *The Art of Roman Britain* (1995). He has just completed a book on the culture of "Roman" Wessex in the 1st Millennium A.D. in a style appropriate to the theme of this volume. Institute of Archaeology, 36 Beaumont Street, Oxford OX1 2PG e-mail: martinhenig@hotmail.com

Stephen Henig read English and History at the University of Wales, Bangor and then taught at a number of schools in the London Area, Gloucestershire and South Wales. He now writes for children. Having lived near Chepstow for more than 10 years he has become very interested in Roman sites in the area (notably Caerwent and Caerleon) and concerned to bring them to life for young enthusiasts. e-mail: c/o Martin Henig

Helen Molesworth read Greats at Christchurch, Oxford and took the Fellowship examination of the Gemmological Association with distinction. She is now working in the jewellery department of Sothebys in Geneva, and assisting research of an important private collection of ancient cameos in the UK. e-mail: helen.molesworth@sothebys.co.uk

Dr Caradoc Peters is Lecturer in Archaeology at Truro College, Cornwall, delivering the University of Exeter "HND in Practical Archaeology" programme. He has worked in a number of countries, primarily in New Zealand and Germany, on a variety of archaeological projects, particularly those pertaining to landscape archaeology. e-mail: caradocp@trurocollege.ac.uk

Dr Kate Prendergast undertook her D. Phil. research in the archaeology of cosmology and ritual in Neolithic Britain at the University of Oxford. She currently works as a Writer/Researcher in human rights and development, and as a freelance writer for a range of publications. e-mail:kate@brodgar.fsnet.co.uk

Dr Sarah Shaw (nee Bremner) has a doctorate in English literature from Manchester University. She is now an independent teacher and researcher. Manor Barn, Elsfield Manor, Elsfield, Oxford OX3 9SP. e-mail: cs@patrol.i-way.co.uk.

Jon Stallworthy, formerly a Professor of English Literature at the Universities of Cornell and Oxford, is now a Senior Research Fellow of Wolfson College, Oxford, and a Fellow of the British Academy. Author and editor of many books, his *Rounding the Horn: Collected Poems* and *Singing School*, a fragment of autobiography, were published in 1998. Wolfson College, Oxford OX2 6UD.

Preface

Some of the papers printed here were given at the Theoretical Archaeology Conference, held at Oxford in December 2000. The session was designed to relate archaeology to the outside world, in an inclusive, rather than exclusive, sense. It asked certain questions, for instance: how is archaeology perceived outside of itself as a discipline? How does archaeology mould daily life, for others and ourselves? However it soon became apparent that what linked all the papers was the way they addressed the imagination, especially the poetic imagination, an entity cognate with Lorca's *Duende*. The sub-title, 'Archaeology and Poetic Imagination' thus seemed inevitable.

It is fitting to begin the volume with part of a new work by a major poet (Jon Stallworthy), together with an explanation of how he came to write a work about the Uffington White Horse. Tessa Farmer, a practising fine artist, shows how death and decay, processes that make archaeology possible, are central to her vision. Christine Finn, in her first contribution explores the making of Jacquetta Hawkes, a very remarkable archaeologist whose poetic vision embraced the whole story of humanity and her/his relation to the planet. Dr Giles Gasper takes us back in time to look at the perception of light in the Twelfth-Century Renaissance. Light is a reflection of the primal light of God and in his first contribution Dr Martin Henig explores the unchanging nature of gods and goddesses in art through many religions, and shows how this unity ultimately reflects Truth itself, the Unchanging Divine Love. By contrast, in his wide-ranging paper, Dr Caradoc Peters takes perhaps a more 'rationalist' approach by showing how different concepts of time have moulded the differing perceptions of human beings to history.

Several writers were fired by the period of Romanticism, a key time for the development of the concept of Archaeology. Lauren Golden excavates within the mind, within the brain, to show the influence of the German philosopher Kant, on the English poets Coleridge and Wordsworth; Dr Sarah Shaw looks at that prime figure in Romanticism, Mary Shelley, and her fictional attempts to restore the dead to life. In his second contribution Dr Henig starts with a poem by Byron and shows how poetry (and by implication the whole of literature) can be excavated by the archaeologist and, indeed, we are all archaeologists whether or not others designate us as such. Nigel Henbest takes us out of this world in a material sense showing how archaeology can even inspire the astronomer.

The past can certainly have new meanings for each generation. Thus Helen Molesworth demonstrates how the garland style in English platinum and diamond jewellery was influenced by Roman art of the Augustan period, and contained within itself a comparison between the Roman Empire and the British Empire. Dr Kate Prendergast takes Stonehenge, that most familiar of archaeological sites, and shows the range of claims as to its meaning, including 'New Age' theories as a sign of health. Imagination is paramount and Stephen Henig, visiting Roman Caerleon, brings the amphitheatre and the Fortress Baths alive for the young visitor. Finally Christine Finn closes the volume by commenting on a remarkable play about the 'Iceman' from South Tyrol, written by the son of a famous Cambridge archaeologist..but this was more than a play about a single find: All human life is here and we are back again at the beginning of our quest.

Christine Finn
Martin Henig
Institute of Archaeology, Oxford

Skyhorse

Jon Stallworthy

When I was twelve, my parents gave me a copy of *Tom Brown's School-days* (to prepare me for my own), and in its opening chapter I read of King Alfred's victory over the Danes at the battle of Ashdown in 871:

'And in this place, one of the two kings of the heathen and five of his earls fell down and died, and many thousands of the heathen side in the same place.' After which crowning mercy, the pious King, that there might never be wanting a sign and memorial to the country-side, carved out on the northern side of the chalk hill, under the camp, where it is almost precipitous, the great Saxon white horse, which he who will may see from the railway, and which gives its name to the vale, over which it has looked these thousand years and more.

I was still a schoolboy when I climbed that hill myself for the first of several family picnics there. If the White Horse made an impression on me, it lay buried for fifty years, before resurfacing in September 1999 as a conflation of two myths. I suddenly saw the White Horse as an English Pegasus, ancient Greek symbol of poetic inspiration.

Turning then to Morris Marples' book, *White Horses and other Hill Figures*, I found in his chapter on 'The Uffington Horse' my own questions voiced: 'Who made it? When? Why?' Marples disputed the local legend (repeated in *Tom Brown's School-days*) that it was a Saxon horse, cut to commemorate Alfred's victory at Ashdown, and said 'there may be something in the suggestion that the horse has a religious significance'. I remembered the anthropologists' belief that a tribe's first poets are its priests, and scribbled in my notebook: 'Could "they" have gone to so much trouble for any reason other than religious?' That was one of several 'Questions for Chris Gosden' (editor, I had learned, of a forthcoming monograph on the Uffington Horse) I jotted down as a skeletal agenda before meeting him.

Our discussion was – for me – immensely useful, answering the second of Marples' questions: 'When?' I learned that Optically Stimulated Luminescence dating of samples from the White Horse's V-shaped chalk-filled trench showed it to have been cut approximately 3,000 years ago. Such a dating supported the hypothetical narrative already taking shape in my imagination.

I saw a lonely figure, lit by lightning, fall to the ground. Other figures cluster round him. He rises unsteadily to his feet, and his lips move. I think I know what he is saying. In later footage, as it were, of the same film, I see a hand engraving a fragment of bone with a flint knife; then other hands with knives of flint and bone peeling back fire-blackened turf from a curving line of chalk 'markers'. The Skyhorse has come down to earth.

I spent New Year's Eve 1999 at his side as, with unblinking eye, he watched the millennia change. By then,

I had heard and recorded in my notebook these first two speakers in what would become an eleven-part polyphonic poem.

I

The first priest
of the White
Horse tells
his son
of his
commission,
c. 1000 B.C.

When the skyhorse jumped out of the sky
when his eye
when his breath
when his teeth
death.

Firebreath then
but no firelight
and women talking.
    - Three days dead
but no deathsmell.
        - Whose death, woman? I said.
Their answer only the sound
as of does in flight
of feet shaking the ground.
Four feet, then many,
and voices I knew well
came near and spoke my name.
    - We saw the skyhorse claim him
with his hooves, his teeth,
and yet he moves.
        - And speaks. What cave
darkens your face?
    - No cave, brother. This is the hill
where you and the skyhorse met,
where he gave us fire,
where he set the mark
of his hoof on your head,
making your eyes dark,
ash-white your hair.

Oh then I heard a voice
I knew and did not know
as mine cry
            Skyhorse,
stargrazer, firebringer,
if you require my eyes
in tribute, gladly
I give them. I will be
your praisesinger.
But if, bestowing light
and dark, you light my eyes
as you have lighted fire,
I and my sons will whiten
the hill's head with your mark,
shadowing your shadow
for all the tribes to praise.

And when the day's eye opened,
mine could see it shine.

II

Priest and
poet,
c. 970 B.C.

The skyhorse calls
for his bondman,
his priest, who lies
in his shadow
and will not rise
until we let
his spirit go.

The trees add their
lament to ours.
He was their friend,
singing their praise.
In tribute now
his trees let fall
a branch, a bough.

So we must go
and gather them,
men shouldering
the gifts of oak
and ash, children
a holly branch
or mistletoe.

And as we build
the horseman's pyre
see the pictures
I shall sing. –
The horse stamping
his hill, bringing
his people fire.

The horse darkens
a man with light,
a praisesinger
he makes his own.
The man shaping
what his eyes saw.
Flint scraping bone.

The skyhorse leaps
from a white bone
to a burnt hill.
His horseman sows
it with white stones.
On the burnt earth
a starhorse glows.

Skinning the hill
between the stones,
the praisesinger
honours the horse
that honours us,
our guardian
and firebringer.

Bring me a seed
of fire to sow.
It will take root
and its flowers tell
whose spirit goes
to the great cave.
Father, go well.

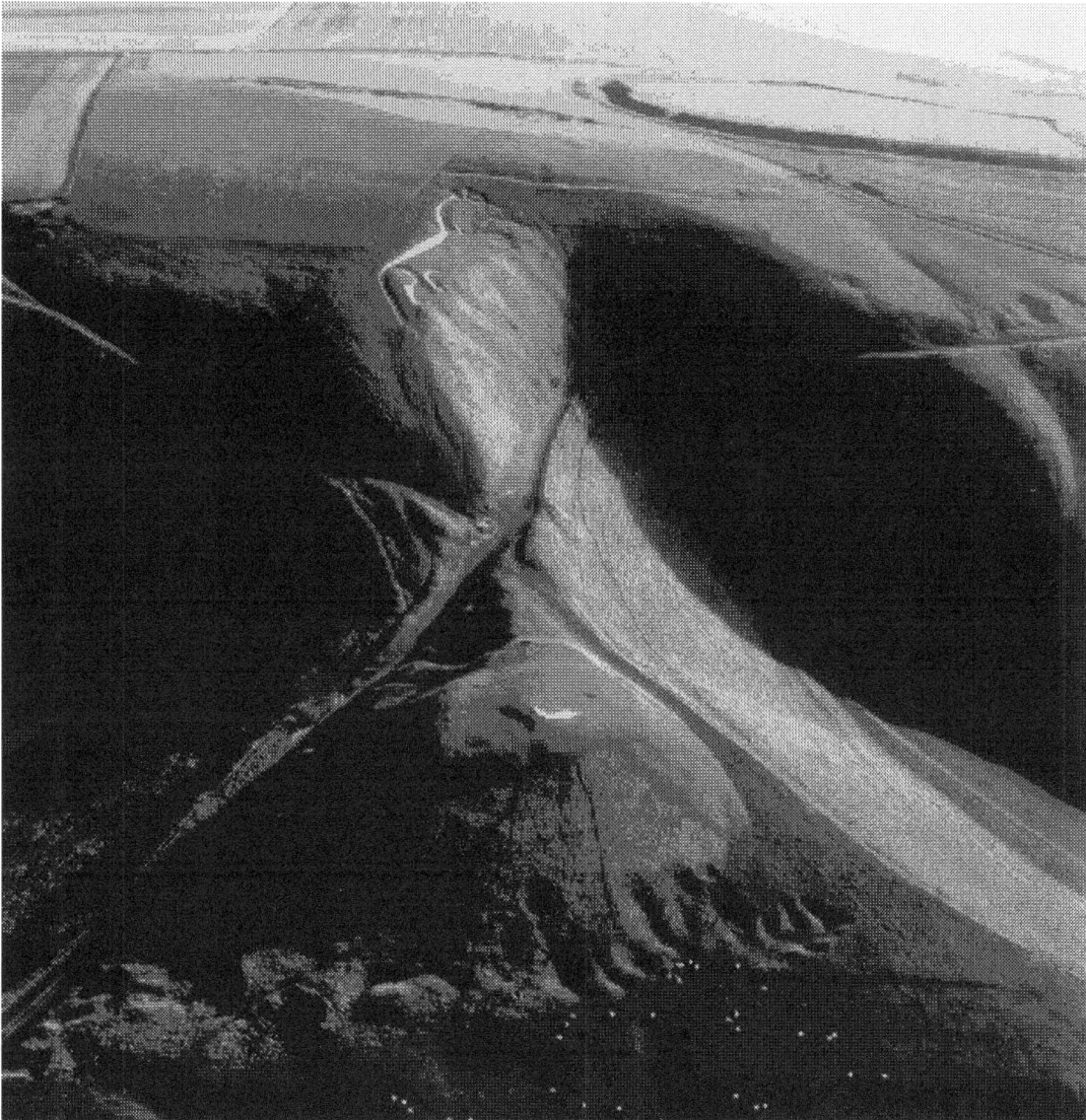

The White Horse and Dragon Hill
© Vale of the White Horse Council and the Oxford Archaeological Unit

To Wander is to Wonder
Archaeology, Art and Nature

Tessa Farmer

'Modern Sculpture is wilfully ignorant'
(Ian Hamilton Finlay, landscapist /sculptor, Nature Over Again after Poussin, p.21)

When using nature as a source to create art there is an obvious danger of superficial and decorative interpretation. I am not averse to producing beautiful work, but I am wary of such associations. Nature's implicit processes of life, death and decay may allow us to side step the issue of beauty as the only interpretation, however they also provoke exploration of further stimulus.

Studying human anatomy was a valuable influence and took my working methods beyond simply 'arranging nature' towards a fusion of anatomy with nature; I began to combine landscape and the skeletal form of the human figure. This proved an effective method to transform natural matter from its inert and passive state. *(Figures: Untitled, Anna, and Head).* When the work is given back to the land this becomes an inherent part of it and the piece may still be deemed superficial if its context is overlooked as being a palimpsest of multiple histories.

After attending a series of lectures, 'Archaeology in context', I became conscious of the cross-pollination that is evident between art and archaeology, and that contemporary art is not as autonomous as is often thought. A spirit of discovery that stems from enquiry about our past is a valuable source for juxtaposing contemporary practice and historical knowledge. Interdisciplinary collaboration allows engagement with the unknown and mysterious intrinsic creativity of all those who want to understand the world, however apparently untranslatable their dialogues. Traces of the past are bound together by the archaeologist in a translation that represents a truth of the past: the artist interprets this information to construct an imaginative representation, reinvested with subjective and poetic meaning that may have been removed through scientific interpretation.

With this insight I intend to inform work that previously was scraping the surface, literally and metaphorically, and adopt archaeological interpretation as a means of integrating art and nature.

In the autumn of this year I will undertake a residency in King's Wood, Challock, Kent. It is an ancient woodland site, now a working forest, producing, beech, fir and pine and sweet chestnut. I intend to use the forest detritus to create a series of unobtrusive pieces situated off the beaten track. Some will be more conspicuous than others, which may never be discovered *(Figures: King's Wood proposal drawings).*

Tiny skeletal fairies will nest, swarm and play amongst partially hidden enclosures and the exposed roots of fallen trees throughout the forest whilst larger ambiguous skeletal creatures materialise from branches and twigs scattered on the forest floor and a giant mass of wooden vertebrae wind through the trees. The most conspicuous piece will be an ancient tree stump crawling with fairies. In fact this tree is so old, the species is not known – it seems alien in its surroundings. Exterior activity will hint at unseen interior activity, inside the tree and the surrounding environment; perhaps it is riddled with passageways like a giant termite hill. Their purpose will be to refocus our vision on those things that we overlook, through overfamiliarity, and to prompt exploration of the ground beneath our feet and to rethink the surrounding environment. I envisage that by elevating the forest debris, that we walk across regardless, so that it draws us back to the surface, will cause the forest floor and its surroundings to become a membrane permeable to various levels of intertwined archaeological interpretation – imaginary/physical, mythical and personal. In artistic terms, I feel that the pieces will be completed on discovery and contemplation. Some may never be found, but all will inevitably return to the life cycle of the forest as nature destroys traces of my intrusion.

The insertion of human like skeletal forms into the forest could be perceived as a comment on environmental decay due to human intervention, however I would rather think of it as a testament to the power of nature, not man. The metamorphosis of rotting detritus and its consequent interruption of the flux of this habitat can only be temporary. Like all life it will eventually return to nature's implicit cycle; beauty is transient and decay awaits us all. The scent of death hangs heavy over my work, although the pieces appear to be very much alive. By stripping away the shells of our existence and exposing our fate, which we attempt to hinder by means of modern day medicine, contemplation is forced of our own mortality, connecting us with the past, with all humanity and with ourselves. We exist for only a moment in time; on death we return to the earth beneath our feet and are lost in another layer of history.

Mythical interpretation of the life-death continuum may help to avoid contemplation of the imponderable shortness of life and the finality of death. The myth of the Green Man dates back to Roman time. Of profoundly pagan association, he is considered to be a forest god, protector of plants and responsible for the continual renewal of the entire living universe. He is often depicted as quite grotesque, with leaves and vines sprouting from his mouth, nose and ears; the essence of him is the cycle of death and rebirth. As myth has it, the death of the Green Man in winter is required to bring about the rebirth of the Green Man of summer. My figures can be interpreted as representative of the Green Man's death and renewal; I will construct and position them in autumn while the trees become stripped bare and by spring they will have been reclaimed by the forest; destroyed by the elements or concealed by the growth of new life.

The animated wooden skeletons echo that transitory moment between life and death that is captured in numerous Iron Age Bog Bodies dug up from peat bogs in Northern Europe during the last two centuries. These deaths were not accidental, and in many finds the bodies had been pinned down in the bog with stakes or branches, it is believed, to prevent the spirits from walking and haunting the living. Evidence suggests that some of the bodies had been buried and speared alive. The skeletons in King's Wood may evoke an association with the bog bodies, as if the sticks that covered and speared them have absorbed their life and their spirits have materialised to haunt the forest as a reminder of the human remains that may lie underneath our paths.

Nearly all trees have some sacred association from ancient times. Beech is said to be concerned with ancient knowledge, and indicates guidance from the past to gain insight; fir manifests high views and long sights with a clear vision of what is beyond and yet to come and pine indicates issues of guilt. Many trees are regarded as having their own personalities, while others are specifically a haunt of fairies or spirits, particularly oak and hawthorn.

Among many explanations for the existence of fairies was the theory that they were spirits of the dead. Like the larger creatures, the fairies appear dead in a physical sense *(Figures: Fairy Swarm, Biker Fairy).* Myth has it that if a person doesn't believe in fairies one will die. Perhaps their skeletal form can be attributed to their transitory state somewhere between imagination and existence, between life and death.

Their miniature human form hints at an analogy of man in the universe, dwarfed by the potentially uncontrollable forces of nature; they will be tiny and insignificant monsters 'frolicking' in the forest, as we do on this planet to our own detriment. Eventually the fairies will fall to their imminent 'death' and decay. We forget that nature can create her own monsters in reaction to human intervention.

I call them monsters because, contrary to popular belief, fairies are not necessarily kindly beings. Mine are visually provocative; they are macabre yet intricately beautiful, combining elements of attraction and repulsion. I want to open the viewer's mind to the possibilities of imaginative interpretation, which all too often is a childhood luxury; to re-ignite a childlike curiosity and provoke all the wonders, hopes, fears and possibilities that disappear as we grow

older. Re-tuning a vivid imagination that is able transform banal objects can illustrate how vast the world can be.

Passers by will stumble across unexpected delights or horrors that intrigue, provoke and question the limits of their imagination and instil a sense of wonder, magic and possibility *(Figures: Flower Fairy, Daffodil, Amaryllis).* In such instances, wandering becomes wondering.

The interdisciplinary juxtaposition of objects in sixteenth century cabinets of curiosity invited viewers to adopt wonder as a valid way of contemplating the unfamiliar. The Renaissance had seen a renewed spirit of enquiry leading to these collections that celebrated the strange, the marvellous and the rare, housing unusual artefacts and human and animal anomalies, for example shrunken heads, mermaids, werewolves, dried kidney stones - the list is endless. The collector's desire was to evoke gasps of wonder from visitors who could view the joy and diversity of the world as microcosm through natural and artificial objects. These displays required active knowledge production and demanded the use of the imagination to perceive their possible interpretation.

Today in an age of sophisticated communication and technology it is possible to believe that we have 'seen it all'. In a society where people are accustomed to provocative and shocking imagery there is a need to reintroduce the idea of magic and restore the spirit of discovery of previous centuries; curiosity leading to a self reflexive engagement with the methods of wonder, rather than wonder as a state of astonishment.

The Ruskin Parasite, an unsightly snake like creature emerged and disappeared sporadically from holes and crevices throughout the Ruskin school of Drawing *(Figures: Ruskin Parasite, Skeleton in the closet).* This creature and the Skeleton in the Closet, in the basement of the building, took the vision of those who observed them beyond the superficial, yet visually transient interior surfaces of the walls, and encouraged reflection of the histories that may lurk within them and the rest of the building. Metaphorically, the Parasite materialised the way in which art students feed off each others imaginations, and the value and rewards of looking beyond the confines of ones own discipline.

" We insist, it seems, on living. Then
again, indifference descends. The roar
of traffic, the passage of
undifferentiated faces, this way and
that way, drugs me into dreams,
rubs features from faces. People might walk
through me...we are only lightly
covered with buttoned cloth and
beneath these pavements are shells
bones and silence. '

Virginia Woolf, The Waves

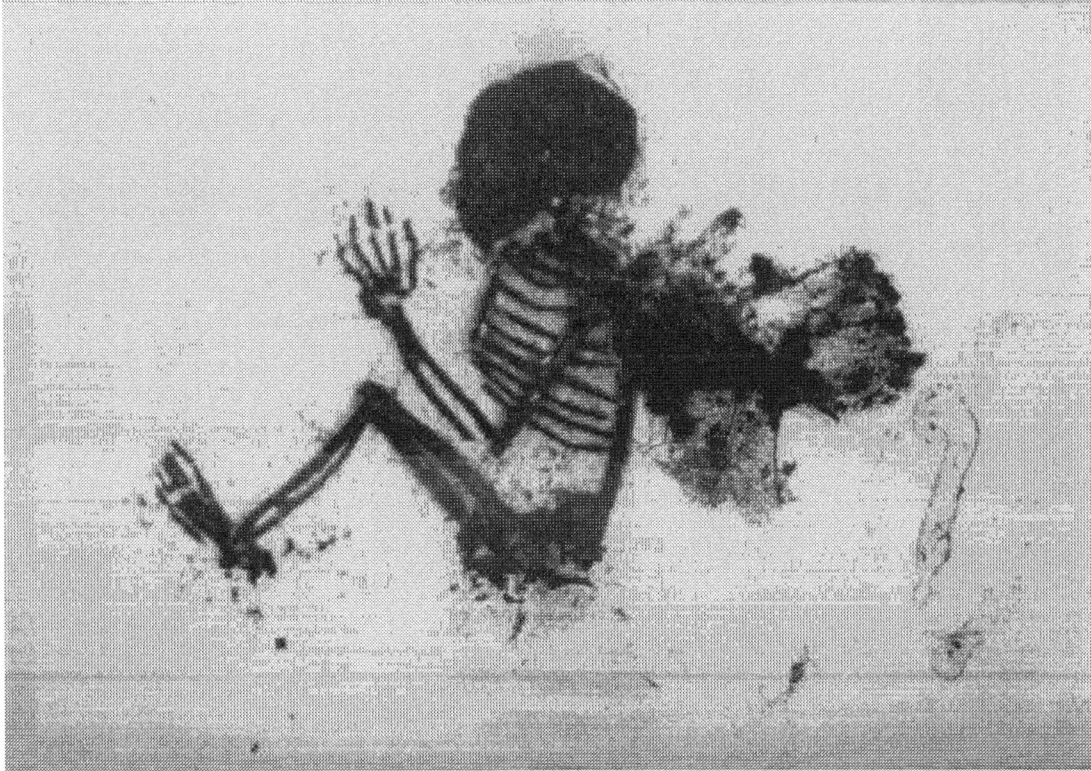

Untitled

Anna

Head

King's Wood proposal drawings

Fairy Swarm

Biker Fairy

Flower Fairy

Daffodil

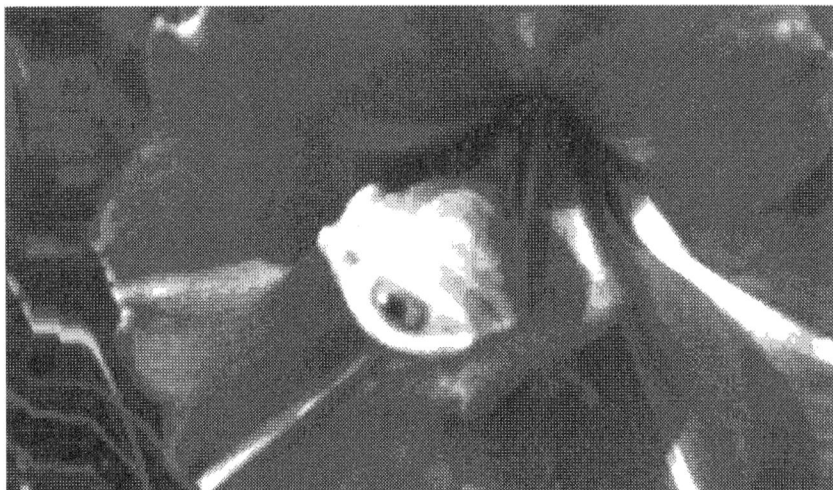

Amaryllis

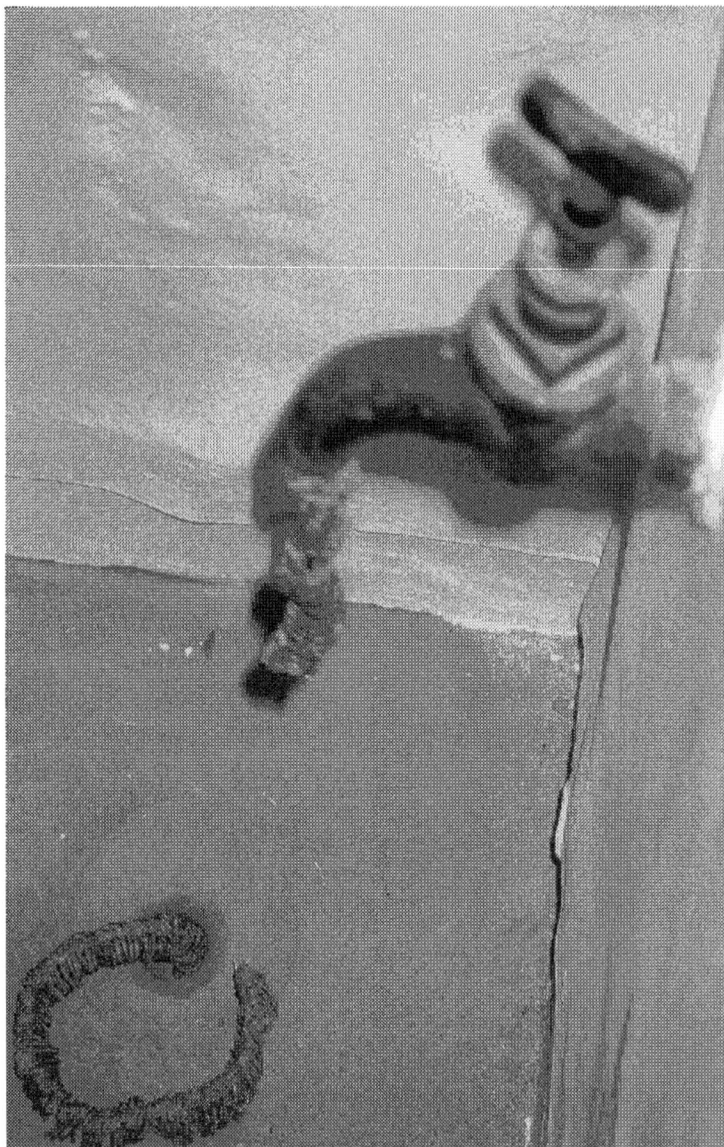

Ruskin Parasite

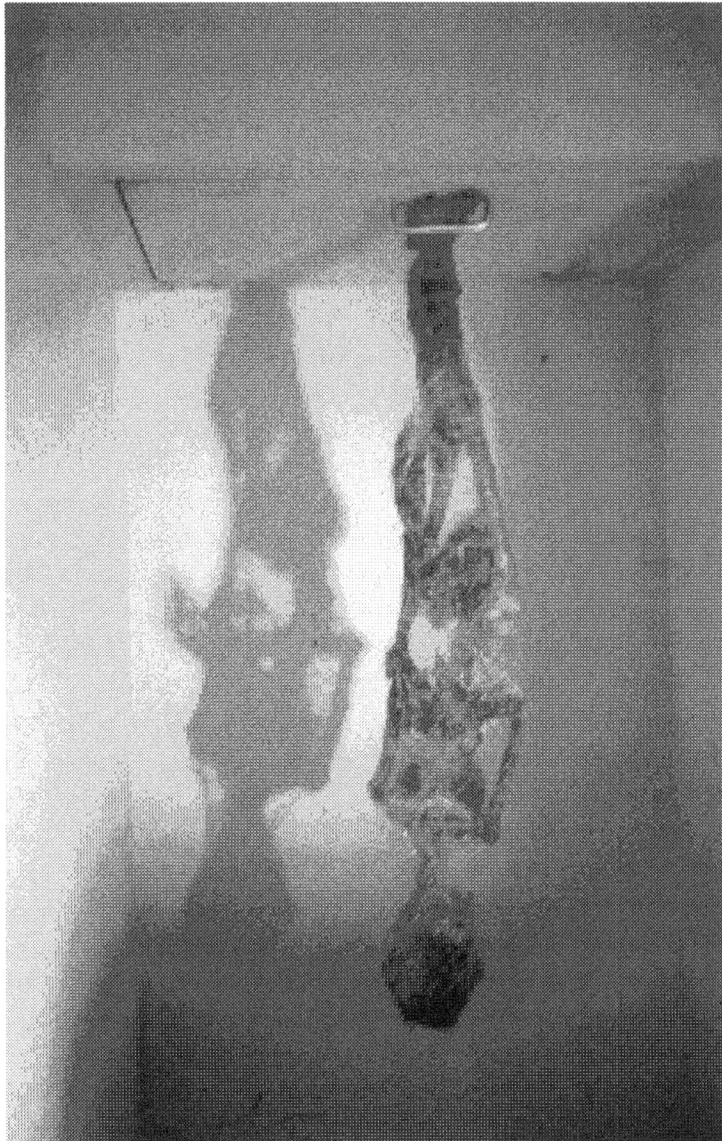

Skeleton in the closet

The pre-history of an archaeologist: Jacquetta Hawkes outside archaeology

Christine Finn

Are archaeologists born or made? Those who have entered the profession, or work alongside it, can often remember the event, or the object, or the place which marked the beginning of their fascination with the past. I pondered this question as I pored over several volumes of photographs taken by a young Jacquetta Hawkes in the process of researching her life and work. As I tried to make sense of them as a narrative, I looked for clues to her formative, and unique, perspective on the past. Is there such a thing as an archaeologist's eye which develops from an early age?

The yellowing prints tumbled out of albums and envelopes, and the enigmatic negatives of prints not yet seen represented, to me, the Ur-glances of an extraordinary archaeologist and writer. The range of photographs, some of which are included here, reveal an early point-of-view, or focus, of a child, or a teenager, not yet practising archaeology, but very much sensitive to the past. In the midst of the pile, some childhood photographs of Jacquetta Hopkins, as she was then, one showing an odd confluence of interests – on a motorbike, with a teddy bear (figure 1). She continued to photograph archaeological sites, excavations and artifacts throughout her working life.

To set the photographs in context, Jessie Jacquetta Hopkins, was born into a traditional Cambridge academic household on the 5th of August, 1910. Her father, Sir Frederick Gowland Hopkins, was a noted scientist, the founding figure of biochemistry. But when, in 1929, he was awarded the Nobel Prize in Stockholm, it was his youngest daughter who shared the limelight. The dark, attractive teenager, poised to go up to Cambridge to study archaeology, caught the attention of the Crown prince of Sweden, himself an archaeologist. He insisted she should have a specially conducted tour of the National Museum. This was an early indication of Jacquetta's unswerving ability to stand out from the crowd; in later life this would win her friends and plaudits, as well as the distinction of being a brilliant but difficult woman.

Jacquetta was a fascinating contradiction: passionate and aloof; alarmingly class-conscious but a staunch supporter of causes on the fringes of society; a detached mother and an overtly sensuous lover who celebrated the presence of male in female, and female in male to a sometimes confusing degree. She could have had a comfortable life as an Oxford don's wife, but chose instead the scandal of divorce, estrangement from her academic peers and life with a significantly older, if celebrated, playwright, which she openly admitted was more sexually fulfilling than her first marriage.

She was the youngest of three children. Her sister, Barbara, was too old to be a childhood companion, and although devoted to her brother, Frederick, Jacquetta's formative experiences appear to have been enjoyed on her own, or with adults such as her nanny, or her mother. It was not a demonstrative household, and Jacquetta noted surprise when her father cried at his mother's death. But it was a happy home, where she described her childhood as 'steeped in sweetness and light and no awareness of harsher ways'.

The Hopkins family was marked by its strong and diligent characters. With his own father dead, Frederick Hopkins had battled to study science against the wishes of his guardian, Uncle James, who considered it an evil force at a time of violent exchanges over science and religion. He eventually trained as a Home Office analyst, and only at 28 did he begin training at Guy's Medical School. Showing the same self-determination as his youngest daughter would need to employ, Frederick worked in a private laboratory in the evenings, gained an external science degree and, when he qualified as a doctor, won a gold medal for chemistry. When he met and married Jessie Ann Stevens in 1898, the couple began their married life at Uncle James'. But they rapidly found independence with an invitation to Cambridge, where Frederick was to become a science Fellow at Emmanuel College.

If Jacquetta's individuality was most pronounced in her lyrical writing which unfashionably, and unwisely for an academic, drew together arts and science, it was rooted in familial traits. Her father's great creative imagination was described by his biographer, Professor Ernest Baldwin, as being 'of such power that it could not fail to influence the thought and activities of everyone who had the good fortune to work in his department'. And there was a poet already in the family: Jacquetta's great-grandfather was the second cousin of Gerald Manley Hopkins.

Jacquetta's own highly developed imagination, seen at its most extreme and controversial in the reflective and controversial veiled autobiography, A Quest of Love, was teased and nurtured throughout her childhood. The inspiration came not from a close relationship with her father, whom she felt was weak rather than gentle, but her own ability to absorb sights and sensations from an early age. She recalled the vivid memory of being an infant in a pram and the 'Tarry smell from those dark boards, the shed. That mysterious breath of out-of-doors on my cheeks. The canopy ripples and stills, ripples again. It ripples against the blueness - the bluest blue....'

Jacquetta's childhood was framed by academia. There was no religious instruction at home, as one of her closest friends, the writer Diana Collins notes: 'Intellectual integrity was an absolute in the Hopkins family'. At Trinity College, Cambridge, where her father was made a fellow and praelecturer, the college statutes were altered to accommodate Hopkins' principled agnosticism.

(Jacquetta's son, Nicolas, from her marriage to the archaeologist, Christopher Hawkes, also received no religious education from his parents and in later life adopted Quakerism). The family's moral convictions were sound, particularly against lying and stealing, which led to great trauma for Jacquetta when she once transgressed them and she admitted becoming confused over the position of 'white lies'. In later life her honesty would be seen as bluntness, her directness as caustic criticism.

Hopkins's Trinity College position, which came with an improved salary, allowed the family to have a house built at 71 Trinity Road, Cambridge. It was close to the laboratory and Hopkins' colleagues were among the callers. Jacquetta was sometimes taken in to the laboratory and it was there that her father told her about atomic fission and its possible dire consequences: possibly the seeds were being sown for Jacquetta's very public involvement with the Campaign for Nuclear Disarmament, 40 years later. The move to Grange Road did not come without cost. The offer of a Trinity College Fellowship came after Jacquetta's father suffered a breakdown prompted by his unrelenting research and the pressures of teaching. Even after he recovered his health, Jacquetta would recall him sitting in the midst of people, scribbling formulae into a notebook. This image of doggedness and concentration, a mark of Hopkins' genius, must have come back to haunt Jacquetta in the throes of her marriage to Christopher Hawkes. His brilliance and fanatical drive also produced what was, in all respects, a breakdown due to overwork. And after his eventual divorce from Jacquetta, a letter from Christopher to his new wife-to-be, Sonia, appears to suggest that he too, had been juggling scientific pragmatism and the instinctive excitement of discovery: '..to archaeology I've been grateful ever since I took it up as a boy; because it's such an endlessly gay and exciting subject...I like gay things and amusing things and interesting things and strenuous things and beautiful things...'.

If Jacquetta's imagination was fired by her ability to absorb and recall, in a Proustian fashion, the sensations of her childhood and her first experiences of self-consciousness, the forming of her intellect also marked out her individuality. She was a loner and a reader with a critical eye for poetry. At Miss Sharpley's school in Cambridge, she preferred the company of a few rather than a crowd, a trait to continue into undergraduate days. Her isolation was often self-induced - she had a passion for tree-climbing. The drive of the woman who was to respond so well in later life to the championing of causes, such as CND and the Homosexual Reform Bill, was seen first here in the kidnapping of 'the pale fragile child of well-to-do parents', snatched at the behest of Jacquetta who felt he needed an afternoon away from his parents.

Jacquetta's love of climbing was matched by that of bird-nesting and then bird-watching, a life-long interest instilled into Nicolas. 'Perhaps it is evoked by the singing, whistling and calling that fall into millions of ancestral ears

and there left images that we all inherit', she wrote in *A Land*. As a young teenager, she became friendly with Emma Turner, an eminent ornithologist and bird photographer, who took her to the Norfolk Broads and the Brecks. When Jack Priestley's second wife, Jane, began an affair with an ornithologist, so easing his divorce and re-marriage to Jacquetta, the irony would hardly have been lost on the pair.

Wayward and independent, the founder of the Trespassers Society was determined not to be a prissy schoolgirl. Diana Collins describes Jacquetta as a tomboy 'who detested dolls and contrived to lose or break any given to her. In a passion of hatred she deliberately smashed a large blue-eyed doll on her mother's rockery.' Diana considers this more the action of a rebel against social stereotyping than the lack of maternal instinct later perceived by Jacquetta. It can be said, however, that Jacquetta's relationship with Nicolas appeared dutiful rather than openly loving. It reflected her own childhood of considered restraint.

When she was nine, Jacquetta Hawkes declared in a school essay that she wanted to become an archaeologist. This development may have been inspired in part by her mother's fascination for the past. There were frequent outings to museums in Cambridge, where Jacquetta was drawn to the exhibits of ancient jewellery and pottery. She was to recall such images later in a poem inspired by gazing on a Celtic brooch, which appears in *Symbols and Speculations* : 'There on the bronze, the line/Cut by brain-held hand/Grips space in its design...' The formation of the poem in 'On staring at a Celtic ornament' was also inspired by Jacquetta's interest in the evolution of human intelligence and early tool technology.

These museum visits were made even more pleasurable by a direct connection with the family home. Among the exhibits was an amber necklace dug out from below a gate-post at the entrance to 71 Grange Road; the house had been built where a Roman road was overlapped by an Anglo-Saxon cemetery. Jacquetta was fascinated by this meeting of cultures across the centuries, and by the realisation that archaeology was concerned with such matters of distinguishing 'things made by one people, or at a particular time, from those made by other people or at a different time.' Reflecting on this, Jacquetta realised an apppreciation of this contrast 'between the soft, hand-shaped pottery of the Anglo-Saxon burial urns and the harsh, striated Roman stuff', placed her at an important intellectual vantage point, one 'at the very root of the simple archaeology then near the beginning of its rapid growth and flowering'. The would-be archaeologist had seen a grave group at the museum and longed to dig deep into the garden herself. When she was denied permission, she mounted a clandestine excavation by torchlight, removing a square foot of turf and coming up with 'only a dessertspoonful of dull earth'.

This connection provides a pragmatic explanation for Jacquetta's early passion for archaeology - 'interest would be too cool a word' - she insisted and it was not wholly satisfactory to her. Instead, she reached down into her unconscious for an explanation. The self-penned preface to A Land, perhaps her most critically acclaimed work, suggests that if the writings did recall her own childhood, it was 'not so much from egotism as from a wish to steal that emotion which uses our own early memories for a realisation of the most distant past...I find I am being led back far beyond the bounds of personality and of my own life'. Her later reading of Jung, which was shared with Priestley, would have helped her articulate her fascination for the past. She was not a wholesale supporter of Freud, however, despite parallels often drawn between his work and archaeology, and indeed his large personal collection of antiquities.

Childhood excursions inspired, in Jacquetta, a connection with the very physicality of archaeology. She returned to this theme frequently as a writer. The Brecks, in the East of England, which she visited with Emma Turner, were a fascination to her because they contained the prehistoric flint mines known as Grimes Graves. The archaeological evidence for Neolithic activity suggests that the digging of shafts into the chalk was achieved with nothing less than antler picks, the flints brought to the surface for reshaping and trading. These tools worked by 'brain-held hand' played on Jacquetta's imagination. Of the prehistoric miners, she noted: in A Land 'They were the first men to cut down through the accumulation of time to reach hidden resources which would then be used to transform the land itself'. In the same work, which fuses geography, geology, history and prehistory, she introduced an element of ethno-archaeology, as she recalled visiting present-day flint-knappers at a cabin 'deep in silica dust and flakes', where the products were gun flints, rather than prehistoric axes.

Grimes Graves gave Jacquetta other impressions which she worked through in later life. She noted that at the bottom of one mine shaft at Grimes Graves, which had failed to strike the flint bed, 'a figure of a goddess was discovered enthroned above a pile of antlers on which rested a chalk-carved phallus...Our Lady of the Flint Mines, it seems, was being asked to cure such sterility.'

Back in Cambridge, Jacquetta's interest in archaeology continued to flourish as she anticipated the thrill of her own finds. In the Museum of Archaeology and Anthropology, she delighted in the prehistoric artefacts suspended in the preserving peat of the Fenlands, such as a perfect shield, which conjured up for her 'visions of Bronze Age chieftains', while an armilla from Gunty Fen was all the potent for her imagination, by its golden curls springing up through the peat. 'Knowledge of such local treasures was beginning to inform and inspire my archaeological consciousness', she said. A meeting with the prehistorian Miles Birkett proved fateful. He told her about a new - and unique - tripos at Cambridge, in Archaeology and Anthropology. In the end, she had to take the exam at home, struck down with influenza and unnerved by a chimney fire. However, Jacquetta's unique

talents were recognised at interview and she was given one of the keenly contested places, but without a scholarship. She would go to Newnham, close to Grange Road, as her sister had done. But Jacquetta resolved to live at college, and began then to cut her family ties. At Cambridge, her participation at last in an excavation led to her meeting, and falling in love with, an aspiring archaeologist named Christopher Hawkes. Jacquetta's future, as a voyeur and communicator of prehistory and the past, was sealed at last.

Jacquetta placed many of her early photographs in albums, identifying place and date in her own hand. They range from the family pet dog in the garden in Cambridge, to birds and buildings and the holiday souvenirs from Rome (figure 2).

The author would like to thank Nicolas Hawkes for permission to reproduce the photographs here.

Figure 1

Figure 2. The photographs of classical sites are shown as they are set out in the bottle-green, tooled-leather album. Jacquetta's own hand informs us in a neat hand-inked label, that they were taken in Rome between April 24th and May 1st, 1929. She was 18 and on a family holiday before going up to Cambridge to read Archaeology and Anthropology. The black and white prints show the Forum, Trajan's Column, Via Appia at Seneca's Tomb, the Temple of Saturn and Arch of Severus, Hadrian's Tomb, a Relief of Ambarvalia Sacrifice at the Forum, and a view from The House of the Vestal Virgins.

Figure 3. Jacquetta Hopkins was studying her beloved archaeology, and her father was a Nobel Laureate. The caption for the view of the Rollright Stones (extreme left) notes only the name of the prehistoric monument; the illustrious Sir Frederick Gowland Hopkins is left here to serve as a human scale.

Towards a Theology of Light in the Twelfth-Century Renaissance*

Giles E. M. Gasper

The term Renaissance is a familiar one within medieval history, and the 'Twelfth-Century Renaissance' the original application of the term to the middle ages. It was first applied to any great effect by the American medievalist Charles Homer Haskins (Haskins, 1927, Swanson, 1999, p. 1ff.) and has recently received a new general discussion by Robert Swanson. Swanson's exciting discussion adopts the same chronology of the 'long twelfth-century' that Haskins advocated, that is, the period c.1050-c.1250, for the the cultural and intellectual changes associated with the Twelfth-Century Renaissance. As far as intellectual life is concerned this allows the development of particular methods of inquiry to be charted from their progenitors in Lanfranc (c.1010-1089) and Anselm of Laon (d. 1117), stopping just before the great *Summae* of the thirteenth century Friars, for example, Thomas Aquinas (c.1225-1274) and Albert the Great (d.1280).

Quite what the focal point of the twelfth-century renaissance should be is a subtle and multi-faceted question: how far, for example, should the lens of the perceived interests of 'The Renaissance' with its emphasis on the Classical past, be used to examine the earlier period. To do so too readily risks anachronism, not least in the definition of the Classical past. However, it is to the intellectual changes that the pre-dominant discussion of the ambit of the term, turns. Swanson in his concluding remarks points to the fact that the 'twelfth-century renaissance' is arguably formed of 'several renaissances'(Swanson, 1999, p. 210), in theology, canon law, and the translation of new texts into Latin from Greek and Arabic. It emerges as centred on educational and theological changes, focused on Paris, and taking place in Latin. Swanson excludes 'wider cultural developments, in the arts, music and vernacular literature' but he does state that 'those evolutions again attest a different renaissance.'(Swanson, 1999, p. 210)

The purpose of the present paper is limited to raising one theme within the long twelfth-century, namely, the treatment and discussion of light. It is a theme of theological importance, to be found in a variety of authors and genres, as well as one which involves texts newly translated into Latin, and it can be seen at play in and around developments diffused from the Paris region. Light is, potentially, a widely suffused theme within the twelfth century renaissance, and one which also integrates, to an extent, architectural changes witnessed during the period.

To this extent, with the interests of this volume in mind, an archaeological perspective proves illuminating. This paper is intended to suggest areas in which this theme of light might be fruitfully pursued and forms the beginning of a broader project with which I am involved.

Without attempting to cover ground that has been covered many times before and in many different contexts, and at the risk of simplification, some general observations on characteristics of the period in question should be made. The period was one of rising confidence, growth and expansion in Western Europe, characterised by Karl Leyser, for example, as 'the ascent of Latin Europe' (Leyser, 1986). Sir Richard Southern memorably described the crucial significance of this period in the history of Western Europe in his celebrated essay *The Making of the Middle Ages*. Chrétien de Troyes, in a phrase quoted by Southern, and many others since, wrote, at the end of the twelfth century, that:

> ...the pre-eminence in chivalry and learning once belonged to Greece. Then chivalry passed to Rome, together with that highest learning which has now come to France. God grant that it may be cherished here, that the honour which has taken refuge with us may never depart from France...of Greeks and Romans no more is heard; their fame is passed, and their glowing ash is dead. (Southern, 1953, p. 16)

To some degree then a consciousness existed in this period of the worth and mettle of its achievements. Southern writes of Chrétien's phrases that: 'these words were written ...about the year 1170: they would have been idle boasts at the beginning of our period [972]. Now they could be spoken with the modesty of achievement and insight.' (Southern, 1953, p. 16)

The achievements of this period are, unsurprisingly, traced in the literary record, and the twelfth century affords copious documentary material. Nevertheless that is far from the whole story. There are aspects of the period whose interpretation is aided by an archaeological perspective. At a general level, for instance, many of the economic and societal changes lie silent, outside the purview of high intellectual texts. As Southern points out 'this silence in the great changes of history is something which meets us everywhere as we go through these centuries' (Southern, 1953, p. 15). Notwithstanding the changes did occur. A huge shift in the use of the landscape and in agricultural technique is to be observed, for instance, in the archaeological record as well as in documentary sources (Bartlett, 1993, pp. 156-166 points to the future potential of medieval archaeology in this period). In a different vein the artistic and architectural developments which grew alongside this intellectual

----
*I am very grateful to Martin Henig for the invitation to give this paper at the Theoretical Archaeology Conference in December, and for the opportunity to expand what was delivered at the conference for this volume.

flowering are well-known, whatever the way they are seen to relate to the theological concerns of the renaissance.

The intellectual developments of the long twelfth century witness the rise of the scholastic method of inquiry, a method which consists essentially of the reconciliation of contradictory statements in the sources of doctrinal and canonical authority. Those sources include the legal pronouncements of Church Councils and the writings of the Church Fathers—those theologians, Greek and Latin, writing in the first five centuries, in the context of a, theoretically, unified church. Peter Abelard's *Sic et Non* is celebrated as an early example of the collection of apparently contradictory statements in the writings of the Fathers. 'By doubting we come to inquiry and by inquiry we perceive the truth' is Abelard's statement in the prologue to his work (Clanchy, 1997, p. 34ff). The same method was employed in the influential canon law collection of Gratian, produced in about 1140. This collection, the *Decretum*, has as its alternative title the *Concordance of Discordant Canons*, a title indicative of the attempt to give clarity to the subject. Peter Lombard's famous *Sentences* completed about a decade later provided a similar guide for theology. It is within this period that it becomes possible to make the terminological distinction between theology and philosophy (Swanson, 1999, p. 103ff), although the two remain inter-related.

This inter-relation is observable in the reception of texts newly translated into Latin, a dominant feature of the intellectual landscape from the mid-twelfth century onwards. The twelfth century saw the first translations of classical Greek philosophy into Latin since the fifth century. Works of Aristotle, and to a lesser degree those of Plato, long hidden to the medieval West, gradually became available and were absorbed into Western thinking. The integration of Aristotelian with Christian thought was to a great extent the task and achievement of the thirteenth century, much as the fact of translation was that of the twelfth. It was not an integration which was always easy, both in terms of textual issues, and the content of the new works. Robert Grosseteste, the powerful and luminescent bishop of Lincoln 1235-1253, noted in his *Hexaemeron*, a study into the first six days of Creation, that there were:

> certain modern writers who, in the teeth of Aristotle himself, and his commentators, and the sacred commentators too, strive to make Aristotle's view, which was heretical, a Catholic one.

Their self-deception, in toiling 'at making Aristotle into a Catholic' is attacked by Grosseteste in no uncertain terms. Such writers

> fruitlessly use up their time and strength of mind, and while they make a Catholic of Aristotle, will make heretics of themselves. (Grosseteste, *Hexaemeron*, I.8.4; Martin, 1996, p. 59)

Grosseteste also took issue with those who used poor translations and faulty texts. The translations of Aristotle in the twelfth century were not directly from Greek, but rather from Arabic. Arabic translations made from greek, from the ninth century were rendered into Latin, often with their Arabic commentaries and commentators, introducing such variously (and usually erroneously) named characters as Averroes, Avicenna, and Alfarabi into the medieval intellectual scene.

It is the Greek philosophical texts which have taken the scholarly limelight, but the twelfth century translators also set to work on theological texts of various Greek Fathers. Some of these texts had been previously known to the West, for many works of Greek Fathers had been translated into Latin in the fourth, fifth and sixth centuries, with more limited translation-efforts in the ninth century. The twelfth century saw re-translations of some of these works. Others were entirely new to the West. Amongst the new translations were homilies of John Chrysostom, the Patriarch of Constantinople at the turn of the fifth century and the *On the Orthodox Faith* of John of Damascus, and amongst the re-translations the writings attributed to Dionysius the Pseudo-Areopagite. Pseudo-Dionysius, to whom I shall return, appears to have been a Syrian author, writing, possibly, in the late fifth century, although debate still exists as to his precise identity. In the Middle Ages the identity was less clearly discerned, the writings identified at one and the same time with Dionysius the Areopagite against whom Paul spoke as recorded in the Acts of the Apostles (Acts 17.34) and Dionysius (Denis) the apostle of France. Patristic texts as much as Aristotelian texts were discussed and absorbed into the frame of intellectual life in the medieval West during the twelfth-century renaissance.

At the centre of the interests of this period lie the ordering of human knowledge and the harmonisation of discordant authorities. Sir Richard Southern seductively described the period from the late eleventh century to the late thirteenth as one in which the hope of coherent and universal knowledge was possible.

> The ground of this hope was that the whole system, in its assumptions, its sources, its methods and aims, expressed a coherent view of Creation, of the Fall and Redemption of mankind, and of the sacraments whereby the redeeming process could be extended to individuals.
> (Southern, 1995, p.3)

Southern goes on to state that

> it was the twelfth-century innovators who first introduced systematic order into the mass of intellectual material which they had inherited in a largely uncoordinated form from the ancient world. The general aim of their work was to produce a complete and systematic body of knowledge, clarified by the refinements of criticism, and

presented as the consensus of competent judges. (Southern, 1995, p. 4)

This vision of systematic knowledge Southern portrays as dissipating and losing its way after the late thirteenth century (Southern, 1995, pp. 51-57).

If order is seen to lie at the heart of much of the twelfth-century renaissance, then light can be seen as playing a significant role in the formulation and development of the interests of the period. Light provides a rich, biblically centred, illustration for order, and for the contingent relation between Creator—the arbiter of order, and Creation. God who dwells in unapproachable light (I Timothy 6.16 '*Qui..lucem inhabitat inaccessibilem*), and is light, allows the illumination of the human mind. In the Incarnation the Light of the World takes on human flesh (John 1.4-9 *Erat lux vera, quae illuminat omnem hominem venientem in hunc mundum*) and gives human knowledge and intellectual growth its focal point. These are all images and elements of thinking pursued during the twelfth-century renaissance. To track the various ways in which light was discussed and understood may reveal much about the dynamics and concerns of the period in question. Light as a theological topic emerges in a number of contexts: in the visual arts and architecture, in the traditions of biblical exegesis, in the *Hexaemeronic* tradition, and in theological speculation.

As far as the latter is concerned, what has been termed 'the metaphysics of light' (Dijksterhuis, 1961, p. 151) is a common enough area of discussion especially with respect to the thirteenth century. It emerges fully fledged in the writings of Robert Grosseteste. Grosseteste's thought on light, both its physical properties and the relation of the light of God to that of creation have received extensive treatment elsewhere (McEvoy, 1982, *in extenso*; Southern, 1992, pp. 136-139, 217-218; MacKenzie, 1996, cc. 2-3), although it might serve a purpose to set Grosseteste's thought alongside other reflections on light produced in the long twelfth century. A connection between light and order is explicit in Grosseteste's late, and significant, treatise *De Luce*, from its opening:

> The first bodily form [*formam primam corporalem*], which some call corporeity, I deem to be light. For light, by itself, spreads itself in every direction, so that a sphere of light, however great you will, is generated instantly from a point of light, unless a barrier obstructs [its progress]....For since light is the perfection of the primary body, which naturally multiplies itself from the primary body, light necessarily spreads itself into the centre of everything. (MacKenzie, 1996, p. 25, p. 28)

As MacKenzie stresses we have in Grosseteste a distinction between the light that God is, and created light; 'light is the sublime conjunction between creation and Creator' (MacKenzie, 1996, p. 41). This is a theme which Grosseteste had broached earlier in his *Hexaemeron*. Light

becomes a powerful tool for Grosseteste to comment and develop his thoughts on Creation.

Light and order are themes prominent also in the writings of Hildegard of Bingen (1098-1179), the celebrated Abbess of Disibodenberg, whose visions, as well as her musical, medical and scientific works, of great power and originality are well-known. Hildegard is the focus of much scholarship, and her 'visions', the writing out of which gave opportunity for her to express in the richest language her experience of the 'living light' (Atherton, 2001, p. xi), have been frequently analysed. Light appears often and centrally in her writings, notably in the *De operatione dei - Book of Divine Works*. The beginning of the Gospel of John provides the fulcrum for the visions set down in this work and Hildegard responds to the light imagery found within that text. The light of God, and the Son of God as the light of the world, are themes upon which she meditates constantly and to which she returns. In Vision Four John the Baptist is discussed, in an exposition of John 1.7, as he who was 'to bear witness to the light, that is to say, to the God from whom all light is enkindled so that all who are inflamed by the Holy Spirit might believe in God.' John 1.9[1] 'That [the Word] was the true light' elicits the following from Hildegard:

> ***Erat lux vera****, quę numquam umbra ulla obumbrata est et cui numquam tempus seruiendi vel dominandi, minuendi seu augendi datum est; sed quę ordinatio omnis ordinationis et lux omnis luminis est ex se lucens. Deus enim numquam in aliquo mane, in ulla aurora surrexit; sed ante euum semper fuit.*
>
> That [the Word] was the true light, that has never been darkened by any shadow and which has never been given a time to serve or to rule, to wane or wax; but which is the ordering of all order and the Light of all lights, giving light out of itself. For God has never arisen on a particular morning or at any dawn, but he was, before that, for ever. (Derolez and Dronke, 1996, p. 256)

The vision of light for Hildegard was both a powerful experience and a stimulating spur to exegesis.

Light could also play a role in the theological speculations of authors for whom it was not so controlling or central a theme. An example is Baldwin of Ford, a rough contemporary of Hildegard, a friend of John of Salisbury, Abbot of the Cistercian Abbey of Forde, bishop of Worcester, and finally, Archbishop of Canterbury from 1184 to 1190. Perhaps best known for his sermons, his Tract 13 *Charitas Dei diffusa est*...(Migne, 1844-1864, t. 204, 535-540) incorporates a section in which light is closely discussed by Baldwin. Corporeal light is contrasted to spiritual enlightenment, and, interestingly, is compared with the action of love, *charitas*. The theology of love was one of the pre-eminent themes explored by Cistercian authors during this century, from St Bernard onwards. For Baldwin to talk of light in this context is therefore potentially striking.

Nevertheless light for Baldwin does not seem to lie at the heart of his theological writings, as it does for, for instance, Grosseteste. The same can be said for the chronologically earlier example of Anselm of Canterbury (1033-1109). Originally from Aosta in the Alps, Anselm spent the majority of his life in the Norman abbey of Bec, where he was successively Prior and then Abbot, before being appointed Archbishop of Canterbury in 1093. Light does not play a controlling part in Anselm's thought, but his early treatise, the *Proslogion*, an exercise in the problems involved in how to speak of, or rather with, God, does have sections in which light is referred to and employed in a theological context.

Anselm explores in this work the unbridgeable chasm between humanity and God, and faces the issue of how, in this situation, it is possible to say anything meaningful about or to God. The long first chapter sees Anselm in poetic language setting out the complete distinction between God and humanity, asking for enlightenment and revelation. God is described later on as 'light and truth' (*Proslogion* 14, Schmitt, 1946-1961, i. 111-112), and the process of understanding is put in terms of divine illumination:

> For how great is that light from which shines every truth that gives light to the rational mind!
> *Quanta namque est lux illa, de qua micat omne verum quod rationali menti lucet!*

The unapproachable light wherein God dwells is used in chapter sixteen as a way for Anselm to express the heights of God and the inability of the human mind to scale them, as well as the fact that everything that Anselm does understand is by virtue of this unseeable light.

> My understanding cannot reach that [light], for it shines too bright. It does not comprehend it, nor does the eye of my soul endure to gaze upon it long. It is dazzled by the brightness, it is overcome by the greatness, it is overwhelmed by the infinity, it is dazed by the largeness, of the light. Oh supreme and inaccessible light, oh whole and blessed truth, how far you are from me, who am so close to you!
> *Non potest intellectus meus ad illam. Nimis fulget, non capit illam, nec suffert oculus animae meae diu intendere in illam. Reverberatur fulgore, vincitur amplitudine, obruitur immensitate, confunditur capacitate. O summa et inaccessibilis lux, o tota et beata veritas, quam longe es a me, qui tam prope tibi sum!* (*Proslogion* 16, Schmitt, 1946-1961, i. 112-113)

This is not a theme which Anselm went on to expound in any of his other texts, but it is a fulsome, if limited application of light imagery to the problems of Creation, and the relation of these to understanding and truth.

Light as a topic of theological speculation can, therefore, be detected in various thinkers throughout the twelfth-century renaissance. Where these thinkers drew their inspiration from is a different question, but light is also a common theme in the writings of the Fathers, including those of the Greek Fathers whose works had been translated into Latin. Light also figures importantly in the Aristotelian corpus, particularly with respect to the *Optics* absorbed in the thirteenth century, although I wish for the present purpose to confine attention to the Fathers. Many of these sources have a potential impact on the understanding of light in a theological context, for example Basil (c.330-379) in the *Hexaemeron*, and Gregory Nazianzen (329/330-389/390) in his *Theological Orations* a number of which had been translated into Latin. One translated Greek source which has received attention, and which has certain links to architectural developments in the twelfth-century renaissance is the works of Pseudo-Dionysius, to both of which areas I will now turn.

The writings of Pseudo-Dionysius have long been identified as carrying significant passages of light imagery. *The Celestial Hierarchy* speaks of the reader calling upon Jesus Christ, who is the light of the Father, through whom we gain access to the Father 'who is the light of all.' Pseudo-Dionysius goes on,

> We must lift up the immaterial and steady eyes of our minds to that outpouring of Light which is so primal, indeed much more so, and which comes from that source of divinity, I mean the Father. (*Celestial Hierarchy*, 1.2; Luibheid, 1987, pp. 145-146)

Other treatises continue his line of thought on light, and especially the emphasis on the primal light of God the Father being mediated to his Creation. In *The Divine Names* God is described as the fount of all and the source to which all things turn in the terminology of light (*The Divine Names*, 4.4-6; Luibhead, 1987, pp. 73-76). Light imagery was not the whole purpose of Pseudo-Dionysius's theological canon, and can be over-emphasised, but equally its place remains important.

The monastery of St Denis in Paris claimed a special relationship with Pseudo-Dionysius in the Middle Ages. The apostle of France was in its view the author of the texts we attribute to Pseudo-Dionysius. In the ninth century the Byzantine Emperor Michael the Stammerer had given a Greek manuscript of the works to the monastery. These were translated twice in the ninth century, badly by Abbot Hilduin, and extremely competently by John Scottus Eriugena. Only in the twelfth century was a new translation demanded, with one supplied by John Sarrazin, 'the Saracen' in the middle years of the century.

At or around the same time the abbey church at St Denis was rebuilt by its then abbot, Suger (c.1081-1151). Suger, a prominent politician who held the regency of France when Louis VII went on the ill-fated second crusade, also wrote a record of this re-building as a well as a series of reflections on the design of the building. Practical aspects of the building work are noted down. For example, Suger recorded his hunt for marble columns for the church.

> Since we found none, only one thing was left to us, distressed in mind and spirit: we might obtain them from Rome (for in Rome we had often seen wonderful ones in the Palace of Diocletian and other Baths) by safe ships through the Mediterranean, thence through the English Sea ad the tortuous windings of the River Seine, at great expense to our friends and even by paying passage money to our enemies, the near-by Saracens. (*Libellus alter de consecratione ecclesiae sancti Dionysii*, 2; Panofsky, 1979, p. 90-91)

Eventually a way around the problem was found, the even nearer quarry of Pontoise found to be both suitable and profitable.

The place of Pseudo-Dionysius within Suger's writing has been a topic of debate. The very positive interpretation of Suger's debt to Pseudo-Dionysius given by Erwin Panofsky, has been criticised, recently, by Burcht Pranger and Lindy Grant (Pranger, 1994, pp. 215-221; Grant, 1998, pp. 22-26). Grant argues against the notion of Suger as an independent theological mind. She refers to the rather 'woolly light symbolism' which appears in the verses inscribed on the bronze doors in the West portal of the Cathedral, as well as to the fact that Suger's reading may not have penetrated to the subtlety of Pseudo-Dionysius's texts (Grant, 1998, pp. 23-24). The earlier work of Grover Zinn pointed to the rather stronger connections between Suger and contemporary theological reflection especially that of Hugh and Richard of St Victor, than any direct link to Pseudo-Dionysius via John Scottus Eriugena (Zinn, 1986, especially pp. 35-37).

Pranger's criticism of Panofsky goes deeper, that there is in that interpretation an attempt to see Suger as a 'respectable' thinker on art operating within a 'Platonic' framework, a position which accords far better with Panofsky's view of the later 'Renaissance' (Pranger, 1994, pp. 215-216, 220). But Suger's contact with any such framework was, in the first place, unlikely to have been direct, and secondly was more likely to have been mediated by other contemporary thought. As Pranger puts it, 'If Neoplatonic at all, Suger's thought, like all 'Platonic' ideas in the eleventh and twelfth centuries, is of a much more fragmentary nature and as such subject to endless variations' (Pranger, 1994, p. 220). This is not to say that Suger did not react to the artistic objects he created and reflected upon, but rather that the reflection need not be of a 'complete referential system, on an organisation of signs and symbols, on a spiritual concept of culture governing the world of matter' (Pranger, 1994, p. 220). It is, as Pranger again observes, the very concreteness of the objects which occupies Suger's thought and inspires him to meditate (Pranger, 1994, p. 221).

Light imagery plays a role in Suger's descriptions of gold and jewellery, the decoration of an earlier church at St Denis are imagined as 'blooming with incomparable lustre and adorned with every terrestrial beauty,' and the size of the church 'reflecting the splendour of gleaming gold and gems to the admiring eyes' (*Libellus alter de consecratione ecclesiae sancti Dionysii*, 2; Panofsky, 1979, p. 86-87). When it came to his own building Suger recorded the careful arrangements of the internal dimensions and the positioning of the chapels,

> by virtue of which the whole church would shine with the wonderful and uninterrupted light of most luminous windows pervading the interior beauty. (*Libellus alter de consecratione ecclesiae sancti Dionysii*, 4; Panofsky, 1979, p. 100-101)

Suger's design, and even some of his windows, can still be seen at St Denis. Whether Suger's thoughts on light can be connected directly to Pseudo-Dionysius is debatable. That there is a documented connection between his church building and thinking on light is less so.

There are few other cases in the Middle Ages in which the thoughts of the patron and/or builder can either be connected to an extant church, or deal with the question of natural light within church design. One other example comes from Norway. Here the dominant building material was wood rather than stone, and the pre-dominant form of church design the Stave Church. Forms of architecture more common to Western Europe are to be found in Norway but not in great number. The Cathedral at Nidaros, (Trondheim), was the only medieval stone cathedral in Norway. The Stave Churches remain far more typical of medieval Norwegian church architecture.[1]

The stave church makes an appearance in a collection of Old Norse homilies, dating from the mid-twelfth century. One of the homilies is dedicated to the design and symbolism of the stave church. Within this homily is a short passage concerned with the positioning of the window in order to let in as much light as possible.

> *A þesso briost-þilli ero dyrr inn at ganga í kirkiu.*
> *ok gluggar þaeir er lysa kirkiuna. þvi at droten*
> *sialfr lysir alla þa er inn ganga í tru hans.*
> On this cross-wall is the doorway which one goes through in order to come into the church, and the small windows which let light in, for the Lord himself illuminates all who go in with faith in him. (Korsili, 1976, p. 25; Salvesen, 1971, p. 104)

Whilst it is not possible to connect this text directly with a patron or donor, it does offer another example of a documented connection between church architecture and a

---

[1] I can claim no general expertise in this area, and am grateful to my friend Svein Gullbekk, of Oslo University in this regard. The translation that follows is mine.

theology of light. Illumination in the physical sense acts as a pointer towards spiritual illumination.[2]

As Suger's description of the interior of his church shows the internal decoration played an important role in the quality of the light within the building. Swanson points out that Suger's stained glass 'certainly made the church's interior more jewel-like, but not necessarily any lighter', (Swanson, 1999, p. 160). Here the point at issue is the interplay of the physical light, and the more metaphysical reflections that it inspires. This is a theme to which jewellery and the minor arts within the twelfth-century renaissance make a significant contribution. Innocent III in May 1198 sent four rings to Richard I of England, and outlined in his accompanying letter the properties of the various stones and metals: gold, emerald [*smaragdus*], sapphire, garnet and topaz. The distinguishing feature of topaz, according to Innocent was its radiance, which he connects with good works, which should shine forth in the world.

> ...and the radiance of the topaz, the practice of good works—of which the Lord says 'Let your light so shine before men that they may see your good works and glorify your Fathers which is in Heaven [Matt. 5.16] (Innocent III, Letter 1, Cheney and Semple, 1953)

The delicate interaction between physical light and theological speculation on light is exemplified by an earlier work of art, the Gloucester candlestick (Stratford, 1984, Borg, 1985).[3] Given to the abbey of St Peter's, Gloucester by Abbot Peter (1107-1113), and later removed to the church of Le Mans, perhaps in the late twelfth century, the candlestick has a famous inscription.

+LUCIS ON(US) VIRTUTIS OPUS DOCTRINA REFULGENS PREDICAT UT VICIO NON TENEBRETUR HOMO

The translation of this inscription has been the subject of scrutiny.[4] Stratford opts for 'This flood of light, this work of virtue, bright with holy doctrine instructs us, so that Man shall not be benighted in vice,' and Borg the simpler, 'The burden of light is the work of virtue. Shining doctrine teaches that man may not be shadowed by vice.' An alternative might be suggested, namely, 'May this mass of light and this work of virtue ablaze with doctrine teach man not to be overshadowed by vice.' A degree of symbolism may also be detected in this between the mass

[onus] and the candle, the work [opus] and the candlestick, and, the doctrine or guide [doctrina] and the candlelight.[5]

The use of light imagery within Christian thought is a constant theme, from the Biblical background onwards. It is not confined to any single period. Within the twelfth-century renaissance however it is a theme which can be found in a variety of forms and deployed in variety of ways. It is a theme which intersects with other theological and intellectual interests of the period. A theology of light in the twelfth century can be usefully sought too outside the documentary evidence of this period, a facet which grants an opportunity to see, in some ways, the practical manifestations of theological thought. In the diverse and often connected ways in which thought on light was developed throughout the twelfth-century renaissance it emerges as a theme worthy of further exploration.

References

Atherton, M., 2001 *Hildegard of Bingen Selected Writings*, translated with an introduction and notes, London

Bartlett, R., 1993 *The Making of Europe Conquest, Colonization and Cultural Change 950-1350*, London

Borg, A., 1985 'The Gloucester Candlestick', in *Medieval art and architecture at Gloucester and Tewkesbury*, British Archaeological Association Conference Transactions, London

Cheney, C.R. and Semple, W.H., eds., and trans., 1953 *Selected Letters of Pope Innocent III concerning England (1196-1216)*, Edinburgh

Clanchy, M., 1997 *Abelard A Medieval Life*, Oxford

Derolez, A., and Dronke, P., eds., 1996 Hildegard of Bingen, *Liber divinorum operum*, Corpus Christianorum Continuatio Medievalis, 92, Turnhout

Dijksterhuis, E.J., 1961 *The Mechanization of the World Picture*, trans., Dikshoorn, C., Oxford

Grant, L., 1998 *Abbot Suger of St-Denis Church and State in Early Twelfth-Century France*, London

Haskins, C.H., 1927 *The Renaissance of the Twelfth Century*, Cambridge, Mass.

Korsili, A., 1976 *Symbolikken i stavkirkeprekenen på europeisk bakgrunn*, Unpubl. Thesis, University of Oslo,

Leyser, K. J., 1986 *The Ascent of Latin Europe: An Inaugural Lecture Delivered Before the University of Oxford on 7 November 1984*, Oxford

Luibhead, C., trans., 1987 *Pseudo-Dionysius. The Complete Works*, Mahwah, New Jersey

McEvoy, J., 1982 *The Philosophy of Robert Grosseteste*, Oxford

MacKenzie, I.M., 1996 *The Obscurism of Light A Theological Study into the Nature of Light, with a*

---

[2] There is a significant literature on the general theme of church building and the capturing, or not, of light, see Georges Duby, *Le Temps des cathédrales : l'art et la société, 980-1420*, Paris, 1976.

[3] My sincere thanks for what follows are due to Kate Heard, St John's College, Cambridge.

[4] As well as a correspondence in the between Neil Stratford and Colin Sydenham in the *Burlington Magazine* in 1984. Sydenham's proposal ran as follows: 'Carrying the candle is the task of righteousness: its light is the Church's teaching, whose message redeems man from the darkness of vice.'

---

[5] I owe this point to Helen Molesworth.

Translation of Robert Grosseteste's <u>De Luce</u> by Julian Lock, Norwich

Martin, C. F.J., 1996 Robert Grosseteste *On the Six Days of Creation, A Translation of the Hexaemeron*, Auctores Britannici Medii Aevi, VI(2), Oxford for the British Academy

Migne, J.P. 1844-1864 *Patrologia Latina*, 221 Volumes, Paris

Panofsky, E., ed., and trans., *Abbot Suger on the Abbey Church of St.-Denis and its art treasures* 2nd edition by Gerda Panofsky-Soergel, Princeton, 1979.

Pranger, B., 1994 *Bernard of Clairvaux and the Shape of Monastic Thought, Broken Dreams*, Leiden

Salvesen, A., 1971 *Gammelnorsk Homiliebok*, Oslo

Schmitt, F.S., 1946-1961, *Sancti Anselmi Opera Omnia*, 6 volumes, Edinburgh

Southern, R,W., 1953 *The Making of the Middle Ages*, London

1992 *Robert Grosseteste The Growth of an English Mind in Medieval Europe*, 2nd Edition, Oxford

1995 *Scholastic Humanism and the Unification of Europe*, Volume 1 *Foundations*, Oxford

Stratford, N., 1984 'The Gloucester Candlestick' in *English Romanesque Art 1066-1200*, eds., Holland, T., Holt, J., Zarnecki, G., Exhibition catalogue for the Hayward Gallery, London, 5 April-8 July 1984, London

Swanson, R.N., 1999 *The twelfth-century renaissance*, Manchester

Zinn, G.A., 1986 'Suger Theology and the Pseudo-Dionysian Tradition' in Gerson, P.L. ed., *Abbot Suger and Saint-Denis A Symposium*, New York, pp. 33-47

The Unchanging Face of God

Martin Henig

These thoughts were occasioned by an (unpublished) symposium organised at the University of Leicester in June 1994,entitled *In the Eye of the Beholder. Representation in Classical Antiquity*. Its theme encouraged us to look beyond the mere technicalities of everyday archaeology such as typology, dating and the comparison of cultures one with another to consider the ultimate meaning of human life and human vision; by implication it encouraged us to link the beholder with the spiritual reality which lies beyond the full comprehension of mortal man. The eyes are, after all, not only 'the doors by which one can pass straight from the body into a man's mind' (Brown 1971,74) but also pathways to the Divine Will. This paper is, then, concerned with the gods (or God or, if one prefers, the eternal and pre-existing *Logos*) quite as much as it is with mankind. My starting point in this inevitably all-too-brief survey will be the votive sculpture of the Roman Cotswolds with which I am most familiar although, as will become apparent, it could have begun with any group of religious sculptures from the Roman Empire, Archaic or Classical Greece, the Byzantine Empire or Medieval Western Europe. Moreover, it seems to me that the vibrant religious art of India is likewise entirely relevant to this theme (Michell 1982), and perhaps images from religious systems which have little or no connexion with those of Europe and Asia. Archaeologists and historians are trained to look for changes, but many of the conditioning factors of human experience in fact remain the same throughout the world and through the centuries and, sometimes, it is right that we should consider these too.

The beautiful landscape of rolling limestone hills covering eastern Gloucestershire and parts of the neighbouring counties of Oxfordshire, Wiltshire and Somerset is, by British standards at any rate, quite rich in sculpture and other evidence of Roman religious activity (Henig 1993). The temple of Sulis Minerva at Bath (Cunliffe and Fulford 1982, nos 3-39), of Mercury at Uley (Woodward and Leach 1993, especially Henig in ch.6) and groups of Mars altars at Bisley and King's Stanley (Henig 1993, nos 48-59) provide a wealth of images which can be supplemented by sculpture from other sites though for the most part they follow the conventional iconographies established through the Graeco-Roman world. Thus representations of Mars (Pl.1), like those of Minerva, generally figure him bearing spear and shield and wearing a helmet (except for two representations of Mars as a bareheaded youth). Mercury is nude, and invariably carries a purse and a caduceus; and he is generally accompanied by his animal familiars, a cockerel and a ram or goat. A few reliefs, notably three from Gloucester (Henig 1993, nos 78-80), show a female consort beside him with in the best preserved instance a sceptre and a bucket of liquid refreshment. This fertility deity, conventionally called 'Rosmerta', has analogies with Fortuna, who is figured either standing or seated on a number of statuettes and reliefs in the region. Another

distinctive deity known from a number of representations in the region (Pl.2; Henig 1993, nos 110-14), as well as from London, is a huntsman who stands frontally accompanied by a hound and in some instances by a stag (see Merrifield 1986). He has borrowed a hat of Phrygian type probably from the Oriental Attis but may have been known by more local names and equated with Apollo as *Apollo Cunomaglus*, the 'hound-prince' at Nettleton Shrub or as Mars, for instance as *Mars Nodens*, at Lydney Park (cf. Boon 1989). The most obvious Celtic aspect in cult iconography is triplication, very probably denoting augmentation of powers This is notable in the case of the Matres at Cirencester (Henig 1993, nos 115-8) and of Mars near Lower Slaughter (Henig 1993,no.131). There are also the well-known Genii Cucullati of the area, little godlings who sometimes accompany a mother goddess (Henig 1993, nos 95-106. The deities portrayed generally stand frontally and thus face the spectator. It is evident at least from the remains of two full sized cult statues, versions of classical prototypes, a Minerva from Cirencester (Henig 1993, no.85) and the Mercury from Uley (Henig 1993, no.62), that this feature remains as constant here as it does in the Mediterranean world.

There are only two exceptions to what may be called the 'formal image' of deity. One is a crude rendering of three scurrying *genii cucullati* from Cirencester (Henig 1993, no.96); the other type is more significant, and is represented by three depictions of a god (Mars?) seated on a horse which is clearly in motion (Henig 1993, nos 123-5). These may be uncharacteristic, but they do show us what gods should be doing in the world. If one looks at local epigraphic sources, deities appear to their worshippers in dreams and visions, strike down malefactors with death, disease, blindness or insanity and recover stolen property (Tomlin 1992; idem in Cunliffe 1988,59-269; idem in Woodward and Leach 1993,113-30;RIB 153). The men and women who prayed so fervently, made sacrifice and commissioned votive altars and reliefs assuredly did *not* expect the gods to remain in one place (Lane Fox 1986,102-67). The situation described here was universal in the Greek and Roman worlds as well as in related cultures such as those of sub-Hellenistic Syria. Whether the deity is the Cotswold Mars, Pallas Athena, Dea Brigantia (Henig 1984,ill.103), Ephesian Artemis, Serapis or Cybele, he or she stands or sits enthroned in frozen grandeur. The power is manifest and mythology tells of how it is used, but here at least it is restrained and silent.

In one obvious respect images did move in a material way: Many were portable objects. There were figurines and metal plaques carried to temples as votives or taken away as souvenirs like the famous silver shrines sold by Demetrius and his friends at Ephesus (*Acts* 19). As a student of glyptics, I am equally familiar with gems carrying the same devices of the major Greek and Roman deities as I am with large-scale sculptures in stone (Henig 1974). Such intaglios were set in the bezels of rings which in fact enshrined the gods and goddesses, allowing the votary to carry them around instead of having to seek them in particular places (Henig 1990). Illustrated here is an images of Jupiter on a gem from Bath (Henig 1974,no.1; Pl.3) and another of Zeus Heliopolitanus, the chief god (Baal) of Baalbeck on an intaglio found at Gadara in Jordan (Henig and Whiting 1987,no.24; Pl.4). Perhaps figures of the gods on coins had a similar function and certainly they provided ready-made amulets for individuals: thus for example the image of Fortuna on the reverse of a bronze *as* of Domitian deliberately placed in the mast-step of a barge excavated at Blackfriars, London (Marsden *c*.1967, 36-7) was surely designed to bring fortune to the vessel. Gems, coins and, of course, portable small bronzes further emphasise the universality of divine powers but again give no clue as to how it was thought to be exercised.

A partial exception is provided by a discrete group of 'active' deities. The famous Poseidon from Cape Artemision (and similar images on coins of Poseidonia) is about to hurl his trident while the Ares being manufactured and assembled on the name vase of the Foundry Painter seems about to slay his adversary (Robertson 1975,pls 57,59). These belong to a particular period of time, early Classical Greece when, in Athens at least, the gods seemed especially close. Even so such pieces are not necessarily cult-images proper and may in fact be regarded as extracts from myth scenes as portrayed in pediments (Athena and Poseidon in dispute on the West pediment of the Parthenon), friezes (such as the gigantomachy of the Siphnian Treasury at Delphi or the Great Altar of Zeus at Pergamum) and, in the minor arts, the familiar portrayals of myth on painted pottery. There is a Roman parallel in the striding type of Mars Gradivus (though this is clearly a figure based on a late archaic or early classical Greek prototype). Even though these figures were never themselves venerated, they do provide examples of action which have so far been lacking. As well as battling with monsters, the gods strike down human malefactors either directly, as Apollo and Artemis shoot down the children of Niobe or, more often, indirectly as Apollo orders the flaying of Marsyas, Artemis directs hounds against their master Actaeon (Robertson 1975, pl.69c) and Dionysus has Lycurgus strangled by the Ambrosia-Vine.

In two similar stories of gods attacking mortals the deities are not directly depicted in art. In the first Attis was driven mad by his jilted paramour Cybele, angered that he had deserted her for the nymph Sangaritis; he castrates himself and dies beneath a pine tree (see Vermaseren 1977). Even better known is the tale of the infant Heracles strangling the serpents sent by Hera to destroy him; this is a curious but important instance of the *failure* of a divine power to quell a mortal - but then Heracles (Herakles) was a son of Zeus (Boardman 1988,827-32)! The difference between divine image and mythological depiction is well shown by

these last two examples. Although Attis was a mortal who died at the behest of the Great Mother, he was resurrected and became a god in his own right, ruling beside her. His imagery is varied according to what concept was to be stressed; as a god he is sometimes a herdsman, perhaps the guardian of the domestic livestock just as his more powerful female consort looked after the whole of wild nature. He is sometimes the young mortal, his trousers unbuttoned and drawn back to show immature genitals. He will grow with the crops and with them be cut. In Britain, as we have seen, he is apparently conflated with a hunter god. All these images, as opposed to myth scenes are static: He does not actually herd sheep or chase deer, still less castrate himself. Heracles is best known through literature and art by way of myths which include his infant prowess and final death, but are centered, above all, on his mighty Labours (Boardman 1990,1-92) when he was under the protection of Athena who significantly stands by him (as on a relief of Hercules evidently killing the Hydra from Corbridge), but never lends her spear or give one of his enemies a timely coup de grace (Pl.5). Like Attis, after his many tribulations, Hercules became a god and his entry into Olympus is sometimes shown on sculpture. He was very widely venerated especially in the Roman Empire, but although almost all his cult images show him wearing the pelt of the Nemean lion and carrying his club, he stands erect and impassive like any other god.

In myth scenes gods and goddesses generally walk or ride in chariots. Horse-riding is the preserve of heroes, especially notable deceased mortals, who are venerated rather than worshipped. Occasionally the distinction between god and hero is blurred as most notably in the case of the Dioscuri. Nevertheless the type which must be regarded as best presenting their divine images shows them as standing frontally holding upright spears, sometimes accompanied by impassive horses. The representations of rider gods from Britain, as mentioned above, show horsemen conflated with Mars (as one inscription makes clear), their monster-slaying activities revealing an earlier ancestry in heroic myth (Ambrose and Henig 1980 and Henig 1984,ill.13; Pl.6); iconographically they may, in fact, be derived from heroic cavalrymen depicted on first-century AD tombstones (Mackintosh 1986). None of the representations is actually a cult image but one is on the side of an altar in the same group as others showing a standing Mars, so just possibly he was envisioned in that way as a god. Certainly in North-West Europe we find one of our more surprising iconographic types. Images of Jupiter seated in a chariot and riding down a giant sometimes replace more normal Jupiter images atop columns (Bauchhenss and Noelke 1981) which may in some instances have been simple votives but in others may have represented sacred trees and have been venerated. If so we end our survey with a possibly unique case of a cult image of a god portrayed in motion.

By and large, however, the situation I have outlined, in which gods appear impassive in art, is hard to refute. Moreover when Christianity eventually replaced Graeco-

Roman religion, the iconographical ground rules remained the same (Volbach 1961). God the Father was seldom depicted, following the earlier Judaic ban on images but Jesus of Nazareth quite soon became the subject of art. At first he appears in symbolic form as the (Good) Shepherd or as a philosopher, but then icons developed of the new young god as world-ruler (Pantocrator) at Ravenna (Volbach 1961,pl.158) and possibly even earlier elsewhere as at Hinton St Mary, Dorset (Toynbee 1964), if this is not in fact the likeness of a contemporary Christian emperor (see below)! These were images falling into a long established mould. Mary, mother of Jesus--'Mother of God', became a mother-goddess of the type of Isis, like her 'star of the sea' and a protector of sailors in navigation, like her clad in blue (Witt 1971,269-81). Also, like her, she suckles an infant son, though here we can point to many other analogues such as the nutrices of north-west Europe (e.g. Henig 1993, nos 117, 118). Illustrated here in a Late-Saxon Virgin and Child relief from Inglesham in north-east Wiltshire (Pl.7), antique not only in the attitude of the Mother, but in the powerful gesture of her Son, already *Cosmocrator*, and the *Manus Dei* above his head likewise originated in Roman art. This sculpture, however, is no earlier than the 9th or 10th century. Even the mortal saints of the Christian church assumed the distance, power and untouchability of the old gods, their pagan predecessors (Brown 1981; Mathews 1993). There were equestrian saints like George; Christopher, the new Hermes-the bearer of the young god, above all the awesome power of Peter, keeper of the keys to heaven, and his companion Paul. There were many female saints each with their attributes, imaged and enshrined in churches throughout Christendom, mostly virgins, many were martyrs; others were holy women...including in England a fair number of Anglo-Saxon princesses. As an Oxonian, it would not do to forget the blessed Frideswide!

Only in myth cycles drawn from the gospels or from saints' lives do we see action and, as in Pagan times, the figures in epic cycles, were not cult images to be worshipped. The passion of Christ or of the saints show the reason for the power but don't show how that power will effect the votary or strike an enemy blind. Punishing malefactors with loss of sight is in fact a popular theme, and an appropriate one to recall in a paper dealing with vision. It is surprising how many of the saints can not only help men but also, like Frideswide, punish transgressions, for example with blindness (Blair 1987). Alban the martyr of *Verulamium* is a case in point for, at the moment of his execution as Mathew Paris shows in a dramatic image, the executioner's eyes fell out. What makes this case especially fascinating is that the cult of Alban seems to have replaced a pagan head cult in Late Roman times (Henig and Lindley 2000, passim). But such violent images are of course adjuncts to narrative not icons. These would always be tranquil and frozen in time and space.

It is easier to describe a phenomenon than to account for it. Clearly both patron and artist, if asked why images designed for worship were so static despite the existence of active myth they would appeal to tradition. Images had always been like this - often even simpler. Such conservatism in action is to be seen in the Byzantine tradition of icon painting even today. Beyond this, they might argue that these static images best expressed the conception of God. Power being exercised would have limited the potential for action. It is not clear that Pallas Athena shown in relief fighting Giants or Persians in Athens, would help the petitioner to Sulis Minerva at Bath seeking health or wishing to recover stolen property. To reveal the divine acting in a specific way limited his power; the Jews knew this very well and by banning all images of their own god, they ensured that he was envisioned as a deity of boundless power. At the other extreme, the Romans had originally venerated some highly specialised deities who were so specialised, so limited in their scope, that no-one in historic times worshipped the god of creaking door hinges or of rust in wheat.

The relationship between deities and temporal power is interesting. In Archaic Greek times under the Tyrants, in the monarchies of the Hellenistic Age, throughout the Roman and Byzantine Empire and in the medieval kingdoms of Western Europe these archetypes mirrored the image of the ruler on earth who was in theory their subordinate. The Ruler cults of Alexander the Great and his successors, the Roman Imperial Cult (Pl.8), the theory and practice of the 'Divine Right of Kings' all had an effect on popular religion for here was power made manifest, gods upon earth whose ministers exercised swift and immediate justice as they sat impassively by. The ruler, whether he was Peisistratos or Richard II lived in 'sacred' surroundings as a sort of god or at least under divine protection:

> For well we know no hand of blood and bone
> Can gripe the sacred handle of our sceptre
> Unless he do profane, steal, or usurp.
> (*Richard II* Act 3, scene iii,79-81),

Trajan was called the *optimus princeps* in direct allusion to Iuppiter Optimus Maximus; Septimius Severus adopted the coiffure of Serapis; Constantine progressed from being the comrade of Sol Invictus to being God's deputy on earth conquering beneath his standard, the *labarum* with its *chi-rho* monogram, a position emphasised by Constantius II and his other successors. The use which Christian rulers were to make of divine sanction is well established in the fourth century as shown in the coinage, such as an issue of Constantius II with the reverse legend 'Hoc signo victor eris'(Kent 1978,no.681) and the dominant chi-rho on some coins of Magnentius (Kent 1978,no.675). The impassive, mask like heads of Constantine (Volbach 1961,pls.16,17 see Pl.9) and of Constantius II (Volbach 1961,pls 18,19) resemble those of divine images and, perhaps, the so-called Christ of the Hinton St Mary mosaic really belongs here: The date would suit Constans or Constantius II. The whole history of the portrayal of Byzantine and medieval monarchy follows the same theme of sacral kingship, drawing on Old Testament myth as well as on earlier

Roman tradition (Alexander and Binski 1987,194-204). Some of the religious *aura* of monarchy remains to this day and in the week of the Leicester colloquium was prominant in the national news. The present Queen of England is closely associated with religion and the church of which she is titular head as Defendor of the Faith, though unlike Henry VIII she has not been portrayed in art enthroned like Solomon (Roberts 1993, 86-7 no.29) nor for that matter, with less Christian hyperbole, has she been flattered as a goddess as was Elizabeth I (Yates 1975)!

Periods of popular or oligarchic rule, for example in Classical Athens and Republican Rome, saw the gods protecting not one man or woman but rather the 'divinity' of the laws of the State. Pallas Athena was in a sense the ruler of Athens as was Jupiter and perhaps also Mars Pater in the Roman Republic. They provided the religious foundation of the state in place of a temporal ruler. The same spiritual sanction is apparent today in the United States of America, where God is seen as the protector of the Constitution, and the Stars and Stripes has a mystical significance which the Union Jack does not have.

Gods, as defined in this contribution, are moulded in the image of man and accord with his psychology. It is legitimate to ask whether divine images are simply political. After all, when Quintilian writes that the beauty of Pheidias' Olympian Zeus added something to revealed religion (*Inst.orat.* xii,51), he is effectively saying that mankind literally carves or casts the gods it needs. In his time these gods included emperors, especially dead emperors. The fact that emperors were only deified after death expresses a caution over the permanence of their all-too-evident power but their relationship with the living ruler was evident . There were obvious advantages in being able to encapsulate authority in this way, as it allowed the populace to be in the presence of the descendants of gods, who would, moreover, one day be gods themselves. However these deities do not occupy the same positions as the Olympians; As *divi* rather than *dei*, they receive neither votive offerings nor, perhaps, real worship as we would understand it (but see Price 1984). The exercise of human and divine power may have formal similarities but there are also differences. If the world of the gods seems to imitate human institutions it can also transcend it.

The gods frequently stand for justice and truth against rulers who have overstepped the mark. The legendary Oedipus and Pentheus were not portrayed in the image of the divine; rather they were destroyed by the gods. The types of Saul, of Xerxes, of Tarquin, of Nero, of Domitian likewise reveal figures who are ultimately far from statuesque; indeed they are as unlike the gods as it was possible to be. They are imagined as the victims rather than as the perpetrators of divine wrath, a reminder to other men that the gods have always punished evil, and especially *hubris*. The Roman *damnatio memoriae* gave symbolic form to the fall and disgrace of the unworthy would-be *divus*. Thus the unchanging face of god can be seen reflected in the visage of the just ruler and the just state,

but essentially it lies beyond the reach of human power, never more so than when the state exceeds its powers. Self-evidently the image of an enthroned or standing god or goddess does not tell us the whole truth about the nature of the divine, but such images have comforted many people over the ages - and still do! The art historian has every reason to be grateful to this popular tradition for its wealth of images.

Of course, there is another more intellectual approach to God, once again with a pedigree that stretches down from antiquity to our own time. Amongst the most penetrating critiques of what constitutes justice and the good life came from the philosophers of Classical Greece, amongst them Socrates and Plato, and their successors down to the end of the Roman Empire, Stoics and neo-Platonists. In common with the Jewish rabbis (who attempted -and failed-to impose the higher reaches of religion on a whole society) they approached the divine in a more abstract and intellectual manner, rather than through the conventional images of popular cult. Their heirs are surely amongst us in Universities and in seminaries, but their views of the divine are too elusive for the humble iconographer; the spiritual quests of philosophers and poets are far too individual for popular art or, indeed, for established religions. Their speculations lead the soul far beyond terms of human reference and language to seek, in the words of George Seferis.

> 'the other life that is beyond the statues'.
> (*The messenger*, v. trans. Rex Warner).

Just occasionally art gives a hint of these speculations of the philosophers. One such image of enlightenment is even to be found in the Cotswold region and was probably first created in Cirencester. The great Woodchester pavement and the smaller version from Barton Farm) (Henig 1995, illus. 106 and 91; Pl.10) show great sweeping registers of animals and birds and rich vegetal friezes around the figure of Orpheus, perhaps here a late Roman version of the huntsman (Pl.2) It reminds us that all living things, indeed the earth, the sun and the stars, gravitate towards the Unchanged and Unchanging Divine Love.

References

Alexander and Binski 1987 J.Alexander and P.Binski,*Age of Chivalry. Art in Plantagenet England 1200-1400*,Royal Academy of Arts, London

Ambrose and Henig 1980 T.Ambrose and M.Henig,'A new Roman rider-relief from Stragglethorpe, Lincolnshire', *Britannia* XI, 135-8

Bauchhenss and Noelke 1981 G. Bauchhenss and P.Noelke, *Die Iupitersäulen* in den Germanischen Provinzen, Beihefte der *Bonner Jahrbücher* 41,Bonn

Blair 1987 J. Blair, 'Saint Frideswide reconsidered', *Oxoniensia* LII, 71-127

Boardman 1988   J. Boardman, 'Herakles', *LIMC* IV, 728-838

Boardman 1990 J. Boardman, 'Herakles (Labours)', *LIMC* V,1-192

Brown 1971 P. Brown, *The world of Late Antiquity from Marcus Aurelius to Muhammad*, London

Boon 1989 G.C. Boon, 'A Roman sculpture rehabilitated: The Pagans Hill dog', *Britannia* XX, 201-217

Brown 1981 P. Brown, *The cult of the saints*, Chicago

Cunliffe 1988 B. Cunliffe, *The Temple of Sulis Minerva at Bath. vol.2 The finds from the sacred spring*, Oxord University Committee for Archaeology, Monograph No.16, Oxford

Cunliffe and Fulford 1982 B.W.Cunliffe and M.G.Fulford, *Bath and the rest of Wessex*,CSIR Great Britain I.2,Oxford

Henig 1974   M. Henig, *A corpus of Roman Engraved gemstones from British sites*, BAR Brit.ser.8, Oxford (second edn.1978)

Henig 1984   M. Henig, *Religion in Roman Britain*, London

Henig 1990 M. Henig,'A house for Minerva: temples, aedicula shrines, and signet-rings', pp.152-62 in M. Henig, *Architecture and Architectural sculpture in the Roman Empire*, Oxford University Committee for Archaeology, Monograph no.29, Oxford

Henig 1993 M. Henig, *Roman Sculpture from the Cotswold Region*, CSIR Great Britain I.7, Oxford

Henig 1995   M. Henig, *The Art of Roman Britain*, London

Henig and Lindley 2000 M. Henig and P. Lindley (eds), *Alban and St Albans Roman and Medieval Architecture, Art and Archaeology* BAA Conference transactions 24, Leeds

Henig and Whiting 1987 M. Henig and M. Whiting, *Engraved gems from Gadara in Jordan. The Sa'd collection of intaglios and cameos* Oxford University Committee for Archaeology, Monograph no.6, Oxford

Kent 1978   J. P. C. Kent, *Roman Coins*, London

Lane Fox 1986 R. Lane Fox, *Pagans and Christians*, Harmondsworth

Mackintosh 1986 M. Mackintosh, 'The sources of the Horseman and Fallen Enemy motif on the tombstones of the Western Roman Empire', *JBAA* CXXXIX,1-21

Marsden *c.* 1967 P. Marsden, *A ship of the Roman period from Blackfriars,in the City of London*, London

Mathews 1993   T. F.Mathews, *The clash of gods. A reinterpretation of early Christian art*, Princeton, N.J.

Merrifield 1986 R. Merrifield, 'The London Hunter-God', pp.85-92 in M. Henig and A. King, *Pagan Gods and Shrines of the Roman Empire*, Oxford University Committee for Archaeology, Monograph no.8

Michell 1982   G. Michell, *In the Image of Man. The Indian perception of the Universe through 2000 years of painting and sculpture*, Hayward Gallery, London

Price 1984 S. R. F. Price, *Rituals and Power. The Roman imperial cult in Asia Minor*, Cambridge

Roberts 1993 J. Roberts, *Holbein and the Court of Henry VIII*, National Galleries of Scotland, Edinburgh

Robertson 1975 M. Robertson, *A History of Greek Art*, Cambridge

Tomlin 1992 R. S. O. Tomlin, 'Voices from the Sacred Spring', *Bath History* IV,7-24

Toynbee 1964   J. M. C. Toynbee, 'A new Roman mosaic pavement found in Dorset', *J.R.S.* LIV, 7-14

Vermaseren 1977   M. J. Vermaseren, *Cybele and Attis. The myth and the cult*, London

Volbach 1961   W. F. Volbach, *Early Christian Art*, London

Witt 1971 R. E. Witt, *Isis in the Graeco-Roman world*, London

Woodward and Leach 1993 A. Woodward and P.Leach, *The Uley Shrines. Excavation of a ritual complex on West Hill, Uley, Gloucestershire: 1977-9*, English Heritage Archaeological Report no.17, London

Yates 1975 F. Yates, *Astraea. The Imperial Theme in the Sixteenth century*, London

Pl. 1. Relief of Mars from Bisley Common, Chalford, Gloucestershire. H.59cm. Stroud Museum (Photo: R.L. Wilkins FSA, Institute of Archaeology, Oxford)

Pl.2. Relief of hunter-god from Chedworth, Gloucestershire. H.45 cm. Site museum (Photo: author)

Pl. 3. Cornelian intaglio of Jupiter from Bath. L.1.1cm.In Roman Baths museum (Photo: author)

Pl. 4. Impression of sardonyx intaglio of Zeus Heliopolitanus from Gadara. L.1.6 cm.
(Photo: R.L.Wilkins FSA, Institute of Archaeology,Oxford)

Pl. 5. Relief showing Hercules slaying the Hydra from Corbridge, Northumberland. H.89 cm. Site museum (Institute of Archaeology, Oxford, archive)

Pl. 6. Relief showing rider-god (Mars) from Stragglethorpe, Lincolnshire. H.74 cm. (Institute of Archaeology, Oxford, archive)

Pl. 7. Relief of Virgin and child in Inglesham church, Wiltshire. Late Saxon (Photo: G.Soffe)

Pl. 8. Dynastic relief from Julio-Claudian monument in Ravenna, showing deified rulers. Ravenna Museum (Photo: author)

Pl. 9. Colossal marble head of Constantine, *c.* A.D. 315-30 in the courtyard of the Conservatori palace, Rome
(Photo: author)

Pl. 10. The great mosaic at Woodchester, Gloucestershire (detail showing friezes). *In situ* but now reburied
(Photo: L. Henig)

Cyberdreaming with Laris Pulenas: an afterlife beyond the Post-Modern

Caradoc Peters

This paper, as the others in this volume do, investigates the contribution of perspectives other than purely archaeological ones to 'excavate' the past (Henig in this volume). Indeed, the past encompasses not just different opinions, but also a vast array of different approaches to describing the passage of time and the human condition. Specifically, this paper looks at the whole question of dimensionality, including that of Virtual Reality and Shamanistic thought, and investigates the possibility of prior ideological labour and dialogue in social transformation, which could be applied to archaeological examples.

Firstly, the question of dimensionality and prior ideological labour will be discussed and then illustrated with examples mainly from British prehistory and Etruscan archaeology.

Extra-dimensional discussion is the prerequisite to action. From the shaman that enters the spirit world through induced trance or communicates with divine beings through avatars, to the modern designer or scientist who tries to pre-empt the future by creating something that the future is generally understood to possess, all periods witness dialogues with other dimensions that are very real and active to their respective populations.

"Cyberdreaming" is an attempt to connect the preplanning of Cyberspace and written documentation with the preplanning of shamans either for use in this world or in spiritual dimensions into which humans would eventually be expected to enter. Many societies, including those practising shamanism, have perceived of dimensions that are parallel to past, present and future (Guenther 1999) – for example, the Yanomano Indians (Chagnon 1996), South African Bushmen (Jolly 1996 and Figure 1) and Australian Aborigines (Goodale 1999).

The nature of the dimensionality can be explained through Superstring Theory in Physics (Davies & Brown 1988; Pierre 1999), where the four 'open-string' dimensions of our everyday experience are supplemented with other 'closed-string' dimensions that exist in parallel but cannot be experienced in an everyday fashion. These 'closed-string' dimensions closed within a fraction of a second of the Big Bang. Although not immediately experienceable, they are necessary to explain the gap between the physics of relativity and the physics of electromagnetism. In the same way, 'other' dimensionality in the human mind is often necessary to explain human actions in the four 'open-string' dimensions (Figure 2.).

In daily life, one experiences three dimensions of space and one of time. People represent these dimensions usually by means of lines. Models of waves for mathematical purposes are linear, even though the waves

are not linear in three dimensions. Lines are easy to understand; easy to construct and deconstruct; and therefore, resorted to in order to help order data that are not static. Time, at least in ordinary human experience, is essentially directional and motive. Time must be an essential element in archaeological theory. This element has presented serious difficulties for both post-processualists and cognitive-processualists. The use of lines in the past may well have been used to illustrate 'open-string' dimensionality, at least in some aspect - for example, the Royal pyramids of Meroe in the Sudan (Figure 3.) or round barrow cemeteries in Britain (Figure 7.).

Time is relative, and this is reflected in other aspects of dimensionality. It is argued here that the rate of cultural change varies according to how dimensionality is perceived. Also, the manner of cultural change is linked to the question of identity itself, which in turn is connected to dimensionality. It is proposed that using this understanding as a guide, a multilinear/multidimensional model of the past could be developed. This would provide an alternative to the period and phase models that continue to be problematic for post-processualists, while providing a firm basis for critical thought, which has been problematic for cognitive processualists.

Applying these ideas to preplanning, it appears that first a society requires an exploration and understanding of space, and then of time. The two are strongly connected in societies with more elaborate forms of preplanning. Identity is also intimately linked to this preplanning. Identity is associated with thought (Descartes) and with duration of thought (Bergson) (Russell 1979, 547-548 & 756-765). Identity can be individual and collective, locative and tative. For example, Fred Smith could see himself as Fred Smith, or as an Englishman, or as a resident of Tunbridge Wells, or as a manager of a local branch of a chain of supermarkets. This idea can be applied to societies in the past.

Three types of dimension need consideration from this perspective: spatial, temporal and 'other' (often spiritual dimensions).

Spatial dimensionality is important in defining identity, and is the dimension that is most easily distinguished. At its weakest, it represents an area necessary for subsistence, perhaps with a spiritual core of sacred sites - called an 'estate' by Stanner (1965), distinguished by changes in ecology, but not strongly defined from neighbouring territories culturally. Such societies are likely to show a strong identification with the nature and natural cycles. This is typical of Mesolithic Europe (*e.g.* Bradley 1998).

Temporal dimensionality shows wider deeper differences

in human perception. At one end of the spectrum, it is seen as a cycle of seasons, repeating continuously with little or no change, as with many hunter-gatherer societies. At the other end, it is a rigidly structured and mapped out sequence stretching out from the distant past through the present even into the future as with 21st century Europe.

Other dimensions, separate from these first two (often, though not always, of a spiritual nature), are parallel both to the spatial and the temporal dimensions. Examples of these are the Dreamtime of Australian Aborigines and the Cyberspace of 21st century USA (see Finn in this volume). These dimensions are not superfluous, aside from any arguments about whether or not they really exist, because problems in the four dimensions of common everyday experience are resolved in such dimensions. Equally importantly, such dimensions are also perceived as real, and as such are given full weight in human dialogue including in the symbolic dialogue of material culture (Rheingold 1994; Turkle 1995).

'Otherworld' dimensionality is so real for many societies that the location of such spiritual dimensions is sometimes seen as having physical, spatial boundaries, such as being under the ground or at the edge of the known world (*c.f.* Homer and Gilgamesh). On the Mappa Mundi in Hereford Cathedral, there are strange beings like people with large feet that could be used to shade themselves, or others with no heads, but eyes and mouth in the chests in Africa, and the Garden of Eden is given a physical location (Koziol 2000).

However, one should not assume that this only has relevance for past societies. The work of many cyberpsychologists and cyberanthropologists, like Turkle (1995), Rheingold (1994) and Escobar (1994), illustrate the complexities of identity and cyberspace. In Sherry Turkle's cyberpsychological study 'Life on the Screen' (1995), one interviewee described Real Life (RL) as "just one more window, and it's usually not my best one", classifying it as just one of a number of real dimensions. In fact many people in modern life, treat different media as separate lives that can provide mutually supporting benefits. For example, Rheingold (1994) describes such behaviour experienced in the WELL, an early virtual community in California. There has even been some consideration of the issues represented by Cyberspace for archaeology, especially when looking at the fundamental question of what makes a community (Jones 1997).

Problems in one dimension can be resolved in another. Levi-Strauss in "The Savage Mind" (1966) shows how gaps in theoretical knowledge needed to operate western technology have been filled by mythological explanations. This 'bricolage' or 'tinkering' provides links to adapt new ideas where obvious connections cannot be found in one's previous experience.

Changes in the relationship between the first two types of dimensionality and the last ('other' dimensionality) occur through exploration and wider contacts, which in turn, are promoted by changing dimensionality. The 21st century view of the past, like that (albeit less accentuated) of the ancient Greeks and Romans, has come about through an exploration of space, and the recording of the passage of time. The latter has led to a wider exploration of time, archaeology, geology and astro-physics for the past, and futures markets, climatic modelling and science fiction for the future. Benedict Anderson (1991) has pointed out that the nations existed in literature long before Napoleon, and that this blueprint was used to create nations in areas outside of the European tradition. Mapping of territory was important in this process too (Anderson 1991; Edney 1997). The growth of mercantilism and capitalism as part of this process led to an increased popular identification with trade, and therefore, standardisation, homogenisation and secularisation, which accompanied the growth in trade.

This has obvious implications if writing and printing are looked at as the continuance of a human trait of using symbols as a means of dialogue and by extension, planning. For another example of this, see Gaspar (in this volume), who shows the connection between the imagery of light in literature and twelfth century architecture. The means of dissemination in time and space will be modified by taphonomic processes and by the effectiveness of the means of spatial dissemination available at any given time.

The use of symbols is of course only as effective as its medium, given taphonomic problems. Thus, the relativity of time mentioned above may be influenced by the medium of discourse. Einstein's Theory of Relativity indicates that time alters according to the standpoint of the observer, and that time is not fixed as might be thought (Davies & Brown 1988; Pierre 1999). Perceived time alters even without the considerations of theoretical physics. For example, the concept of the "Old Family", referring to wealthy landed gentry or patrician classes in towns, occurs because those families can point to a longer record of existence through monuments and documents, even though peasant families may have a longer history in the area (Figure 4.). This is a distortion of perceived time.

Writing can be used to distort time in other ways too: for instance, by universalising it as in the case of recent IT technology (*c.f.* Sandbothe 1998). Monuments and writing slow time down. For example, relatively short periods such as the Roman period or the Mediaeval period were seen as longer than pre-Roman times in Britain by antiquarians because the monumental and written evidence available for the former periods was greater (Daniel 1981; Trigger 1989). In addition, because time in such literate and monument-building periods is perceived as slower, the record of change can be seen and acted upon to produce more change. Thus paradoxically, change is quicker and more frequent.

Some periods or indeed social groups do not use monuments or writings, which underline or even underpin such symbolic forms of control and negotiated change.

Nevertheless, dimensionality is still readable through the available symbolic evidence.

Using a few case studies, these ideas of dimensionality can provide alternative ways of investigating and classifying societies from different times without reference to a standard Western chronology.

The Mesolithic period offers little in the way of cultural differentiation across Britain relative to later periods. Part of this is due to taphonomic reasons, though this would have been the case even in the period itself. Ethnographic comparisons would suggest a cyclic sense of time, and indeed, the archaeological evidence at sites like Star Carr (Clark 1952) and the Oronsay sites (Mellars & Wilkinson 1980) tends to support this.

Planning is likely to have been on a seasonal basis, rather than long-term. The way in which raw materials are little altered from their natural state, for example in human burials at Téviec (Figure 5), and the burial of dogs in the same fashion as for humans (*e.g.* Bradley 1998), leaves the impression of an identification with nature and the natural cycles.

There could potentially be problems with the idea that hunter-gatherers such as those in the Mesolithic could be classified merely on the basis of their economy. Hunter-gatherers are unified by the type of economy, but not by any thing else necessarily. There are a great variety of forms of hunter-gatherer society (*c.f.* Gamble 1999, Layton 1986, Service 1971) from relatively egalitarian through to what might be considered chiefdomships. However, the dimensional model provided here does not rely on the broad technological or economic classifications common in prehistory as Table 1 shows. The cave art of the Upper Palaeolithic, for example, appears as more 'open-stringed' than the Mesolithic (*c.f.* Leroi-Gourhan 1993).

In contrast to the Mesolithic, Bronze Age burial mounds, especially where arranged in lines (Figure 7), could well have had a similar effect to the genealogical tables mentioned above (*c.f.* Figure 4), in marking out the long existence of at least certain types of ritual if not of chiefly lineages (Barrett 1994). Lines of henges (Burl 1997) might also relate to the long existence of a hierarchy (Figure 6.) as part of the ideological discussion.

The use of artificial symbols (and synthetic symbols in the grave goods) in the Early Bronze Age is in marked contrast to the Mesolithic period mentioned previously. Identification here could be linked to trade and warfare, which is symptomatic of the increasingly 'open-stringed' nature of Early Bronze Age hierarchies. The relative similarity of such monuments across Eurasia (and even down to North Africa) (Mallory 1989) suggests that the identification is less locus-based than the previous phases of the Neolithic. Spatial awareness as part of a wider trade network for instance would lead to greater exchange of ideas and facilitate cultural change.

The monument-building, as mentioned earlier, causes the perceived time to be slow and long in the Early Bronze Age, compared with the fast short, more cyclical time of the Mesolithic. The pace of technological and cultural change is much faster than in the Mesolithic. In fact, the pace of such change is faster than the previous Neolithic phases -for example, changes in pottery, metallurgy, and weaponry. The slower time and greater length of time perceived, allows the consideration of time past, and therefore, a symbolic dialogue to take place in which future change can be planned. In this context, the Middle Bronze Age changes may be more explicable. Bradley (1998), for instance, notes structural and symbolic similarities between the old and the new monument types found at that time.

In these last examples, the processes of change are examined, and then mechanisms for the changes are suggested in order to demonstrate how the idea of "cyberdreaming" or dimensionality may have worked in practice.

The dialogue in symbols is the archaeological key to this 'otherworld' dimensionality. The role of other dimensions as evidenced in symbols could have been as virtual "chat-rooms" in which not only mortal human beings could have taken part, but also spirits, ancestors, and divine beings. Just as futures markets function because of at least some positive feedback or return, so these dimensions were credible because a positive result was perceived. The dialogue itself perhaps made a successful outcome more likely. Another factor may be that symbols do not always behave as their creators originally intend and therefore can acquire a sense of independent power and will. For example, the cross, which was intended as a symbol of ultimate punishment, has become for Christians a symbol of salvation.

In Etruscan archaeology, the interplay between the dead ('otherworld') and the living (the four everyday dimensions of time and space) evidenced in funerary architecture provides an excellent instance of this dialogue due to their tombs clear links with the world of the living. Indeed, the tombs of the Etruscans have long been seen as copies of the actual homes of living people. This Durkheimian view is almost certainly wrong, at least when looked at from the point of view of an Etruscan of the time. No society that actually believes in its religion thinks that their mortal society instructs (as opposed to discusses with /negotiates with/ or even, is instructed by) their divine guardians. Logically, it is *vice versa*.

The earlier Etruscan view of the Afterlife is of a happy and prosperous relief from the mortal world (Bonafante 1986, 271). This changes after interaction with the Greeks and their religion into a place of woe and sorrow. For example, the dress and attributes of the demon Vanth in Etruscan tomb paintings are derived from the Greek Fury, Lyssa, as represented on south Italian vases (Bonafante 1986, 267).

However, the wealth and luxury in Etruscan tombs survives this Hellenization. One would expect the dwellings of the necropolis to be better than those of the living. The ostentation of the necropolis would be even more possible, when one compares costs. It would be much cheaper indeed to furnish a tomb with carved representations of luxury goods and furnishing than to provide a home of the living with the actual items themselves.

The wealth and technology of Greeks would have been difficult to understand when compared with a supposedly superior Etruscan Afterlife that did not include these aspects of Greek culture. This may have spurred on a virtual debate in Etruscan religion, whereby aspects of Greek religion and technology were grafted on to the existing Etruscan religion before eventually being incorporated into mortal Etruscan culture. An example of this is the Greek town planning, which is seen first in the necropolises of older towns (2nd half of the 6th century onwards) such as Banditaccia, Cerveteri (Caere) and Crocefisso del Tufo, Orvieto, prior to this occurring in the towns of the living, starting with new foundations such as Marzabotto and Spina at the turn of the 6th and 5th centuries (Barker & Rasmussen 1998, 131 & 151-158; Scullard 1998, 205).

In this way, the way in which Greek symbols could be incorporated into a dialogue with a spiritual dimension, permitted the adoption of Greek ideas, and moreover, found suitable ways in which to adopt those ideas without destroying the Etruscan sense of identity. The alternative would have been the abandonment of an identity, which maintained a political, social and economic system, leading to uncertainty and crisis.

The action of symbols apparently independent of living people can be linked to the idea that the 'otherworld' can represent a wider notion of what a community actually consists of: namely, that the dead in many societies form part of the group identity. The Etruscan example might be compared with Quentin Jones' study of cyberarchaeology, where the notion of 'community' is a deeply contested issue due to the lack of a location in the usual four-dimensional sense (Jones 1997).

Another example of symbols taking an active role (*c.f.* Hodder 1982; McLuhan 1964) is the way in which Bronze Age hilltop enclosures lead to Hillforts in the Iron Age, especially the Late Iron Age. The hilltop enclosures are often suggested as having beginnings as small settlements (Pearson 1993). Corney (2000) has suggested that these enclosures begun as enclosures for livestock (*c.f.* Cunliffe 1991, 41) or ceremonies, and not as forts. He provides evidence, such as hut circles outside the enclosures, sparse settlement, and large unsettled areas inside the enclosures. There have even been suggestions that enclosures on Dartmoor may have been connected with the storage of tin (Gerrard 1997, 47). It could be that the presence of an enclosure containing valuables, such as cattle or trade

items would encourage attack. This might have led to the modification of enclosures into a fortification - an eventuality unforeseen by the societies that first created them.

Thus, the idea of 'cyberdreaming' involves the realisation that dimensionality beyond the four dimensions of common experience is vital to the understanding of processes in the archaeological record. Whether the above examples succeed is less important than the need to debate matters beyond simple chronological processes and look at the basic dimensional structures within which societies have operated and do operate.

A system of classification (see Table 1) of Prehistory, Cartesian Protohistory and Bergsonian Protohistory is proposed to divide up British Prehistory (and potentially other prehistories). Protohistory is used in the francophone sense (*e.g.* Lichardus & Lichardus-Itten 1985) of indicating something of the nature of the society rather than of the sources of evidence available. History itself is taken here in this sense too. Linear (or cyclical) dimensions need to be envisaged for each, according to the type of dimensionality experienced by the given society. The adjective 'Cartesian' is used where there is a growing sense of an identity separate from nature, but where there is little sense of the passage of time outside of cyclical time. 'Bergsonian' is used where there is a growing sense of the passage of time through, for example, lineages. The difference between the two can be illustrated by looking at the Inuit, who do not arrange time along lineages. In Inuit society, for example, children inherit the names of deceased relatives, so they are not just themselves but also their deceased relative alive once more (Brody 2001, 11-14). Even people's lives are cyclical in this 'Cartesian' society.

When applying this system, one should look at the spatial levels appropriate to each case. For example, 17th century England would be appropriate, but obviously not Neolithic England. Within 17th century England, small spatial units down to individual level would also be appropriate, as well as Christian dimensions of Heaven and Hell (and Purgatory amongst Catholics), a past and a future (albeit weakly defined compared to the 21st century version).

This would not replace present day reconstructed narratives of the past, but would provide better insights into the thoughts and minds of past generations. People act on perception, not on absolute reality, if such exists. A cure may have been found for a disease, people in the past may have used the cure, but that does not mean to say that people in the past had our explanation for the cure. In fact, it may be that they used the cure unknowingly, and explained patients' recovery by reference to some other action taken.

Archaeology has in the past, and will hopefully continue to benefit from 'outside' contributions. Archaeology till recently has avoided opinions from outside academia

(Shanks & Tilley 1992). It may also be time to consider whether both the conventional 'rational' explanations and the spiritually based explanations of the past are as radically different from one another as might be thought. Archaeologists could well reflect on how far the difference may be due to modifications in 'other' dimensionality.

Laris Pulenas, as an Etruscan priest (Pallottino 1978, 200 & 219), would have attempted to define the will of the Gods, and would have attempted to put this will from an unexcavatable dimension into reality. Much of the human past was enacted in alternative 'closed-string' dimensions. Not to investigate this dimensionality is to ignore much of the past if not most of it.

Table1.
Classification of the Human Perception of the Past

Prehistory	Cartesian Protohistory	Bergsonian Protohistory	History
Cyclical time Space too 'closed-string' natural in character	Cyclical time Space 'open-string' culturally defined	Time beginning to be 'open-string' or linear Space 'open-string'	Time and space culturally defined and structured
Strong sense of natural 'other' dimensionality	Strong sense of natural 'other' dimensionality	Strong sense of natural 'other' dimensionality	Culturally defined 'other' dimensionality - Secularisation
Lower Palaeolithic	Upper Palaeolithic (areas of cave painting)	Some regions of the Late Neolithic	Some regions of Roman Britain weak sense of history
Middle Palaeolithic	Early Neolithic	Early Bronze Age	The overall entity of Roman Britain
Upper Palaeolithic (areas without cave paintings)	Middle Neolithic	Some regions of the Late Iron Age	Some areas of Mediaeval Britain weak sense of history
Mesolithic	Some regions of the Late Neolithic	Some regions of Roman Britain	Post-Mediaeval Britain
	The Late Bronze Age	Early Mediaeval Britain	Industrial Age Britain
	Some regions of the Iron Age	Most of Late Mediaeval Britain	The Future

Bibliography

Anderson, B. 1991. *Imagined Communities*. Revised edition. London: Verso.

Barrett, J.C. 1994. *Fragments from Antiquity*. Oxford: Blackwell.

Barker, G. & Rasmussen, T. 1998. *The Etruscans*. Oxford: Blackwell.

Bonafante, L. 1986. 'Daily Life and Afterlife', pp.233-278 in L. Bonfante (ed.) *Etruscan Life and Afterlife*. Detroit: Wayne State University Press.

Bradley, R. 1998. *The Significance of Monuments*. London: Routlege.

Brody, H. 2001. *The Other Side of Eden: hunter-gatherers, farmers and the shaping of the world*. London: Faber and Faber.

Burl, A. 1997. *Prehistoric Henges*. Princes Risborough: Shire.

Chagnon, N.A. 1996. *The Yanomamo*. New York: Harcourt Brace. Clark, J.G.D. 1952. *Prehistoric Europe: The Economic Basis*. Methuen: London.

Corney, M. 2000. "Iron Age Hillforts". *Lecture given to the Cornwall Archaeological Society*. 04/00.

Cunliffe, B.W. 1991. *Iron age communities in Britain*. London: Routledge.

Daniel, G. 1981. *A short history of archaeology*. London: Thames and Hudson.

Davies, P.C.W. & Brown, J. (eds.) 1988. *Superstrings: A Theory of Everything?* Cambridge: Cambridge University Press.

Edney, M.H. 1997. *Mapping an empire: the geographical construction of British India, 1765-1843*. Chicago: Chicago University Press.

Escobar, A. 1994. "Welcome to Cyberia: Notes on the Anthropology of Cyberculture". *Current Anthropology* 35: 211-231.

Fagan, B.M. 1998. *People of the Earth*. 9th edition. New York: Longman.

Gamble, C. 1999. *The Palaeolithic Societies of Europe*. Cambridge: Cambridge University Press.

Gerrard, S. 1997. *English Heritage book of Dartmoor*. London: Batsford.

Goodale, J.C. 1999. 'The Tiwi of Melville and Bathurst Islands, north Australia' pp. 353-357 in R.B. Lee & R. Daly (eds.). *The Cambridge Encyclopedia of hunters and gatherers*. Cambridge: Cambridge University Press.

Guenther, M. 1999. 'From totemism to shamanism: hunter-gatherer contributions to world mythology and spirituality' pp. 426-433 in R.B. Lee & R. Daly (eds.). *The Cambridge Encyclopedia of hunters and gatherers*. Cambridge: Cambridge University Press.

Hodder, I. 1982. *Symbols in action*. Cambridge: Cambridge University Press

Jolly, P. 1996. "Symbiotic Interaction between Black Farmers and South-Eastern San." *Current Anthropology* 37: 277-305.

Jones, Q. 1997. "Virtual-Communities, Virtual Settlements & Cyber-Archaeology: A Theoretical Outline". *Journal of Computer-Mediated Communication* 3 (3). [WWW] http://www.ascusc.org /jcmc/vol3/issue3/jones.html (15/03/01)

Koziol, G.G. 2000. "Hereford Cathedral: Mappa Mundi" in *History 155A & 155B: Europe in the Middle Ages*. [WWW]. http://ishi.lib.berkeley.edu/ history155/slides/mappamundi/ (20/11/00).

Layton, R. 1986. "Political and territorial structures among hunter-gatherers." *Man* 21: 18-33.

Leroi-Gourhan, A. 1993. *Gesture and speech*. Cambridge: Cambridge University Press.

Levi-Strauss, C. 1966. *The Savage Mind*. London: Weidenfeld & Nicolson.

Lichardus, J. & Lichardus-Itten, M. 1985. *La Protohistoire de l'Europe*. Paris: PUF, Coll. Nouvelle Clio.

Mellars, P.A. & Wilkinson, M.R. 1980. 'Fish otoliths as evidence of seasonality in prehistoric shell middens: the evidence from Oronsay (Inner Hebrides). *Proc. Prehist. Soc.* 46: 19-44.

Mallory, J.P. 1989. *In Search of the Indo-Europeans: language, archaeology and myth*. London: Thames and Hudson, 1989

McLuhan, M. 1964. *Understanding Media: The Extensions of Man*. New York: McGraw-Hill.

Pallottino, M. 1978. *The Etruscans*. Revised edition. Harmondsworth, Middlesex: Pelican.

Pearson, M.P. 1993. *English Heritage book of Bronze Age Britain*. London: Batsford.

Péquart, M. & Péquart, S.J. 1954. *Hoëdic, deuxième station-nécropole du Mésolithique côtier Armoricain*. Antwerp: De Sikkel.

Pierre, J.M. 1999. "SUPERSTRINGS!" Physics Department University of California, Santa Barbara, CA 93106-9530 [WWW] http://www.physics. ucsb.edu/~jpierre/strings/index.html (20/11/00)

Rheingold, H. 1994. *The Virtual Community: Homesteading on the Electronic Frontier*. London: Secker & Warburg

Russell, B. 1979. *History of Western Philosophy*. London: Book Club Associates.

Sandbothe, M. 1998. "Media Temporalities in the Internet: Philosophy of Time and Media with Derrida and Rorty". *Journal of Computer-Mediated Communication* 4 (2). [WWW] http://www. ascusc.org/jcmc/vol4/issue2/sandbothe.html (15/03/01)

Shanks, M. & Tilley, C. 1992. *Re-Constructing Archaeology: Theory and Practice (Second edition)*. London: Routledge.

Scullard, H.H. 1998. *The Etruscan cities and Rome*. Baltimore: John Hopkins University Press.

Service, E.R. 1971. *Primitive social organization: an evolutionary perspective*. 2nd edition. New York: Random House.

Stanner, W.E.H. 1965. "Aboriginal-territorial organisation: estate, range, domain and regime." *Oceania* 36:1-26.

Trigger, B.G. 1989. *A History of Archaeological Thought*. Cambridge: Cambridge University Press.

Turkle, S. 1995. *Life on the Screen: Identity in the Age of the Internet.* New York: Simon and Schuster.

Woodward, P.J. 1991. The South Dorset Ridgeway. *DNH & AS Monograph Series* No. 8. Dorchester: Dorset Natural History and Archaeology Society.

Figure 1. South African cave paintings. After Jolly (1996, Figure 2.)

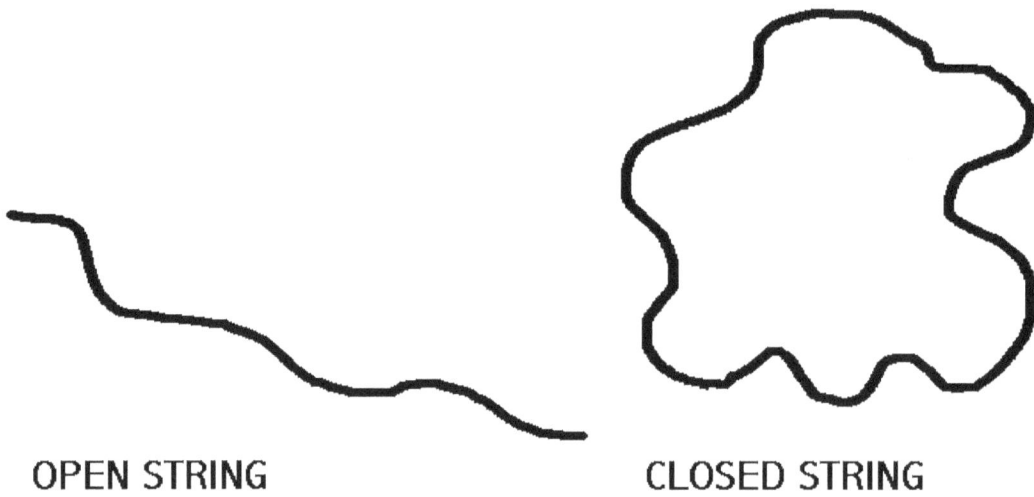

OPEN STRING

CLOSED STRING

Figure 2. Open strings have a tendency towards linearity, though the degree of linearity varies from one type of dimensionality to another. Closed strings are self-contained, are parallel to everyday experience, and are cyclical in nature.

Figure 3. Royal pyramids at Meroe, Sudan. After Fagan (1998, Figure 16.11)

The English Royal Line of Descent (Short Version)

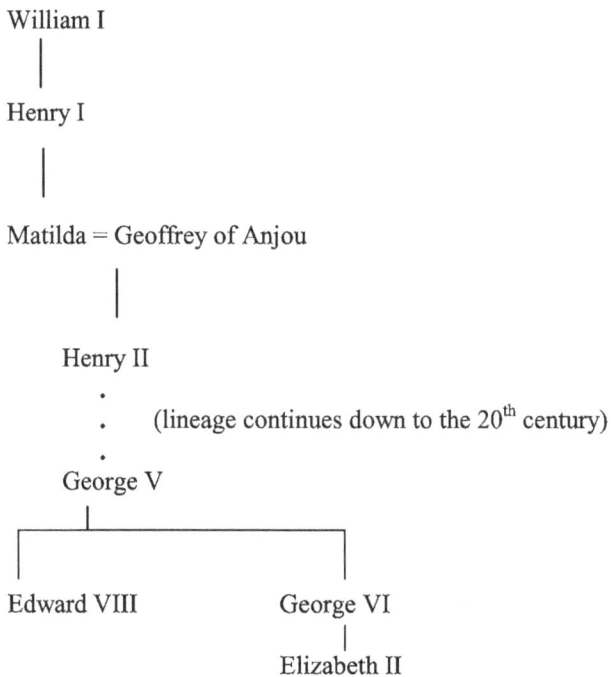

William I
|
Henry I
|
Matilda = Geoffrey of Anjou
|
   Henry II
.
.   (lineage continues down to the 20th century)
.
   George V
|

Edward VIII   George VI
|
Elizabeth II

Figure 4. Lineages, such as this one (which includes the use of numerals for additional effect), add a sense of time depth, and thus seniority in terms of property and other rights.

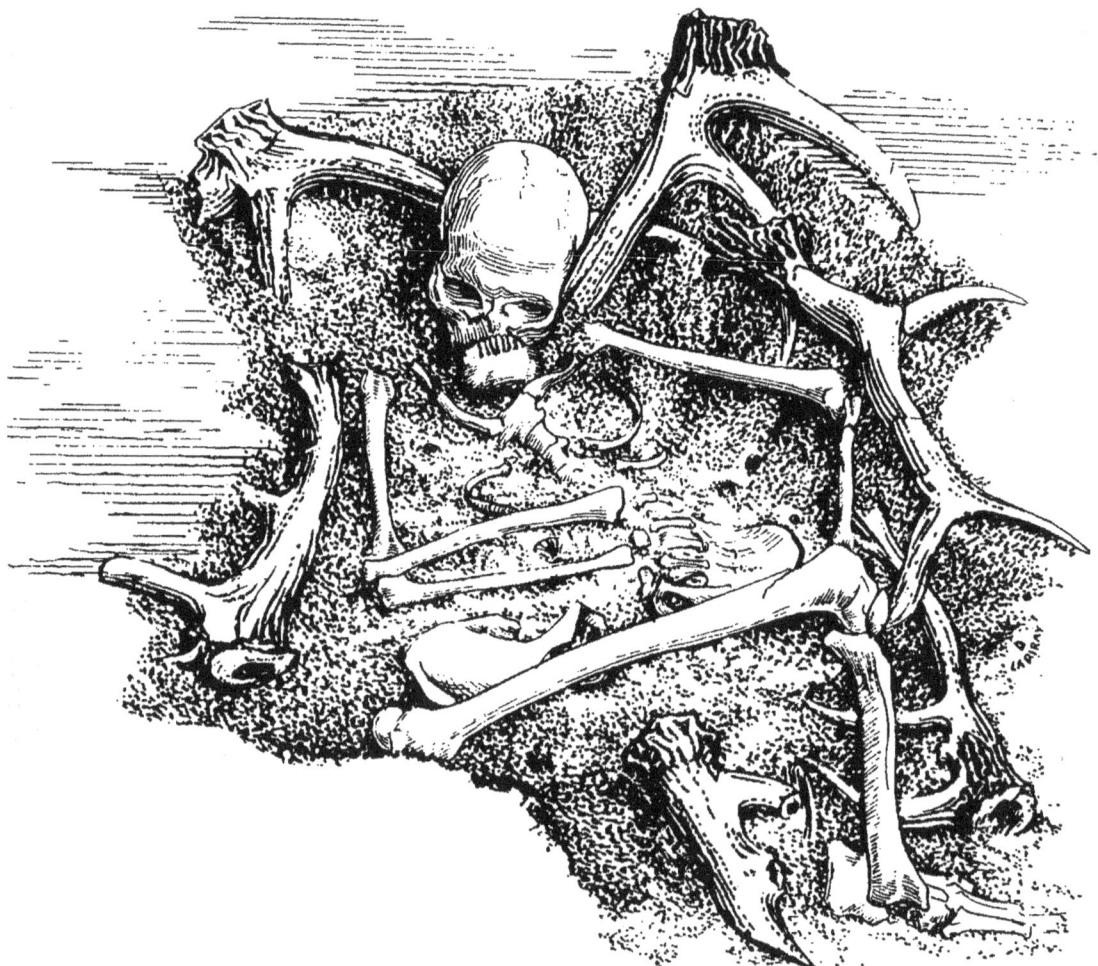

Figure 5. Mesolithic burial from Hoëdic, Brittany complete with red deer antler.
After Péquart & Péquart (1954, Figure 41.)

Figure 6. The Priddy Henges, Somerset, from the north-northeast (Photograph: Cambridge University)

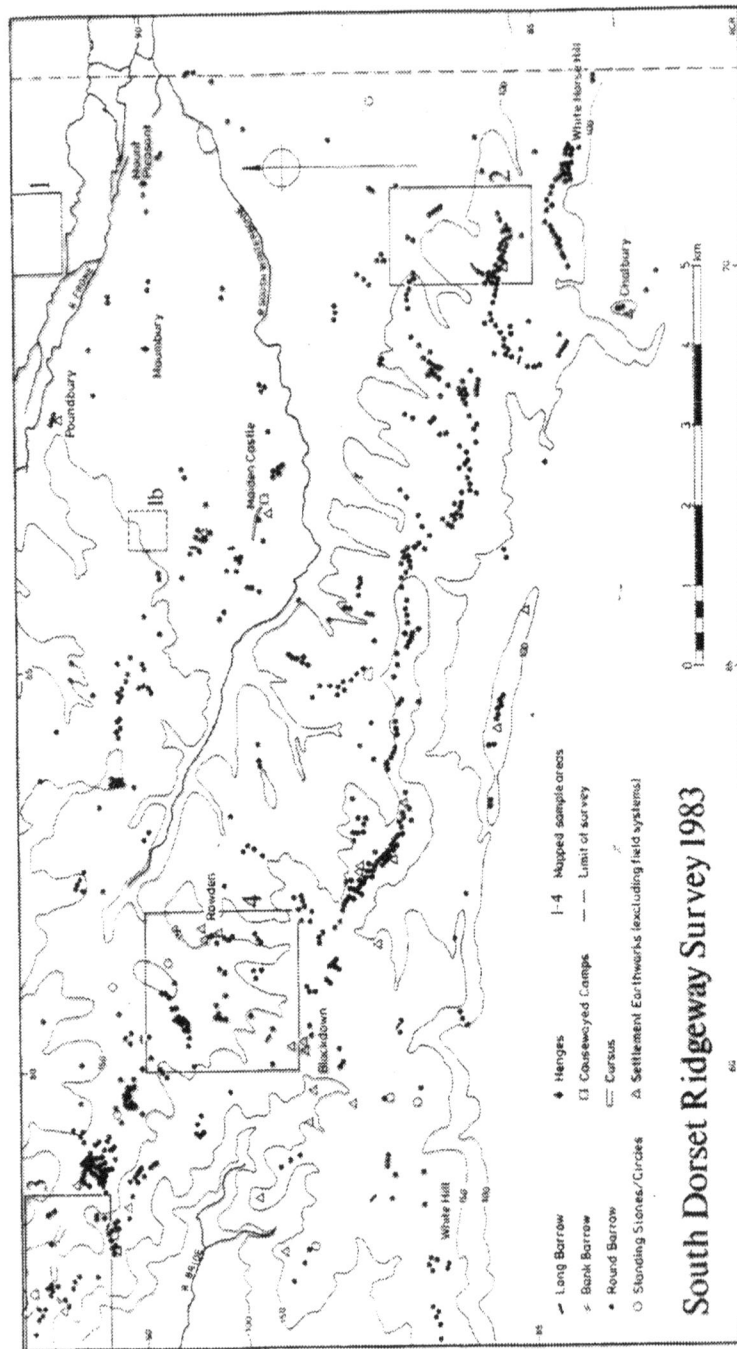

Figure 7. The South Dorset Ridgeway Survey 1983. After Woodward (1991, Figure 2.)

Excavating the Imagination: The Cognitive Archaeology of the Romantics

Lauren Golden

I meant what I said, and at the age of nearly four-score, I have something else, and more important to do, than to write a commentary on my own works. Immanuel Kant[1]

Introduction

The discussion of the imagination and its role in creativity has a monumental history, often negative and sometimes positive, but found major acceptance in the writings of the Romantics, Coleridge being one of its main defenders. Coleridge cites the above statement of Kant in discussing the criticism of Kant's First Edition (1781) of the *Critique of Pure Reason*. The criticism of the first *Critique* that Kant received, was primarily concerned with the emphasis he placed on imagination as the operation of the mind that makes reason possible, an emphasis he subsequently toned down in the Second Edition. Coleridge, unlike other interpreters of the *Critique of Pure Reason* (not only contemporaries of Kant, but even those of today) who have seriously misunderstood Kant's argument about the role of imagination as the *basis* of all cognition[2], seems to have caught on to the controversial theory Kant was proposing. Coleridge states that: "The few passages that remained obscure to me, after due efforts of thought…and the apparent contradictions which occur, I soon found were hints and insinuations referring to ideas, which Kant either did not think it prudent to avow, or which he considered as consistently *left behind* in a pure analysis, not of human nature in toto, but of the speculative intellect alone."[3]

Interestingly, Coleridge does not name exactly what these "hints and insinuations" are[4] but, this passage is just before his discussion of the imagination as a "plastic power" and the importance of the visual symbol, i.e., imagery, for "An IDEA".[5] Coleridge, quite specifically sees the power of imagination as having a 'plastic' quality and, indeed, invents his own word to describe this power: "Esemplastic".[6] Coleridge admits a direct correlation between this word and *Einbildungskraft*: "How excellently the German word Einbildungskraft expresses this prime & loftiest Faculty, the power of coadunation, the faculty that

forms the many into one, *in eins Bildung*. Esenoplay…is contradistinguished from the fancy or mirrorment, repeating simply or by transposition."[7] Further, he identifies the sophistication of visual thinking, where "all symbols involve an apparent contradiction"[8] and this is made possible by the productive power of imagination.[9] Clearly, Coleridge understood both the import and the controversial nature of Kant's theory of imagination, which that imagination is *the* a priori mental structure of the brain and mind that enables *all* thought and consequently, creativity.

In all other writings, even the most recent, nowhere are the operations of the imagination referred to directly as relating to 'cognition' let alone as 'thinking'. Terms and phrases for imagination and its attributes include various permutations of image, presentation, creative act, power, primary, secondary, act of mind, capacity, faculty, unifying - the list is endless, but all amount to the same thing, that imagination, is still, however, elevated, a subsidiary operation of the mind.[10] These terms emphasize that imagination is somehow separated from the act of 'thinking',[11] which is always related to consciousness, self-consciousness, understanding and reason, attributes that are considered qualifiers of the *human* mind. Therefore, for all theorists examining what it is to be *Homo sapiens sapiens*, the role of the human imagination has been 'fly in the ointment' of the dominant Cartesian, logocentric paradigm.

So often the operation of the imagination is related to the 'arts' - those human activities that produce wondrous

---

[1] Cited in Coleridge, S. T., *Biographia Literaria*, [1817] ed., Shawcross, J., Oxford, 1907, 2 vols., I, IX, p.101.

[2] See Golden, L., 'An Historical Enquiry concerning the Imagination in Philosophy, Art History and Evolutionary Theory', unpublished Doctoral Thesis, University of East Anglia, 2001.

[3] Coleridge, [1817], 1907, I, IX, p.99.

[4] Shawcross considers this whole episode to be referring to Kant's writings on Religion. See, Coleridge, [1817], 1907, Notes, p.100, pp.245-246. However, on a close examination of Coleridge's text there seems to me to be much more evidence that what Coleridge is discussing is the controversy surrounding Kant's exposition of imagination. On this controversy, see, Golden, *op. cit*; Heidegger, M., *Kant and the Problem of Metaphysics*, Indianna, 1962, *passim*, esp., p.192; Kearney, T., *The Wake of Imagination. Ideas of Creativity in Western Culture*, London, 1988, pp.194-5; Avens R., *Imagination is Reality*, Texas, 1980, pp.14-15.

[5] Coleridge, [1817]. 1907, I, IX, p.100.

[6] 'Esemplastic' - to shape into one. Coleridge, *op.cit.*, I, IX, p.107. See also, Richards, I. A., *Coleridge on Imagination*, London, 1952, p.76; Engell, J., *The Creative Imagination*, Cambridge MA. & London, 1981, p.224 & p.345.

[7] Coleridge, S. T., *The Notebooks of Samuel Taylor Coleridge*, ed., Coburn, K., 3 vols., London, 1973, vol. III, February-June, 1813, entry 4176.

[8] Coleridge, [1817], 1907, I, IX, p.100.

[9] *Ibid.*, II, XIV, p.12.

[10] It would be fruitless to give examples here for each of these terms, but they will be observable in quotations used throughout this text. However, a worthy example, can be found in Engell, especially as he uses Heisenberg's Uncertainty Principle as a way of explaining imagination, in a passage that is commenting on Coleridge (who, himself, demonstrates the problem with terms), uses many of the terms above, not only to describe Coleridge, but also his own ideas on Imagination. See, Engell, 1981, 'Imagination's Image of Imagination', pp.346-347. So far, I have not come across any scientific research concerning the mind, be it paleoarchaeology, cognitive science or neuroscience that considers imagination as a fundamentally important aptitude for all further cognitions.

[11] In some ways, there is one exception: E. L. Murray, *Imaginative Thinking and Human Existence*, Pittsburgh, PA, 1986. Obviously the title claims imagination as thinking, but the framework of the book is within the context of psychology. Therefore, imaginative thinking is not discussed as a structure of the brain, rather, imaginative thinking is proposed as an alternative form of thinking to that which is logical or rational. See, *ibid.*, pp.28-37.

products that have no 'logical' explanation for their creation. This is linked to the idea of imagination as an irrational human attribute of mind that is as far away from logic, reason and science as can be possible. However, Charles Darwin, one of the greatest scientists, was an observer extraordinare, whose scientific activities were enabled by employing imaginative comparison throughout his life, as his detailed journals, papers and books testify, ranging from the study of the way worms react to sound and music from the piano[12] to observations comparable to those made by modern social anthropology.[13] Importantly, the theory of evolution proposed by Charles Darwin is an example *par excellence* of an exploitation of the imagination. Although he could not prove that evolution had taken place or that the method of evolution was by 'Natural Selection' (crucial evidence on the precise mechanisms underlying 'Natural Selection' only became available with Crick and Watson's discovery of DNA in 1953), nevertheless, he literally rewrote human history and the biological sciences.[14] Darwin himself stated that "The Imagination is one of the highest prerogatives of man"[15] and that "we should bear in mind that the activity of the mind in vividly recalling past impressions is one of the fundamental…bases of conscience."[16]

This very same ability was to lead Darwin to throw light on the 'origins of man', arguing that human beings were *descended* from apes, an heretical proposition that required a creative and extreme imagination. In *The Descent of Man*, published in 1871, he came to the startling conclusion that: "It is therefore probable that Africa was formerly inhabited by extinct apes closely allied to the gorilla and the chimpanzee; and as these two species are now man's nearest allies, it is somewhat probable that our early progenitors lived on the African continent than elsewhere."[17] For Darwin, wonder and curiosity manipulated by imagination elicited, perhaps, from him, what may be considered, the most important scientific theory in human history, thus far.

The human brain and mind is survival mechanism predisposed to face the unknown. The need for this mechanism to remain active far outweighs any period experienced by humans, of seemingly effortless basic survival, in comparison with the millions of years of body and brain evolution and subsistence existence of our evolutionary ancestors. Change is a constant that the evolving brain had to adapt to in order to survive. Therefore, the need for awareness of the unfamiliar in a survival situation is a body and brain function of such magnitude that it could be proposed that the *Homo sapiens sapiens* brain and mind will create ways in which to exercise this activity. Imagination is a facilitator of survival strategy, where encountering a new survival situation relies on applying past experience and knowledge in a new way to contend with an unfamiliar situation. A modern example of this survival body and mind mechanism can be observed, for example, with Einstein, who used and broke with Euclidean science in order to conceive his theory of relativity. Likewise, Picasso used his awareness of visual perception to create a new way of seeing. This could be seen as a human need to make the familiar strange in order to exercise a survival need to be aware of the unfamiliar. It could be said that another name for this behaviour of the awareness of difference is 'Creativity'.[18]

However, this idea is not new and can be found in the writers of the eighteenth-and early nineteenth-century. The ability to make the familiar unfamiliar, as a basis of creativity was particularly exalted by the Romantic Poets.[19] Coleridge, in agreement with Wordsworth, describes the aim of poetry, in the *Biographia Literaria*, as: "to give charm of novelty to things of every day, and to excite a feeling analogous to the supernatural, by awakening the mind's attention from the lethargy of custom, and directing it to the loveliness and wonders of the world before us; an inexhaustible treasure, but for which, in consequence of the film of familiarity and selfish solicitude we have eyes, yet see not, ears that hear not, and hearts that neither feel nor understand."[20]

Accounts of the origin and cause of 'creativity' have a long history[21], but in terms of an approach of cognitive archaeology it could be said that Alberti is the earliest explanatory example. Alberti ascribes the origin of art to the human ability to see images in natural formulations.[22] Later, Giorgio Vasari in his *Vite*, although he begins in the

---

[12] Darwin, C., *The Formation of Vegetable Mould, through the Action of Worms, with Observations on Their Habits*, (First Published, London, 1881), in eds., Porter, D. M., & Graham, P. W., *The Portable Darwin*, Harmondsworth, 1993, pp.521-553, pp.530-531.

[13] Darwin, C., *The Expression of the Emotions in Man and Animals* [first published 1872], 3rd edition, with Introduction, Afterword and Commentaries by Eckman, P., London, 1998; *A Biographical Sketch of an Infant*, London, 1877.

[14] The literature on Charles Darwin's life, works and subsequent effects on science is vast. For a general introduction to Darwin, historical context and development of his theories in the Twentieth Century, see, Appleman, P., ed., *Darwin. A Norton Critical Edition*, New York & London, 1979; Oldroyd, D. R., *Darwinian Impacts. An Introduction to the Darwinian Revolution*, Milton Keynes, 1980. See further, White, M., & Gribben, J., *Darwin. A Life in Science*, London, 1996; Desmond, A., & Moore, J., *Darwin*, Harmondsworth, 1991. For an excellent elucidation of his theories, see, Cronin, H., *The Ant and the Peacock*, Cambridge, 1993; Lowenberg, B. J., "The Mosaic of Darwinian Thought", in Appleman, 1979, pp.211-219, esp. pp.211-212; Randall Jr., J. H., "The Changing Impact of Darwin on Philosophy", in Appleman, 1979, pp.314-325.

[15] Darwin, C., *The Descent of Man, and Selection in Relation to Sex*, 2nd edition, London, 1906, p.113.

[16] *Ibid.*, p.935.

[17] *Ibid.*, 1906, p.240.

---

[18] See, Golden, *op. cit.*

[19] Abrams, M. H., *The Mirror and the Lamp: Romantic Theory and the Critical Tradition*, Oxford, 1971, pp.40-42.

[20] Coleridge, [1817], 1907, II, XIV, p.6. See further, Abrams, 1971, pp.377-384, pp.406-408 & pp.411-414.

[21] For example, see Hesiod, *Theogeny*, 211-32; Philostratus, *Imagines*, trans., & eds., Page, T. E., Capps, E., & Rouse, W. H. D., The Loeb Classical Library, London & New York, MCMXXXI, I, 294k, 1-12; Graves, R., *The Greek Myths*, Harmondsworth, 1962, 13a.

[22] Alberti, in *On Sculpture*, describes the origins of art as stemming from the ability to see images in a tree trunk or a lump of earth. See Alberti, *On Painting and On Sculpture: The Latin Texts of* De Pictura *and* De Statua, ed., Grayson, C., London, 1972, pp.117-142 & I, p.121.

'Preface' with an account of God's creativity that is endowed in humankind *via* grace[23], he quickly moves on to consider "Nature herself"[24] as the source for creativity, and further, creativity is hinted as being an innate 'natural' ability in humans, no matter how uneducated, where "simple children, crudely brought up in the woods and prompted by their liveliness of mind, have begun to draw by themselves, using as models those beautiful pictures and sculptures in Nature."[25] In his general introduction to the *Vite*, he reflects that the origin of the urge to create was an innate part of human nature where, "our earliest ancestors, who stood nearer to the beginning of all things and the divine Creation, and were thus more perfect and endowed with mental vigor, discovered those noble arts by themselves."[26] It is tempting to interpret Vasari's idea of "our earliest ancestors" who are closer to "the divine Creation" within a biological evolutionary framework, where, perhaps, their 'mental vigor' reflects the constant need for awareness in arduous survival conditions. Indeed, throughout Vasari, this 'mental vigour' is in constant use by artists who engage in the faculty of pattern recognition almost constantly.[27] More recently, this faculty was investigated through the Rorschach ink blot tests,[28] and even Descartes describes this particular visual cognition:

> We must at least observe that no images have to resemble the objects they represent in all respects...resemblance in a few features is enough, and very often the perfection of an image depends on its not resembling the object as much as it might. For instance, engravings, which consist merely of a little ink spread over paper, represent to us forests, towns, men and even battles and tempests. And yet, out of an unlimited number of different qualities that they lead us to

conceive the objects, there is not one in respect of which they actually resemble them, except in shape.[29]

Perhaps, in some way, Vasari could be seen as a precursor of neuropsychology, for, embedded in his theory of artistic creation, which rests upon inner vision "...wonderful and divine thoughts"[30] can be perceived the functions of the brain that are important for survival; imagination and pattern recognition.[31]

Immanuel Kant, Nature and the Archaeology of the Mind
Kant, in the *Critique of Judgement* (1790), continues his cognitive archaeology of the mind (as in the first edition of *Critique of Pure Reason*), employing the scientific understanding of his time. Here, he concentrates on human creativity, excavating *a priori* aesthetic cognitions, which today might be explained in terms of the evolution of the human brain.[32] He argues that the apprehension of the sublime[33] - the beautiful - cannot be bound or confined by 'concepts' and what is required is an mental operation for which there is no constraint, namely the imagination: "As the subjective universal communicability of the mode of representation in a judgement of taste is to subsist apart from the presupposition of any definite concept, it can be nothing else than the mental state present in the free play of imagination and the understanding."[34] Such judgements of the sublime are also connected with the bodily senses that are attended to by the imagination: "The feeling of the sublime is a pleasure that arises only indirectly, being brought about by the feeling of a momentary check to the vital forces followed at once by a discharge all the more powerful...but dead earnest in the affairs of the imagination."[35] These 'vital forces' are part of a universal response (perhaps, here, just a Western one) to the 'beautiful' that involves an *a priori* (transcendental) aesthetic predisposition,[36] which Kant places in the class of "synthetical *a priori* judgements".[37] This is made possible: "Only where the imagination in its freedom stirs the understanding, and the understanding apart from concepts puts the imagination into regular play, does the

[23] Vasari, G., *The Lives of the Artists*, Oxford, 1991, pp.3-4.
[24] *Ibid.*, p.3.
[25] *Ibid.*, p.4.
[26] Cited in Kriz, E., & Kurtz, O., 1979, p.34, from, Vasari, G., [1550], *Vite de piu eccellenti pittore, scultori, ed architetti*, 9 vols., Con nuove annotazioni e commenti di G. Milanesi, Florence, 1878-85, 1:221.
[27] Onians, J., & Collins, D., "The Origins of Art", in *Art History*, 1, 1978, pp.1-26. For various accounts on artists seeing patterns and images in natural formations, see, Kriz, E., & Kurz, O., 1979, pp.45-7. Vasari reports that Piero di Cosimo stared at vomit, finding patterns and images, "imagining that he saw there combats of horses and the most fantastic cities and extraordinary landscapes ever beheld", and further, "he cherished the same fancies of clouds." See, Vasari, G., *Lives of the Painters, Sculptors and Architects*, Everyman's Library, New York, 4 vols., 1963, II, p.177. Leonardo recommended interpreting damp spots on walls, see Leonardo da Vinci, *On Painting*, ed., Kemp, M., New Haven & London, 1989, p.222. See also, Gombrich, E. H., *Art and Illusion*, London, 1993, pp.159-161. Alberti, in *On Sculpture*, describes the origins of art has being able to see images in a tree trunk or a lump of earth. See Alberti, "De statua", in *On Painting and On Sculpture: The Latin Texts of De Pictura and De Statua*, ed., Grayson, C., London, 1972, pp.117-142 & I, p.121.
[28] Gregory, R. L., *The intelligent eye*, London, 1970, p.38; *The Oxford Companion to the Mind*, Oxford & New York, 1987, pp.646-647; *Mirrors in Mind*, New York, 1997, pp.67-71 & pp.260-261. The ability to organise vague perceptions into a coherent whole was also developed in Gestalt Theory. See Gregory, 1970, pp.19-21; *Eye and Brain. The psychology of seeing*, London, 1977, pp.9-10; 1997, pp.215-216. See also, Gombrich, 1993, pp.155-157.

[29] Descartes, R., *Dioptrics*, in eds., & trans., Anscombe, E., & Geach., P. T., *Philosophical Writings*, 1963, pp.241-256, Discourse IV, pp.243-4.
[30] Cited in Kriz & Kurtz, 1979, p.48, from Vasari, Milanesi, 1878-85, 2:204.
[31] Onians, & Collins, 1978.
[32] See, Golden, *op.cit.*
[33] Kant, I, *Critique of Judgement*, trans., Meredith, J. C., Oxford, 1952, Part I, 14. See also, *ibid.*, 25.
[34] Kant, [1790], 1952, Part I, 9. See also, *ibid.*, 25-27. Also, Zammito, J. H., *The Genesis of Kant's Critique of Judgment*, Chicago & London, 1992, p.117-118; Banham, G., *Kant and the Ends of Aesthetics*, London, 2000, pp.54-55; Guyer, P., "Pleasure and Society in Kant's Theory of Taste", in Cohen, T., & Guyer, P., eds., *Essays in Kant's Aesthetics*, Chicago & London, 1982, pp.23-54, pp.23-25; Makkreel, R. A., *Imagination and Interpretation in Kant*, Chicago & London, 1990, pp.52-3.
[35] Kant, [1790], 1952, Part I, 23. See also, Makkreel, 1990, p.98.
[36] *Ibid.*, Part I, 37-39. See also, *ibid.*, Remark 1; Remark 2 & 58. See also, Zammito, 1992, p.92.
[37] *Ibid.*, Part I, 36. See also, Banham, 2000, p.100.

representation communicate itself not as thought, but as an internal feeling of a final state of the mind."[38]

Kant is trying to explain the idea that humans have an 'innate' sense of beauty, and he relates this to what he has described as 'finality' - being.[39] The most perfect example of the state of 'being' is Nature and is, therefore, employed in Kant's definition of 'Fine Art': "A PRODUCT of fine art must be recognized to be art and not nature. Nevertheless the finality in its form must appear just as free from the constraint of arbitrary rules as if it were a product of mere nature."[40] This judgement is a response where: "To enable me to estimate a beauty of nature, as such, I do not need to be previously possessed of a concept of what sort of thing the object is intended to be, i.e., I am not obliged to know its material finality (the end), but, rather, in forming an estimate of it apart from any knowledge of the end, the mere form pleases me on its own account."[41]

Kant seems to be striving to explain an abstract notion of pleasing forms, which are inherent in Nature and unrestricted by artificial rules and regulations, to such an extent that they mirror the qualities of *a priori* imagination. Consequently, this similarity between Nature and the human imagination facilitates, one could say, unconsciously, a human recognition of 'beautiful art'. Therefore, this notion can, perhaps, have a foundation in the biological and natural realm that is in a recognition of a state of 'finality' - 'being', "hence the finality in the product of fine art, intentional though it may be, must not have the appearance of being intentional, i.e., fine art must be clothed *with the aspect* nature, although we recognize it to be art."[42]

For Kant's the human response to 'beautiful art', which elicits the 'judgement of taste', is an unconscious response that is not manipulated by artificial rule and reason[43] but, is an aesthetic predisposition of a universal pleasure that is communicable,[44] which is, *a priori*, embedded within the

mind and its mental structure. Kant names this structure the '*sensus communis*'[45] that is not an intellectual but an *a priori* judgement of taste,[46] "the faculty of estimating what makes our feeling in a given representation *universally communicable*, without the mediation of a concept."[47]

Kant also attempts to explain the cognitive properties of 'genius'[48], which he describes as the "spirit, in an aesthetical sense" that "signifies the animating principle in the mind".[49] In effect, this aesthetic animating principle (spirit), is, by Kant's own description, none other than the imagination: "The imagination (as a productive faculty of cognition) is a powerful agent for creating, as it were, a second nature out of the material supplied to it by actual nature."[50] Importantly, imagination has the ability to surpass nature, that which can be experienced, and this is crucial for creativity.[51] Imagination cognizes beyond the limits of experience, and Kant stresses that the talent for art, which elicits such an aesthetic response from the viewer, cannot be learnt or made manifest by employing rules or "mechanical imitation."[52] Rather it is a product of imagination that can apply experience in a new way, which is, therefore, the basis of what we call creativity: "The product of a genius…is an example, not for imitation…but to be followed by another genius - one whom it arouses to a sense of his own originality in putting freedom from the constraint of rules so into force in his art, that for art itself

---

[38] *Ibid.,*, Part I, 40. See also, *ibid.,* 58.

[39] Zammito, 1992, pp.99-100. Further, In J. H. Bernard's translation, 'finality' is translated as 'purposiveness' (sic), which probably reflects more accurately Kant's meaning of 'finality'. See, Kant, I, *Critique of Judgement,* trans., Bernard, J. H., in eds., Hofstadter, A., & Kuhns, R., *Philosophies of Art & Beauty. Selected Readings in Aesthetics from Plato to Heidegger,* Chicago, 1976, pp.280-243, I, 10-11, pp.293-295, p.293. I have chosen to use the Meredith translation but 'purposiveness' is employed by many commentators on Kant and as such should be considered, here, the meaning of 'finality'. On 'finality' (purposiveness) see, Zammito, 1992, pp.90-91 & pp.95-105; Cohen, T., "Why Beauty is a Symbol of Morality", in Cohen & Guyer, 1982, pp.221-236, pp.231-232; Guyer, P., *Kant and the Claims of Taste,* Cambridge, MA., & London, 1979, pp.211-220.

[40] Kant, [1790], 1952, Part I, 45.

[41] *Ibid.,* Part I, 48.

[42] *Ibid.,* Part I, 45. See also, Zammito, 1992, pp.130-136, esp. p.135.

[43] *Ibid.,* Part I, 46.

[44] *Ibid.,* Part I, 37-38. There are problems with Kant's idea of universal communicability, but if Kant's *a priori* claim to universality of what is pleasurable is seen as his struggle to demonstrate that human cognition has a fundamental basis that he calls a 'mental state', see, *Ibid.,* Part I, 9, which today would be considered as an evolutionary cognitive brain

structure, then the problems of 'communication' begin to disappear, as they are, therefore, communicable because all human brains have the same cognitive structure. On the problem of 'universal communicability', see, Guyer, in Cohen & Guyer, 1982 pp.43-50. In my opinion, Guyer's partial solution is problematic as he starts to base this communicability on "an empirical interest in communication, as the basis of society", and Kant is quite clear that the aesthetic judgement is not empirical. See, Guyer, *ibid.,* pp.49-50. A similar approach to mine, which emphasizes the sensory perceptions and psychological responses as the structure through which the pleasurable and aesthetic beauty are engendered, can be found in, Aquila, R. E., "A New Look at Kant's Aesthetics" in Cohen & Guyer, 1982, pp.87-114, esp., pp.90-93 & pp.113-114.

[45] Kant, [1790], 1952, Part I, 40.

[46] *Ibid.,* Part I, 40.

[47] *Ibid.,* Part I, 40. See also, Banham, 2000, pp.101-102; Makkreel, 1990, pp.162-6; Kemal, S., *Kant and Fine Art,* Oxford, 1986, pp.183-4.

[48] Kant, [1790], 1952, Part I, 49.

[49] *Ibid.,* 1952, Part I, 49.

[50] *Ibid.,* Part I, 49. See also, Makkreel, 1990, pp.119-120. Banham resists this obvious statement by Kant by stating that it is the 'spirit' that does the work and the imagination just "presents ideas". Banham is separating imagination from spirit and they are, here, obviously one and the same thing. See, Banham, 2000, p.111. Although Banham goes on to conclude that Genius is the power of imagination, it is for him, clearly not a cognition, for, as he states, "With the imagination we create 'another nature' and free ourselves from the determinations which follow for orders of cognition." Further, imagination becomes an 'idea', not a cognitive faculty. See, *ibid.,* p.112. The difference between Banham and myself, is that I interpret Kant's exposition of imagination as a visual cognition that 'presents' "a multiplicity of partial presentations" that *results* in ideas. See, Kant, [1790], 1952, Part I, 49.

[51] Kant, [1790], 1952, Part I, 49. Zammito does not seems to recognize Kant's meaning that imagination is crucial for 'creativity', but rather that it is crucial for 'Reason'? Granted, Kant can be difficult at times to make sense of his nuances, but here, Kant is extremely clear. See, Zammito, 1992, pp.139-140 & p.284.

[52] Kant, [1790], 1952, Part I, 49. See also, Zammito, 1992, p.144.

a new rule is won - which is what shows a talent to be exemplary."[53]

Thus, the cognition of imagination enables creative activity,[54] where "such representations of the imagination may be termed *ideas*", which in turn "furnish an *aesthetic idea*."[55] Here, Kant is clearly referring to visual thinking, and this is important. Kant describes this visual cognition thus:

> Those forms which do not constitute the presentation of a given concept itself, but which, are secondary representations of the imagination, express the derivatives connected with it, and its kinship with other concepts, are called (aesthetic) *attributes* of an object, the concept of which, as an idea of reason, cannot be adequately presented. In this way Jupiter's eagle, with the lightning in its claws, is an attribute of the mighty king of heaven, and the peacock of its stately queen. They do not, like *logical attributes*, represent what lies in our concepts of the sublimity and majesty of creation, but rather something else - something that gives the imagination an incentive to spread its flight over a whole host of kindred representations that provoke more thoughts than admits of expression in a concept determined by words.[56]

Importantly, what Kant is explaining here, is how the imagination, in its ability for "unbounded expansion", is a powerful method of conceptualization, and further, it is "a creative activity" that "puts the faculty of intellectual ideas (reason) into motion."[57] This is a positive assertion of the power of mental imagery and visual thinking. Also, regarding words and language, the success of poetry and rhetoric is dependent on this visual cognition that is universal and, therefore, universally communicable.[58] On discussing the effectiveness of a particular poem, Kant states, "the imagination (in remembering all the pleasures of a fair summer's day that is over and gone - a memory of which pleasures is suggested by a serene evening) annexes to that representation, and which stirs up a crowd of sensations and secondary representations for which no expression can be found."[59] Further, Kant attempts to describe and clarify this complex and elusive visual thinking, which has an unlimited power of cognitive 'representations' - images -: "the aesthetic idea is a representation of the imagination, annexed to a given concept, with which, in the free employment of imagination, such a multiplicity of partial representations

are bound up, that no expression indicating a definite concept can be found for it."[60]

Genius, therefore, is the employment of this visual cognition "in a certain relation...which science cannot teach nor industry learn"[61] resulting in the expression (genius and art) of an aesthetic idea. For Kant, without the benefit of neuroscience, whilst clearly recognizing imagination as a productive use of cognition, could not go so far as to name it 'visual cognition' (a paradigm elusive to him). However, that Kant is clearly struggling to reach such a conclusion is apparent in an example of nebulous writing in which he falls back on the notorious use of 'thing':

> For to get an expression for what is indefinable in the mental state accompanying a particular representation and to make it universally communicable - be the expression in language or painting or statuary - is a thing requiring a faculty for laying hold of the rapid and transient play of the imagination, and for unifying it in a concept (which for that very reason is original, and reveals a new rule which could not have been inferred from any preceding principles or examples) that admits of communication without constraint of rules.[62]

This passage, as well as the form of visual cognition described by Kant in his example of 'Jupiter's eagle', demonstrates Kant's radical acknowledgement of the supreme importance of imagination and visual thinking; the power of the symbolic[63] (aesthetic idea),[64] which language is incapable of matching; imagination is an "indefinable" power' that provides the "multiplicity of partial representations", which are crucial for genius; the "talent" of the "soul".[65]

Kant, by including the biological, is providing a 'natural' context: "the subjective finality of nature"[66] for the notion of the universality of *a priori* aesthetic judgement, which can only be resolved by seeking "in the supersensible the point of union of all our faculties."[67] For Kant, that the aesthetic judgement must be considered *a priori* means that the "aesthetic idea cannot become a cognition, because it is an intuition (of the imagination) for which an adequate concept can never be found."[68] This provides a mental

---

[53] Kant, [1790], 1952, Part I, 49.
[54] *Ibid.*
[55] *Ibid.*
[56] *Ibid.*
[57] *Ibid.*
[58] *Ibid.*
[59] *Ibid.* See also, *ibid.*, 53.

[60] *Ibid.*, Part I, 49.
[61] *Ibid.*
[62] *Ibid.*
[63] Although Kant does not use 'symbolic' here, it is clearly what he means. See, *ibid.* However, Kant does clarify this meaning of the symbolic, later. See, *ibid.*, 59. Zammito, too, identifies that the symbolic is what is being discussed. See, Zammito, 1992, p.286 & fn.62. Further, see, Makkreel, 1990, pp.122-9.
[64] See also, Kant, [1790], 1952, Part I, 49. Later, Kant again emphasizes the superiority of the visual over other senses, see, *ibid.*, Part I, 53.
[65] Kant, [1790], 1952, Part I, 49.
[66] *Ibid.*, Part I, 57, 340, 1. See also, *ibid.*, 58.
[67] *Ibid.*, 57. See also, *ibid.*, Remark 2.
[68] *Ibid.*, Part I, Remark 1. See also, Makkreel, 1990, p.119.

freedom, which is crucial to the step that Kant takes to make the idea of *a priori* morality (freedom of will) inherent in human aesthetic judgement.[69] Thus, art, is a reflection of the supersensible aesthetic idea that is integrally moral and free where, like Nature, it does not function in terms of an objective end[70] but rather has the "capacity for originating in free activity aesthetically final forms, independently of any particular guiding ends."[71] The inclusion of the 'Critique of Teleological Judgement' in his argument, which deals with the *systema naturae*, from which the source of universal aesthetic judgement and morality can be found, the connection between human aesthetic predisposition and the natural world, for Kant, is a logical one: The finality in nature is "relative to comprehensibility - man's power of judgement being such as it is - and to the possibility of uniting particular experiences into a connected system of nature".[72]

Kant achieves this by considering man as an animal and as a species,[73] and thus, seamlessly incorporates the 'finality' of man in the 'finality' of nature, where, as in nature, there is "a primordial organization, an indeterminable yet also unmistakable function",[74] so in man there is "a causality according to ends - a creative understanding - to account for their intrinsic finality"[75] and this 'finality' underlies the reflective and the aesthetic judgement.[76] Thus, human intrinsic finality, analogous with nature, provides Kant with a foundation and context for human behaviour[77] Kant argues that happiness is not man's ultimate purpose (finality of being) but "the mere idea of a state"[78] that is "the material subjectivity of all his earthly ends."[79] Therefore, 'happiness' cannot provide "absolute worth" and, it is only in the "freedom" and "good will…as a moral being that man can be a final end of creation."[80]

Morality, therefore is the *a priori* cognitive condition that enables man to make sense of his purpose and that informs the moral aesthetic: "For theoretical reflective judgement an intelligent world-cause was sufficiently proved by physical teleology from the ends of nature."[81] He further states that "in all probability, it was this moral interest that first aroused attentiveness to beauty and the ends of nature."[82] However, Kant argues that it is human cognitive

inclination that facilitates a physical teleological analogy, which allows for the notion of a Supreme Being.[83] The 'cause' of the analogous conception of a Supreme Being involves a "latent anthropomorphism"[84] that is facilitated by consciousness of separation from the natural environment, which is the origin of human morality and free will: "The moment mankind began to reflect upon right and wrong - at a time when men's eyes as yet cast but a heedless regard at the finality of nature, and when they took advantage of it without imagining the presence of anything but nature's accustomed course - one inevitable judgement must have forced itself upon them".[85] Kant argues that this 'inevitable judgement', the notion of right and wrong, is the product of a "voice within" that states that there must be a consequence of behaviour - "that it must make a difference."[86] The cognitive origin of morality is a problematic subject, even for evolutionists today[87] but, for Kant the answer was simple; that such an "irregularity" i.e., no right and wrong in the natural world was "revolting to the human mind."[88] One of the most remarkable aspects of Kant's proposition for the origin of morality and the idea of a Supreme Being - God - is that he sees them as constructs of the human brain, the 'supersensible', developed in response to environmental experience: "there is only one principle upon which they could even conceive it possible for nature to harmonize with the moral law dwelling in them. It is the Supreme Cause ruling the world according to moral laws"[89] and, it "was this moral interest that first aroused attentiveness to beauty and the ends of nature."[90]

Although Kant does not specifically say so, what he must mean here is that the notion of morality - right and wrong, good and bad - implicitly carries with it the conception of what is beautiful. That is, the good, as morally right, is what is beautiful and this is, importantly, within the context of the 'finality' - being - in nature, what the human brain and mind has subjectively imposed upon the natural world and what underlies reflective and aesthetic judgement.[91] Kant was not arguing simply that the beautiful is good or vice versa, but that the cognitive structure of the brain and mind is predisposed toward

[69] *Ibid*. Part I, Remark 1; Part I, Remark 2; 59 & 60. See also, Zammito, 1992, p.89 & p.93.
[70] Kant, [1790], 1952, Part I, 58. See also, *ibid*., Introduction, II.
[71] *Ibid*. Part I, 58 & 59. See also, Zammito, 1992, pp.287-291.
[72] Kant, [1790], 1952, Part II, Introduction. See also, Abrams, 1971, pp.207-208.
[73] *Ibid*., 21 & 22.
[74] *Ibid*., 20.
[75] *Ibid*., 21.
[76] Zammito, 1992, pp.105-195 & p.221.
[77] Zammito states that, "Kant essentially established that aesthetics was only a propaedeutic concern leading to anthropology… ." See, Zammito, 1992, p.3.
[78] Kant, [1790], 1952, Part II, 22.
[79] *Ibid*. See also, Zammito, 1992, pp.328-329.
[80] Kant, [1790], 1952, Part II, 25. See also, *ibid*., 26 and generally, *ibid*., 22-27. See also, Zammito, 1992, pp.92-93 & pp.332-341; Banham, 2000, pp.181-185; Makkreel, 1990, p.137; Kemal, 1986, pp.140-2.
[81] Kant, [1790], 1952, Part II, 27.
[82] *Ibid*., Remark.

[83] *Ibid*., 27. See also, Makkreel, 1990, p.140; Kemal, 1986, pp.144-7.
[84] Kant, [1790], 1952, Part II, 27. It is important to point out that Kant sees this anthropomorphism as a cognitive construct that does not justify anthropomorphic representation of the Supreme Being. See, *ibid*., 28.
[85] *Ibid*., Remark.
[86] *Ibid*.
[87] To some extent this has been resolved by the theories of reciprocal altruism, first proposed by Charles Darwin in *The Descent of Man*, as a means of ensuring survival of the human species. See also, Cronin, 1993, pp.325-379; Ridley, M., *The Origin of Virtue*, Harmondsworth, 1997, pp.51-84.
[88] Kant, [1790], 1952, Part II, Remark.
[89] *Ibid*. See also, Zammito, 1992, pp.105-105 & pp.226-227. There is a problem with Kant's argument in that he does not really explain an origin for such conception of morality other than from a "supersensible source". See, Kant, [1790], 1952, Part II, 30.
[90] Kant, [1790], 1952, Part II, Remark.
[91] *Ibid*., Part I, 23. Further, *ibid*., Introduction, IX, 196, 15-14. See also, Zammito, 1992, pp.152-153 & p.222; Cohen, in Cohen & Guyer, 1982, pp.233-235.

giving attention to the 'thing-in-itself'[92]; an *a priori* cognition that deals with the natural world.[93] Thus, the physical teleology[94] provides an analogy that explains the human relationship with natural world that allows the incorporation of emotions and, therefore, morality, which is evident in the freeing power of imagination, where: "Both the admiration for beauty and the emotion excited by profuse variety of ends of nature, which a reflective mind is able to feel prior to any clear representation of an intelligent author of the world, have something about them akin to *religious* feeling."[95] This critique of aesthetic judgement had considerable influence on the Romantics and the development of the 'Pathetic Fallacy'.

The Romantic Cogntition
Perhaps the most impressive example of a romantic and scientific archaeology of the mind that includes the imagination is Erasmus Darwin, the grandfather of Charles Darwin. Erasmus had proclaimed the supremacy of the mediating power of imagination in the advertisement to his poem, *The Botanic Garden*, published in 1791, stating that his enterprise was to, "inlist the Imagination under the banner of science; and to lead her votaries from the looser analogies which dress out the imagery of poetry, to the stricter ones which form the ratiocination of philosophy."[96]

In the 'Preface' to his later poem, *The Temple of Nature*, (published posthumously in 1803), Erasmus states that, "its aim is simply to amuse by bringing distinctly to the imagination the beautiful and sublime images of operations of Nature in the order, as the Author believes, in which the progressive course of time presented them."[97] Thus, Erasmus recognizes the power of imagination as a form of thinking,[98] giving it a crucial role in his evolutionary account of humankind that begins with the origin of microscopic life from the primeval soup:

Organic life beneath the shoreless waves
Was born and nurs'd in Ocean's pearly caves;
First forms minute, unseen by spheric glass,
Move on the mud, or pierce the watery mass;
These, as successive generations bloom,
New powers acquire, and larger limbs assume;
Whence countless groups of vegetation spring,
And breathing realms of fin, and feet, and wing.[99]

to that of the complex and upright human being:

Imperious man, who rules the bestial crowd,
Of language, reason, and reflection proud,
With brow erect who scorns this earthly sod,
And styles himself the image of his God;
Arose from rudiments of form and sense,
An embryon point, or microscopic ens![100]

The Temple of Nature prioritizes the power of the imagination[101] and links its power quite clearly with curiosity[102] and reason. However, although he recognises the power of imagination and its role in facilitating comparison, he does not see it as cognition. Instead, he names this 'unknown' operation of the mind 'Intuitive Analogy'. Intuitive, in this case, implies an inborn and essential mental function that, as will become apparent, is, for Erasmus, a faculty critical for survival and responsible for aesthetic pleasure, which enables the comparison of an "incongruous idea with our previous knowledge of nature and reject it"[103]; the familiar and the unfamiliar.

He holds that it is curiosity and the desire for "the pleasure of novelty" that "is produced by the exertion of our voluntary power in comparing uncommon objects with those that are more usually exhibited[104]...leads to explore the works of nature" and motivates "those who travel to foreign regions."[105] Further, novelty and variation, which stimulate curiosity, are deemed essential for aesthetic pleasure: "There is nevertheless, an excess of the repetition of the same or similar ideas, which ceases to please, and must therefore be excluded from compositions of Taste in painted landscapes, or in ornamented gardens; which is then called formality, monotony, or insipidity."[106]

Erasmus asks why it is that novelty - or the unfamiliar - is essential for such aesthetic pleasure, and in his answer acknowledges a certain biological imperative with what he calls the "excitation of ideas"[107]: "all our new train of ideas, whether those of imagination or perception; which by comparing them with our former experience preserves the consistency of the former, by rejecting such as are incongruous; and adds the credibility of the latter, by their analogy to objects of our previous knowledge: and this exertion is attended with pleasurable sensation."[108] Further, Erasmus, in many ways, could be considered a

---

[92] Kant, [1790], 1952, Part I, Remark 2. See also, *ibid.*, Introduction, IX, 196, 15-14.
[93] Kant, [1790], 1952, Part I, Introduction, V. See also, Henrich, D., "Beauty and Freedom", in Cohen & Guyer, 1982 pp.237-257 & p.243.
[94] Kant, [1790], 1952, Part II, *passim*, but see, esp., 26 & General Remark on Teleology.
[95] Kant, [1790], 1952, Part II, General Remark on Teleology, 482, fn.1. See also, Banham, 2000, pp.189-190. See also, Crawford, D. W., "Kant's Theory of Creative Imagination", in Cohen & Guyer, 1982 pp.151-178 & p.178.
[96] Cited in , McNeil, M., "The Scientific Muse: The Poetry of Erasmus Darwin", in ed., Jordanova, L., *Languages of Nature. Critical Essays on Science and Literature*, London, 1986, pp.164-203, p.165.
[97] Darwin, E., *The Temple of Nature*, [1803], A Scholar Press Facsimile, London, 1973, Preface.
[98] McNeil, in Jordanova, 1986, pp.183-185.
[99] Darwin, E., [1803], 1973, Canto I.

[100] Darwin, E., [1803], 1973, Canto I. See also, *ibid.*, 'Additional Notes', p.38. Here, in the last two passages, his hypothesis on the development of different species is extremely close to the Darwinian theory of evolution. Erasmus includes in his theory, reproduction and adaptation by chance in relation to the environment, where: "with frequent additional improvements; which the preceding parent might in some measure have acquired by his habits of life or accidental situation."
[101] Darwin, E., [1803], 1973, Canto II.
[102] Darwin, E., [1803], 1973, 'Additional Notes', pp.81-84.
[103] Darwin, E., [1803], 1973, p.82. See also, McNeil, in Jordanova, 1986, pp.189-190.
[104] Darwin, E., [1803], 1973, 'Additional Notes', p.83.
[105] *Ibid.*, p.81.
[106] *Ibid.*, p.86.
[107] *Ibid.*, p.86.
[108] *Ibid.*, p.86.

precursor of neuroscientific theories, particularly that of neuroscientist Antonio Damasio who argues that feelings and emotions are a body and brain survival function.[109] In describing the effect of novel ideas he writes that they, "affect us with surprise, or incongruity, or novelty, are attended with painful or pleasurable sensation; which we mentioned before as intermixing with all catenations of animal actions, and contributing to strengthen their perpetual and energetic production; and also exciting in some degree the power of volition, which also intermixes with the links of the chain of animal actions and contributes to produce it."[110] For Erasmus, curiosity, the desire for novelty and imagination ('Intuitive Analogy') are all interlinked, a sort of 'Trinity' of cognition. Further, that these are based in the working and survival functions of the body and brain, an 'excitation' of volition, which is intermixed with the "catenations of all animal actions". These body and brain operations underpin and activate aesthetic pleasure and in discussing landscape, the 'Picturesque' and the 'Romantic', he concludes if the "combination of novelty and repetition exists on a larger scale with more projecting rocks, and deeper dells, and perhaps with a somewhat greater novelty than repetition, the landscape assumes the name of ROMANTIC; and if some of these forms or combinations are much above the usual magnitude of similar objects, the more interesting sentiment of SUBLIMITY becomes mixed with the pleasure of the romantic."[111]

Erasmus, here, seems to suggest that the highest accolade that we can make of art - that it is Sublime - is facilitated by the necessity of the mind to be aware of, and to consider, the unfamiliar. This is a mental operation involving what Erasmus names the 'Intuitive Faculty', but is, in fact, quite straightforwardly, the power of imagination to manipulate mental imagery for comparison, where:

> The impatient Senses, goaded to contract,
> Forge new ideas, changing as they act;
> And in long streams dissever'd, or concrete
> In countless tribes, the fleeting forms repeat.
> Which rise excited in Volition's trains,
> Or link the sparkling ring of Fancy's chains.[112]

Erasmus' essential curiosity of the mind and scientific approach to creativity owes much to the Natural Scientists, who examined and classified the natural world in intricate detail. Carolus Linnaeus, *Systema Naturae* (1735), Buffon, *Histoire Naturelle* (1749-1804), who expounded a gradation of forms with humans at the top of 'The Great Chain of Being',[113] Jean Baptiste Lamarck, *Philosophie*

Zoologique (1809), who was the first to person to employ the term 'biology' and explored how *living* organisms interacted with their environment[114] and George Cuvier, *Leçons d'Anatomie Comparée*. These naturalists were compelled in their endeavours by immense curiosity to understand the workings Nature[115] and, while, in many respects, influenced by the French Enlightenment that had perceived nature as a machine,[116] their investigations and theories spawned the anti-mechanistic Natural Philosophy, which embraced the notion of Nature as a unitary organism. The terminology of the natural scientists was adopted by philosophy and both disciplines at this time are almost inseparable, demonstrating a two-way process of influence.[117] This interdisciplinary intellectual environment had an immense influence on eighteenth-and nineteenth-century ideas on creativity and aesthetics.

Man was considered to be part of this magnificent organism of Nature, reflecting its power for self-creation and expression. Natural Philosophers, like the Naturalists, sought to discover a unifying order in the world, but significantly, considered imagination as important for cognition, in conjunction with sense and reason.[118] Imagination was also endowed with an elevated status, in that it was perceived to be essential for an empathetic understanding that could reveal truth.[119] Inherent within this philosophy was the concept of *Entwicklung*[120] - development - where 'evolution' meant the unfolding[121] of the inherent 'design' in Nature. Goethe, for example, was concerned to find the archetypes of natural phenomena, but such discovery could only be made by considering man as part of nature, part of the realm of science and natural studies, a process that is facilitated by imagination, which enables "a large overview of the living world and its laws."[122] Hegel described as a process of 'becoming', the

---

Boorstin, 1984, pp.446-459; Steadman, P., *The evolution of designs. Biological analogy in architecture and the applied arts*, Cambridge, 1979, pp.19-26. For the theory of 'The Great Chain of Being', see, Lovejoy, A. O., *The Great Chain of Being. A Study in the History of an Idea*, Cambridge, MA., 1970. For the eighteenth century biology, see, *ibid.*, pp.227-41; Haber, F. C., "Fossils and Early Cosmology", in Glass, B., Owesi, T., & Strauss Jr, W. L., eds., Forerunners of Darwin: 1745-1859, Baltimore, 1959, pp.3-48 & pp.37-43; Lovejoy, A. O., "Buffon and the Problem of Species", in Glass, *et al.*, 1959, pp.84-113 & pp.88-90.

[114] Oldroyd, 1980, pp.29-37.

[115] For an excellent appraisal, see, Glass, B., "Hereditary and Variation in the Eighteenth Century Concept of the Species", Glass, *et al.*, 1959, pp.144-72.

[116] Oldroyd, 1980, pp.349-350; Tarnas, R., *The Passion of the Western Mind*, London, 1996, pp.267-271 & pp.275-290; Shand, J, *Philosophy and Philosophers*, Harmondsworth, 1994, pp.157-158; McNeil, in Jordanova, 1986, pp.166-173 & pp.200-202.

[117] Oldroyd, 1980, pp.49-58, pp.96-97 & pp.345-350; Tarnas, 1996, pp.366-387; Shand, 1994, pp.176-202; Brann, 1991, pp.99-107 & pp.519-520; Abrams, 1971, pp.159-167 & p.185-187; Desmond & Moore, 1982, p.43.

[118] McNeil, in Jordanova, 1986, pp.183-185; Engell, 1981, pp.3-8, p.226 & p.263.

[119] Engell, 1981, p.258

[120] See, Oldroyd, 1980, pp.49-52.

[121] Oldroyd, 1980, pp.50-52. See also, Hofstadter & Kuhns, 1976, p.345 & pp.378-379.

[122] Cited in, Engell, 1981, p.283, from a conversation between Goethe and Eckerman on January 27, 1830. Source not given. On Goethe's archetypal

---

[109] See, Damasio, A.R., *Descartes' Error. Emotion, Reason and the Human Brain*, London, 1996..

[110] Darwin, E., [1803], 1973, 'Additional Notes', p.32.

[111] *Ibid.*, p.87.

[112] Darwin, E., [1803], 1973, Canto III.

[113] Oldroyd, 1980, p.29 from Lamarck de, J. B. P. A. de Monet, *Philosophie Zoologique, ou Exposition des Considérations Relatives à l'Histoire Naturelle des Animaux*, 2 vols., Paris, 1809, Preface. See also,

way the human mind, intellect and spirit evolve towards self-knowledge and the unity of the Absolute Idea (the telic agent transcending the dualism of the subject and object that allows for the understanding of reality).[123] Significantly, like Kant and Erasmus Darwin, Hegel's philosophy of the 'Absolute' is pivoted on the notion of polarity and the awareness of difference.[124] This principle involves a consciousness of the separation of one thing from another. Then, the next stage, the unity of knowledge, self-revelation and truth can be achieved, and this is facilitated by images, what he called the "gallery of pictures"[125] that are the basis for conceptualization and Absolute Being.[126] This unity, *via* polarity, is achieved by imaging - a form of visual thinking, where consciousness is "so affirmed that its being has the character of something presented, and this union of being and thinking is expressed as what is in fact, viz. - imagining (Vorstellen)."[127]

Schelling, too, designates imagination, in *Transcendental Idealism*, as enabling us "to think and couple together even what is contradictory",[128] thus facilitating ultimate knowledge - the 'Absolute' (or God)[129]: "In the world made concretely manifest, there is from the inner being of the Absolute, which itself is the eternal forming-into-one [*In-Eins-Bildung*] of the universal and particular, an emanation in reason and imagination, both of which are one and the same",[130] which is the basis for all Art and Beauty[131]: "It is the poetic gift, which in its primary potentiality constitutes the primordial intuition, and conversely, what we speak of as the poetic gift is merely productive intuition, reiterated to its highest power. It is the one and the same capacity that is active in both, the only one whereby we are able to think and couple together even what is contradictory - and its name is imagination."[132]

Imagination, for these philosophers, was the faculty that facilitated comprehension of the unity of Man with the Natural world that includes a scientific *systema naturae*.[133] The imagination, in having the power to unfold, to be a self-creating mechanism, reflected the biological system of the Natural World; the macro-and microcosm[134]:

> As the sun stands freely in the heavens, joining and uniting all in the power of its clear light, so the soul of eternal nature stands in the interlinkage [of being] itself as the unity and, so to speak, as the divine imagination of that linkage, free and unbounded, as the origin of all feeling existence, which in visible nature pulsates as the heart. And, moving and circulating everything in nature's holy body, it gives rise to each impulse in the intimacy of creation. [135]

Natural Philosophy sought to employ imagination, through it's seemingly *infinite* powers, as a faculty for attaining spiritual enlightenment, considering the workings of Nature and Man as a reflection of the cosmic mind, where human imagination is, indeed, as omnipotent in its possibilities[136]; a way in which to unite the mystical and scientific and discover an immanent teleology.[137] Indeed, Schelling claims that the "productive and synthetic imagination is the organon and pinnacle of all philosophy"[138] in no way subservient to reason. Fichte, too, in *The Vocation of Man*, states that the imagination facilitates "the very possibility of our consciousness, our life and our being" and Reason.[139]

However, in many ways, what is an important development in these philosophical approaches during the eighteenth-and early nineteenth-century is the consideration of Man and the Natural World as coalescent[140] (as opposed to Man occupying a superior position in a hierarchical 'Great Chain of Being'), a view

forms and the role of imagination in their discovery; see also Tarnas, 1996, p.369, p.376 & p.378; Brann, 1991, p.99.

[123] Kaminsky, J., *Hegel on Art*, New York, 1970, pp.19-23 & pp.44-47; Hegel, G. W. F., *The Phenomenology of Mind*, [1807], trans., Baille, J. B., London & New York, 1971, Translator's Introduction, pp.26-29 & pp.38-39; Preface, p.96; Tarnas, 1996, pp.380-381; Shand, 1994, pp.178-190.

[124] Hegel, [1807], 1971, p.149 ff. & p.206-213, pp.617-620 & *passim*. See also, Tarnas, 1996, p.379; Shand, 1994, pp.183-185.

[125] Hegel, [1807], 1971, p.335.

[126] *Ibid.*, pp.329-336 & pp.766-768. See also, Brann, 1991, pp.103-107.

[127] Hegel, [1807], 1971, pp.624-625. See also, *ibid.*, p.762, pp.765-767, pp.773-785 & ff.

[128] Schelling, F. W. J., *Transcendental Idealism*, [1800], trans., Heath, P., & Introduction by Vater, M., Virginia, 1978, Prt.VI, 3, p.230. See also, Warnock, M., *Imagination*, London, 1976, p.92.

[129] Schelling, [1800], 1978, Introduction, 4, p.13, Prt.IV, Corollaries, p.176. See also, Engell, 1981, p.305, pp.309-312, esp. p.312 & pp.316-318; Brann, 1991, 1991, p.703; Gelernter, M., *Sources of architectural form. A critical history of Western design theory*, Manchester & New York, 1995, pp.196-198.

[130] Cited in Engell, 1981, p.325 from Schelling, F. W. J., *Sämmtliche Werke*, ed., Schelling, K. F. A., 14 vols., Stuttgart & Ausberg, 1856-1861, V, p.361.

[131] Schelling, [1800], 1978, Introduction, 4, p.14, Prt.VI, 2, pp.225-8 & Prt.VI, 3, pp.229-233, esp., pp.230-232. See also, Engell, 1981, pp.301-302, pp.307-309, pp.319-320 & pp.325-327.

[132] Schelling, [1800], 1978, Prt.VI, 3, p.230.

[133] *Ibid.*, pp.175-177; Desmond & Moore, 1982, p.85, pp.96-97 & p.202; Engell, 1981, pp.332-335.

[134] See especially, Schelling, [1800], 1978, Prt.III, IV, pp.120-129, esp., pp.122-124. See also, Abrams, M. H., *Natural Supernaturalism. Tradition and Revolution in Romantic Literature*, New York & London, 1973, pp.67-68 & pp.296-297; Oldroyd, 1980, pp.52-53 & pp.310-311; Engell, 1981, pp.304-305 & pp.312-316.

[135] Cited in Engell, 1981, p.304 from Schelling, F. W. J., *Sämmtliche Werke*, ed., Schelling, K. F. A., 14 vols., Stuttgart & Ausberg, 1856-1861, VII, p.202. See also, Engell, 1981, pp.316-318.

[136] Hegel, G. W. F., *Philosophy of Fine Art*, trans., Bosanquet, B., London, 1886, Introduction, III, pp.55-57. See also, Kearney, 1988, pp.180-181; Abrams, 1971, p.22.

[137] Schelling and Hegel are prime examples: Schelling, [1800], 1978, Prt.V, pp.215-18; Hegel, [1807], 1971, p.295 ff. See also, Tarnas, 1996, pp.372-373 & pp.378-381; Shand, 1994, p.182; Abrams, 1973, pp.177-192.; Abrams, 1971, p.185-187.

[138] Cited in Kearney, 1988, pp.180-181; Abrams, 1971, p.178, from Schelling von, F., *Sämtliche Werke*, Stuttgart, 1885, III, pp.349 ff. See also, Schelling, [1800], 1978, Introduction, 4, pp.13-14. See further, Engell, 1981, pp.320-323.

[139] Cited in Kearney, 1988, p.178, from Fichte, J. G., *The Vocation of Man*, trans., Smith, W., Open Court, 1965, p.141. See also, Engell, 1981, pp.217-218 & pp.225-231. On the elevated status of imagination with regard to Reason, see, Kearney, 1988, pp.180-181.

[140] Abrams, 1971, p.52; McNeil, in Jordanova, 1986, pp.197-200.

to the extent of which leads to the development of the 'Pathetic Fallacy'. As Schelling stated that: "So long as I myself am identical with nature I understand what living nature is as well as I understand my own life...As soon, however, as I separate myself...from nature, nothing more is left to me but a dead object."[141]

The influence of this idea, a form of spiritual evolution, on the Romantic poets was enormous,[142] combining science, imagination and feeling.[143] Although it has been traditionally argued that the Romantics in their spiritual yearnings were anti-scientific,[144] what seems to have been overlooked is the evidence that demonstrates a significant influence on their writings, both of natural science in general and, in particular, of eighteenth-century ideas concerning the 'evolutionary' ideas behind biological and geological enquiry.[145]

A major example of such an influence in the Romantics was the idea of the struggle of primal man in terms of an evolutionary cognitive and spiritual journey - the *Weg*.[146] There is a pervading notion of the evolutionary model throughout these works,[147] for example, Schiller wrote in his essay of 1790, *Something Concerning the First Human Society, according to the Guidance of the Mosaic Records* that "Man was destined to learn to seek out, by means of his own reason, the condition of innocence which he now lost, and as a free, reasonable spirit, to return to that place whence he had started out as a plant and creature of instinct: from a paradise of ignorance and bondage he was to work up, even if it should be after a thousand years, to a paradise of knowledge and freedom; one in which he would obey the moral law of his heart just as he in the beginning had obeyed instinct, and as plants and animals still obey it."[148]

Although the cognitive excavations of the imagination by the Natural Philosophers and the Romantics was by no means the sophisticated archaeology of Kant's *Critique of*

Pure Reason,[149] his influence is clear in the appropriation of the superior 'productive' imagination[150] in contrast to 'fancy'.[151] Coleridge, in his famous passage from the *Biographia Literaria*, confirms the essentiality and unifying power of the productive divine-like imagination; the power of visual thinking:

> The IMAGINATION then, I consider either as primary, or secondary. The primary imagination I hold to be the living Power and Prime agent of all human Perception, and as a repetition in the finite mind of the eternal act of creation in the infinite I AM. The secondary Imagination I consider to be an echo of the former, coexisting with the conscious will, yet still as identical with the primary in the *kind* of its agency, and differing only in *degree* and in the *mode* of its operation. It dissolves, diffuses, dissipates, in order to recreate; or where this process is rendered impossible, yet still at all events it struggles to idealize and unify. It is essentially vital, even as all objects (*as* objects) are essentially fixed and dead.[152]

Wordsworth, too, describes quite clearly, the imagination as a cognitive power equal to that of God:

> That through the growing faculties of sense
> Doth like an agent of the one great Mind
> Create, Creator and receiver both,
> Working but in alliance with the works
> Which it beholds.[153]

Natural Philosophy and its exploration of the workings of the mind and the role of imagination achieved a profound

---

[141] Cited in Abrams, 1973, p.181 from Schelling von, F., *Ideen zu einer Philosophie de Natur*, (1797), *Sämtliche Werke*, Stuttgart & Ausburg, 1858, Pt.I, Vol. II, pp.57-8. See also, Abrams, 1973, p.238-242; Engell, 1981, pp.301-303 & pp.314-316.

[142] Abrams, 1973, pp.192-307; Zammito, 1992, p.14.

[143] Engell, 1981, pp.3-10 & p.127.

[144] Tarnas, 1996, pp.366-387; Shand, 1994, pp.366-378. Abrams, recognises a 'scientific' approach in the Romantics, but does not directly state an influence from natural science, see, Abrams, 1973, pp.170-171; Abrams, 1971, p.101. For an account of the differing opinions regarding the notion of truth and the nature of imagination in terms of poetry versus science, see, Abrams, 1971, pp.298-335; McNeil, in Jordanova, 1986, pp.192-193.

[145] See, Abrams, 1971, p.12, p.38, p.117, p.124 & pp.168-177; Abrams, 1973, p.270. See also, Bowra, M., *The Romantic Imagination*, Oxford, 1988, pp.22-24.

[146] There is no need to repeat here what has been elucidated already by Abrams. See, Abrams, 1973, p.192, p.213, p.215, p.218, pp.228-235 & *passim*.

[147] Abrams, 1973, *passim*, especially, pp.153-163, pp.181-190, pp.206-208, p.219 & p.265-269. On applying an evolutionary model to the origin and development of poetry, see, Abrams, 1971, pp.70-84.

[148] Cited in Abrams, 1973, p.207, from Schiller von, F., *Sämtliche Werke*, ed., Güntter & Witowski, G., (20 Vols.; Leipzig, n.d.), XVI, pp.142-144. See further, Abrams, 1973, pp.206-217; Engell, 1981, p.223

[149] For agreement with this opinion, see, Kearney, 1988, pp.179-180; Abrams, 1971, p.58.

[150] For example, Schelling and Coleridge: Schelling, [1800], 1978, *passim*; Coleridge, [1817], 1907, Introduction, pp.xxx-xxxiv, pp.xli-xlv, p.l, pp.lvii-lix & *passim*; I, IX, pp.99-101. See also, Brann, 1991, p.505; Coburn, K., Foreword, in Richards, 1952, pp.15-17. In his seminal work, Abrams describes, in the Preface, the mind as "a radiant projector which makes a contribution to the objects its perceives." He later qualifies that this is made possible by Imagination. Therefore, Imagination is quite clearly seen to be by the Romantics as a cognitive faculty. See Abrams, 1971, Preface & p.56. See also, Engell, 1981, p.118 & pp.138-139.

[151] On the distinction between 'fancy' and imagination, see, Hill, J. S., ed., *Imagination in Coleridge*, London & Basingstoke, 1978, pp.22-33 & *passim*. There was some debate regarding the difference between 'fancy' and 'imagination' among the Romantics, particularly between Wordsworth and Coleridge. See, Coleridge, [1817], 1907, Introduction, pp.xxxi-xxxiv, pp.xliv-xlv, pp.xlix-l, pp.liii-liv, pp.lxvi-lxviii & *passim*; I, IV, 22, pp.60-65, XII, 3-26, p.194 & XIII, 5-25, p.202; Richards, 1952, pp.30-31, pp.57-59 & pp.72-99. However, the predominant approach was the elevation of the 'productive' imagination. On this debate see, Abrams, 1971, pp.177-183. On hostility to imagination as fancy, perceived as a 'deceiver' in this period, see, Brann, 1991, pp.690-692. For a brilliant exposition of Coleridge's 'Fancy and Imagination', see Barfield, O., *What Coleridge Thought*, London, 1972, pp.69-91. For a general survey of 'fancy and imagination', see, Engell, 1981, pp.172-183 & pp.229-31.

[152] Coleridge, [1817], 1907, I, XIII, p.202. See also, Warnock, 1976, pp.90-92; Brann, 1991, pp.507-509. Further, see, Richards, 1952, pp.82-94.

[153] Wordsworth, W., *The Prelude*, 1805, II, 256. See also, Engell, 1981, pp.274-276.

effect on the Romantics.[154] Coleridge in his account of literary invention,[155] gives to the mechanism a pivotal role, where, "the rules of the IMAGINATION are themselves the very power of growth and production."[156] Also of importance was the notion of polarity, as emphasized by the Natural Philosophers. Coleridge, for example, regarded the creation of art and originality as only achieved through polarity and the synthesizing nature of imagination: "The poet...diffuses a tone and spirit of unity that blends, and (as it were) *fuses*, each into each, by that synthetic and magical power, to which we have exclusively appropriated the name of imagination. This power...reveals itself in the balance or reconciliation of opposite or discordant qualities.[157]

Fichte, too, recognizes the importance of the imagination for the apperception of polarity and the subsequent cognitive realization of synthesizing creation: "Imagination is the power of spacing those oppositions that can be neither dissolved not eliminated from theoretical knowledge. Imagination is the spacing of truth."[158] The productive imagination is considered supreme in its power for synthesis; of images, emotions and ideas.

Kant's *Critique of Judgement* (1790) was also highly influential on this approach to the role of imagination.[159] As discussed, Kant afforded a greater *freedom* to the imagination: describing the "free play of imagination" as one that it is not constrained by external reference. For the Romantics, this aspect of imagination supported vision as the grandest of the senses[160] that could be embraced by the very character of poetry, which allows for the evocation of 'freer' images and visual interpretation as opposed to prose, which exercises a more precise control over the visual and imaginative response to the language, which is constrained by a linear sequence of words.[161] Thus, Kant's

'freer' imagination, as described by his image of 'Jupiter's eagle', becomes the champion of human freedom and of artistic expression in direct opposition to Plato's warning against the imagination.[162] Hegel affirms the exalted position of the freeing powers of imagination in *The Philosophy of Fine Art*, where "the source of artistic creations is the free activity of fancy, which in her imagination is more free than nature's self."[163]

For Kant, this 'free' form of imagination is confined to the world of art but, within that confine, imagination is the stepping stone to the infinite and the sublime. Kant's emphasis on the importance of feelings and emotions, as excited by imagination, as the basis for an 'Aesthetic Judgement'[164] and, his eventual analogy of such judgement with morality[165] influenced not only Natural Philosophy but also the Romantic's views[166] concerning the nature of creativity and the spiritual journey.[167] Inherent in this philosophy is a pursuit of mental freedom which leads toward truth and the Divine, a pursuit that is made possible by the freeing self-creating god-like redemptive power of imagination.[168] Wordsworth, in *The Prelude*, echoes this

---

[154] There is no need to repeat here what Abrams had already lucidly demonstrated. See, Abrams, 1971, pp.159-262. See also, Kearney, 1988, pp.181-185; Engell, 1981, pp.vii-viii, p.3 & *passim*.

[155] For example, see, Coleridge, [1817], 1907, I, p.167, II, XV, pp.16-18 & XVII, p.65. See also, Richards, 1952, p.12 , pp.52-53& p.119; Abrams, 1971, pp.167-183; Barfield, 1972, pp.44-45, pp.60-62, pp.67-68, pp.131-143 & *passim*. Coleridge explored biological science and the notion of evolution more extensively in an essay published posthumously in 1848: *Hints Towards a More Comprehensive Theory of Life*. On this work, see, Barfield, 1972, pp.45-68.

[156] Coleridge, [1817], 1907, II, p.65.

[157] *Ibid.*, XIV, p.12. Further, on polarity, see, Coleridge, *ibid.*, I, XIII, p.196 &, XIII, p.197. See also, Barfield, 1972, pp.30-40; Warnock, 1976, pp.93-94; Engell, 1981, p.223.

[158] Cited in Sallis, J., *Spacings-of Reason and Imagination in Texts of Kant, Fichte, Hegel*, Chicago, 1987, p.64. See also, Engell, 1981, pp.223-231.

[159] On this influence, see, Kearney, 1988, pp.177-181; Abrams, 1971, p.27.

[160] Coleridge writes that, "Mr Wordsworth, if ever a man did, most assuredly does possess, 'The Vision and the Faculty Divine'"; Coleridge, [1817], 1907, II, XVIII, p.45. See further, Bowra, 1988, pp.1-3; Brann, 1991, pp.477-480.

[161] It is important to consider that the affect of this philosophy of the imagination on the writings and poetry of the Romantics, regarding the exalted state of imagination and its ability for reaching the sublime, would have a monumental influence on prose, producing radical and more poetic and free approaches to prose that can be identified in the works of

Proust and Joyce. On Proust and Joyce, see, Brann, 1991, pp.483-486 & pp.742-747. On the problematic nature of verbal vision, see, Brann, 1991, pp.465-482. This debate is, of course, linked to the famous concept of Horace's 'Ut Pictura Poesis'. See, Horace, *Ars Poetica*; Leonardo, *Paragone*; Lee, R. W., "Ut Pictura Poesis: The Humanistic Theory of Painting", in *The Art Bulletin*, 22, 1940, pp.197-269; Brann, 1991, pp.474-482.

[162] Kearney, 1988, pp.174-177; Brann, 1991, pp.99-107 & pp.97-99. For Kant's 'Jupiter's eagle', see, Kant, [1790], 1952, I, 49 and above.

[163] Hegel, 1886, Introduction, I, p.9.

[164] Kant, [1790], 1952, Part I, I.

[165] Kant, [1790], Part I, Remark 2; 59 & Appendix; Part II, *passim*. See also, Brann, 1991, pp.97-98. It is interesting to note that, as early as 1744, Akenside had stated that, "There are certain powers in human nature which seem to hold a middle place between the organs of bodily sense, and the faculties of moral perception: they have been called by a very general name, the Powers of Imagination." Cited in, McNeil, in Jordanova, 1986, p.184 from Akenside, M., *The Pleasures of Imagination. A Poem in Three Books*, London, 1744, p.5. See also, Engell, 1981, pp.301-305.

[166] On imagination and feelings for poetry, see, Abrams, 1971, p.22-24.

[167] Kearney, 1988, pp.178-179 & pp.181-185; Brann, 1991, p.500; Zammito, 1992, pp13-14 & pp.342-346. The influence of Kant can be observed throughout Hegel's *Philosophy of Fine Art*, particularly concerning human cognition and finality in nature, bodily senses, emotions and feelings, imagination, the supersensible, freedom and morality. However, it must be stated that Hegel concentrated on the ability of art to instruct. For influence of Kant, see, Hegel, G. W. F., *Philosophy of Fine Art*, trans., Bosanquet, B., London, 1886, Introduction, esp., I, pp.2-4, pp.12-13; III, p.60, pp.66-67, pp.73-74, p.96, pp.100-101 & pp.107-116; Schelling, [1800], 1978, Prt. I, 2, p.31 & *passim*.

[168] This is especially apparent in the writings of William Blake, who assigns to the imagination (*Urthona*) a redemptive faculty through which the highest arts can be attained and nature, man and god are unified by the creative power of imagination. See, Abrams, 1973, pp.120-121, pp.186-187, pp.256-264 & p.340; Engell, 1981, pp.244-256 & pp.312-313; Bowra, 1988, pp.3-4, p.8, pp.13-14, & p.32-36; Brann, 1991, pp.509-510; McNeil, in Jordanova, 1986, pp.191-193. For discussion of imagination as the faculty that facilitates divine revelation and salvation, see, Tuveson, E. L., *The Imagination as a Means of Grace: Locke and the Aesthetics of Romanticism*, Berkeley, 1960; Engell, 1981, pp.220-223 & pp.259-260. Engell sums the situation up thus: "These views [on imagination] show why, for many Romantics, salvation and imagination become virtual synonyms." Engell, 1981, p.222. See also, Kearney, 1988, pp.178-179 & pp.184-186.

quality of the Imagination, designating it as the highest form of Reason:

> In that breach
> Through which the homeless voice of waters rose,
> That dark deep thoroughfare had Nature lodg'd
> The Soul, the Imagination of the whole.
> This spiritual Love acts not nor can exist
> Without Imagination, which in truth,
> Is but another name for absolute strength
> And clearest insight, amplitude of mind
> And Reason in her most exalted mood.[169]

For Wordsworth, imagination is the creative force that motivates all actuation of being, and which exemplifies the recurrent theme in the Romantics of the unification of Man with Nature *via* the God-like creative imagination.[170] Indeed, for Shelley, imagination is not only served by reason but represents that highest animating quality - the spirit:

> Reason is the enumeration of quantities already known; imagination is the perception of the value of those quantities both separately and as a whole. Reason respects the differences, and imagination the similitudes of things. Reason is to imagination as the instrument to the agent, as the body to the spirit, as the shadow to the substance.[171]

The importance of emotions and feelings being stimulated in order to facilitate a moral enlightenment is not to be underestimated[172] and this is made possible, "through the medium of the vision and the imaginative idea."[173] Coleridge states that:

> Poetry…avails itself of the forms of nature to recall, to express, and to modify the thoughts and feelings of the mind…Now so to place these images [of nature] totalized, and fitted to the limits of the human mind, as to elicit from, and to superinduce upon, the forms themselves the moral reflexions to which they approximate, to make the external internal, the internal external, to make nature thought, and thought nature, - this is the mystery of genius in the Fine Arts.[174]

Indeed, Shelley, in his *A Defence of Poetry*, declared that, "Poetry, in a general sense, may be defined as the 'experience of the imagination'"[175] and that 'experience', according to Coleridge, is an imagination that works in conjunction with the body;[176] "that reconciling and mediatory power, which incorporating the Reason in Images of the Sense, and organizing (as it were) the flux of the Senses by the permanence and self-circling energies of the Reason, gives birth to a system of symbols, harmonious in themselves, and consubstantial with the truths, of which they are the *conductors*."[177] In other words, it is imagination that facilitates human cognition of the world.

Conclusion

The Romantics endeavoured to understand the workings of the human mind and prioritized the imagination. Although they did not have the benefit of the research that the brain sciences provide us today, nevertheless they attempted a form of cognitive archaeology in order to understand the elusive quality of human creativity. They also investigated the operation of the imagination much more fully in relation to the senses and the body. Hegel's statement in *The Phenomenology of Mind* reflects this 'holistic' view. He states that "the self-reflected being of mind in the brain itself is merely a middle term between its pure essential nature and its bodily articulation, an intermediate link, which consequently must partake of the nature of both, and thus in respect of the latter must also again have it in actual articulation."[178] This belief he also applied to creativity. In his *Philosophy of Art*, he employed a saying of Terrence[179] for his argument about what constitutes art: "Homo sum: humani nihil a me alienum puto".[180] Hegel's purpose in using Terrence's words was to imply that *everything* that is to do with the human being is reflected in art and, the imagination is essential for "artistic semblance rests on the fact that all reality must, for man, pass though the medium of the vision and imaginative idea; and it is only after such a passage that it penetrates the emotional life and will."[181]

Few writers, even now, are prepared to consider such an approach concerning the cognitive function of imagination. One *possible* exception is S.M. Kosslyn, who, in *Ghosts in*

---

[169] Wordsworth, W., *The Prelude*, 1805, XVI, 190. For further discussion of Wordsworth's redemptive imagination see, Abrams, 1973, pp.117-122.
[170] Abrams, 1971, pp.64-69 & pp.103-104; Engell, 1981, pp.267-271 & pp.316-318; Bowra, 1988, pp.19-20, pp.82-83 & pp.101-102; Gelernter, 1995, pp.157-161.
[171] Shelley, P. B., "A Defence of Poetry", (1821) in *Shelley's Critical Prose*, ed., McElderry Jr, B. R., University of Nebraska, Lincoln, 1967, pp.3-37, p.4.
[172] Abrams, 1971, p.15, p.20, pp.54-55.
[173] Hegel, G. W. F., *The Philosophy of Fine Art*, in Hofstadter & Kuhns, 1976, pp.382-445, *Introduction*, III, 3, b, p.417. Again, I have used this translation in place of Bosanquet's.
[174] Coleridge, [1817], 1907, II, On Poesy or Art, p.254 & p.258. See also, Engell, 1981, pp.338-340.

[175] Shelley, P. B., "A Defence of Poetry", (1821) in *Shelley's Critical Prose*, ed., McElderry Jr, B. R., University of Nebraska, Lincoln, 1967, pp.3-37, p.4. See also, Engell, 1981, pp.256-264.
[176] Engell, 1981, p.343 & pp.348-350.
[177] Cited in Engell, 1981, p.338 from Coleridge, S. T., *Statesman's Manual*, ed., White, R. J., p.29.
[178] Hegel, [1807], 1971, pp.353-354. This passage is Hegel's alternative to phrenology, which he then goes on to 'debunk'. It is still a remarkable for its forward thinking, especially in the light of present-day Neuroscience. While I would in no way support phrenology it is interesting to note that skull casts of hominids do reveal developments in brain structure and therefore cognitive ability, such as that of 'Broca's Area' and its relationship to language.
[179] "I am a man; there's naught which touches man that is not my concern." Terrance, *Heautontimorumenos*, Act I, sc. I., 25.
[180] Hegel, 1886, Introduction, III, p.87.
[181] I have used a different translation to that of Bosanquet. See, Hegel, G. W. F., *The Philosophy of Fine Art*, in Hofstadter & Kuhns, 1976, pp.382-445, *Introduction*, III, 3, b, p.417.

the Mind's Machine, includes a chapter entitled 'Visual Thinking', demonstrating quite clearly how mental imagery facilitates symbolic association and abstract thinking.[182] However, nowhere is the term 'imagination' employed. One other theorist, J.C. Eccles, does actually *infer* a close connection between imagination and cognition in his use of the phrase "imaginal thinking" but, this is not explicit.[183] Problematically, almost all of the scientific research concerning mental imagery and the imagination is explored in relation to language operations[184] and, this is clearly of limited use as a basis for reflecting on the role of the *visual* process of cognition in human thinking. However, the cognitive neuroscientist, S.M. Kosslyn states that, "One of the reasons I find imagery an exciting topic is that it is likely to be one of the higher cognitive functions that will be firmly rooted in the brain."[185] Importantly, Leda Cosmides and John Tooby have been funded by the Guggenheim specifically to research the neuroscience of imagination. They propose that, "We think that the human mind is permeated by an additional layer of adaptations that were selected to involve humans in aesthetic experiences and imagined worlds."[186]

There is still a pressing need for a cognitive archaeology of the imagination in order to fully understand its function in the human brain and, why human beings are especially creative. The theorists of the Romantic period, a title which belies their scientific approach, did so, and it is now possible to excavate their ideas with the sophisticated archaeology of the brain sciences. Consequently, it may then be possible to revisit Kant's cognitive theory that the imagination is not a *construct* but the *basis* of the mind, which will lead to a greater understanding of the wonder of humanity; imagination, creativity and art.

---

[182] Kosslyn, S. M., *Ghosts in the Mind's Machine. Creating and Using Images in the Brain*, New York & London, 1983, pp.177-193.

[183] Eccles, 1991, p.138.

[184] For a brief précis, see, Kosslyn, S. M., *Image and Brain*, Cambridge MA, 1994, pp.2-4. One brief example of the language orientation of image perception research is as follows. Subjects were asked to identify unfamiliar shapes, but with each picture was presented a word, which half of the time identified the picture and the other half did not. PET scan imaging was used. See, Kosslyn, 1994, pp.252-253 & pp.264-266. Eccles also identifies this problem: Eccles, J. C., *Evolution of the Brain. Creation of the Self*, London & New York, 1991, p.231. See also, Brann, E. T. H., *The World of the Imagination. Sum and Substance*, Lanham, Maryland, 1991, pp.486-7.

[185] Kosslyn, 1994, p.1.

[186] Tooby, J., & Cosmides, L., "Does beauty build adapted minds? Toward and evolutionary theory of aesthetics, fiction and the arts". To be published in *SubStance*, special issue on Imagination and the Adapted Mind, ed., Abbott Porter. Tooby & Cosmides kindly sent me a copy of the draft of this paper.

Time travel and archaeology:
Two stories of reanimation by Mary Shelley

Sarah Shaw

It is a curious feeling giving a paper at a conference on a subject in which one is profoundly unqualified. I have to state here that on those grounds I am definitely an outsider, but one who admires deeply the whole archaeological process: the one time I worked on an extended dig I was really impressed by the careful preparation, discipline and sheer physicality involved in the whole exercise of rummaging and trowelling in the soil for remnants of the past.

This image came to my mind when asked to do this paper, for excavations occur constantly in the literary world too. Sometimes an ancient myth or story type seems to resonate with the literary sensibility of a particular time, and we find endless reworkings and recreations around a theme which embodies contemporary preoccupations and fears. Authors and poets have freedoms the archaeologist does not and may dig around and borrow as they please: but if a theme is to have any life it needs to be refashioned and pushed into a new a shape and literary form. In the early nineteenth century the myth of Prometheus, the figure who steals fire from the gods, provided a precise description of the lonely search that characterised the Romantic mind and in the poetry, drama and fiction of some of the major writers of the period he is examined and remoulded in a modern way as a warning to the poetic and scientific impulse where man, though "part divine" is acting as a "troubled stream from a pure source."[1] The kind of story that I would like to examine is one which is less well known but also has a touch of the Promethean in its account of a transgression of the usual rules that govern our existence. This is the tale of a human body - either that of a corpse or a sleeper - that is literally revived or reawakens, to act in the present and to perceive the world through the lenses and physical perceptions of a time that has gone.[2] It exercised a particular fascination on the nineteenth-century literary imagination, and also represents a development of a story type of some antiquity. Such a figure can speak with a voice we are usually denied hearing: and like other romantic heroes he is in a position which can irreparably separate him from peers and usual human comforts. I propose to focus on two tales by Mary Shelley, which were unpublished in her lifetime and which are now largely ignored. These provide us with early experimentation with a motif which by the end of the century had become one of the most popular forms of literary "time travel" from one historical period to another.[3]

Those familiar with modern cinema will of course recognise the motif in other forms, which have now become so familiar we do not really question their origins at all. A dinosaur, or an embalmed mummy, or a historical personage, is reawakened or reconstituted and is confronted with the developments of the modern world. Indeed in the twentieth century the unpackaging of a past "body" has usually had menacing overtones: the past figure can be a sinister embodiment of fears about the powers of another age, as in all those Boris Karloff films, or a monstrous reawakening of the terrors of past, as in the film 'Jurassic Park' (1993), where dinosaurs are reconstructed: the combined forces of archaeology and science have often in their short history been regarded in the modern popular imagination as awesome and potentially malevolent in their effects.[4] Throughout the end of the twentieth century we have been endlessly preoccupied with recreating the past - and visiting the future - and all forms of time travel are now depicted in films, plays and novels. There is something about the collision of two ages that usually makes for creative storytelling, as the contradiction of two historical periods meeting often sparks the drama and humour that arises out of incongruity. It has to be said that banality often intrudes: in the film I saw last week Napoleon, Abraham Lincoln and Joan of Arc all end up in an American diner, dedicated converts to a life of radio music, eating hamburgers, and, in Joan of Arc's case, to the prospect of becoming an aerobics teacher.[5] We find some comedy in early stories of this type, but they express no such optimism in the beneficial effects of "progress". They do though share a comparable sense of the creative possibilities of bringing past and present together. For this reason I think they make an intriguing study: we see the impulses that generated new forms in this type of tale, and help to explain its longstanding appeal.

---

[1] Lord Byron, 'Prometheus', from *The Prisoner of Chillon and Other Poems* (1816), 11.48-9, See also Perey Bysshe Shelley, *Prometheus Unbound; A Lyrical Drama in Four Acts* (1820) and Mary Shelley, *Frankenstein; a Modern Prometheus* (1818).

[2] In one version of the story which featured in Roman mythology, Prometheus is said to have breathed life into humans as Prometheus Plasticator. For discussion of this see MK Joseph ed, *Frankenstein or the Modern Prometheus* (London, New York and Toronto 1969), vii-xv (edition used in references).

[3] They are collected in C.E.Robinson, *Mary Shelley: Collected Tales and Stories* (1976), referred to here as MSCT. See below for references for each tale.

[4] The revived mummy is now a stock folk villain and at the time of writing this paper up the film 'The Mummy Returns' (2001) is proving to be a box office hit. 'The Mummy' (1932), starring Boris Karloff, is the prototype, made in the wake of excitement about King Tutenkamun's tomb, which was soon followed by 'The Mummy's Hand' (1940), 'The Mummy's Tomb' (1942) and 'The Mummy's Ghost' (1944).

[5] In 'Bill and Ted's Excellent Adventure' (1988). Other time-travel stories proper are too numerous to mention, but have included H.G. Wells' *The Time Machine* (1895), Edith Nesbit's *The Story of the Amulet* (1906) and, at the end of the twentieth century, the long-lived television series Dr Who.

Legendary sleepers

Writers of the romantic period exploited heavily the themes of folklore amidst a general revival of scholarly and literary interest in fairytales, *volkssagen* and mediaeval legend, and shaped them to suit their own preoccupations and needs.[6] Such figures as the Wandering Jew, condemned to wander through eternity until the final day of judgement and the hapless imbiber of the *elixir vitae*, unable to throw off the curse of immortality, all represented further variations on the idea of the mortal who has trangressed some fundamental law of existence that unites him with his fellow men.[7] Some authors, such as G.Croly in *Salathiel, a Story of the Past, the Present and the Future* (1827) and the unknown writer of *Memoires du Juif Errant* (1777), make their lonely heroes observers of historical change, a factor which reinforces their popularity in fiction at a time when history and archaeology were undergoing significant advances.[8] In *St Leon; a Tale of the Sixteenth Century* (1799) Mary Shelley's own father, William Codwin, had already created such a hero, whose immortality enables him to watch the movement from one historical period to another, but always as an outsider, bereft of family and friends.[9] I think there can be few modern scholars in any research into human history who do not feel some affinity with such figures!

The idea that a person could be awakened from a long sleep and from apparent death is a motif of this kind, and has occurred in many cultures, and periods of history. Its most famous treatment is in the Bible in the assurance that the dead will rise at the second coming.[10] It is however primarily folktales which contribute to the development of this kind of tale in the nineteenth century.[11] The legend of Briar Rose, or the Beauty of Sleeping Wood, is found throughout central Europe, which involves an unnaturally long sleep that is said to occur on the basis of a spell or enchantment at the hands of a supernatural agency such as a fairy.[12] A comparable enchantment is the centuries long sleep which folktales attribute to King Arthur and his knights, who, it is said will awaken should the inhabitants of this land ever fall victim to outside attack: again some supernatural force is involved in effecting this. Variations of this tale have occurred throughout the British Isles, involving various ancient heroes who sleep beneath the country hidden in caves.[13] These warriors seem embodiments of some sort of protective properties of the land itself, which may be released to defend the inhabitants of this island should it ever fall under threat. The seven sleepers were said to be persecuted Christians whose sleep of three hundred years enabled them to escape persecution until Christianity had been accepted and they could practise their religion without fear - an equally effective means of describing a spirit that needs to lie dormant until the time and setting are sympathetic and ready to accept it.[14] In 1813 another form of story was recounted as a hoax enacted in a drama based on an Oriental tale: it relates the story of Nourjahad, a Persian who is cured of his wish for immortality when the sultan replaces the people of the court to convince him that he has slept for decades.[15]

It is these last two versions of the motif which were said by the author involved to be the inspiration for her reworkings of the theme.[16] As we shall see however her two short works show how she tailors an old story to suit the day's preoccupations with archaeological research, historical change and a sense that the present has in some way dislocated itself from the past, and may need to be reminded of the values and ideals which had animated the cultures of historical periods before its own.

'Valerius, the Reanimated Roman'

The first story was written early in 1819, during a stay in Rome.[17] It is a neglected oddity amongst Mary Shelley's work that is given only passing mention by Mary Shelley's

[6] This vast subject has been the subject of exhaustive research, most notably by Mario Praz. See A. Davidson trans., *The Romantic Agony* 1933, 23ff, 51ff and 187ff.

[7] Variations on the idea of the lonely immortal, the Wandering Jew, form an interesting counterpart to the tale of suspended sleep. This is also a motif of some antiquity. Roger of Wendover records in *Flores Historiarum* that a Greater Armenian archbishop, visiting England in 1228, claimed to have met Pontius Pilate's doorkeeper, Cartaphilus, condemned to stay on earth for taunting Christ as he carried the cross. See *New Encyclopedia Britannica*, 30 vols (1975) X, 536 and G.K. Anderson, 'The Neo-Classical Chronicle of the Wandering Jew', *PMLA*, 63 (1948), 199-213.

[8] Croly's hero records for instance changes in the detail of Restoration theatre; in the French work Ahasucrus the Jew meets a variety of such legendary figures as Prester John. Other examples of the genre include E.F. Franke's *Die Ahasveriade* (Dresden 1838) and John Galt's *The Wandering Jew* (1820). For archaeological study at this time see P.E.Cleator, *Archaeology in the Making* (New York and London 1976), 31-7,72-81 and 92ff and G.Daniel, *A Hundred and Fifty years of Archaeology*, 2nd ed. (Trowbridge and Esher 1975),16 -56.

[9] The novel is dense with historical detail and consciousness of change from one period to another: it describes tournaments, revolts in Hungary and the Spanish Inquisition. See in particulars *St Leon: A Tale of the Sixteenth Century*, with introduction by J.Beekett and foreword by D.P.Varma (New York 1972), 164.

[10] King James Bible, Corinthians, 1, 15.

[11] See S.Bremner, *The Fiction of Time Travel in the Nineteenth Century*, unpublished doctoral dissertation, Manchester, 1983.

[12] For discussion see Jack Zipes, *The Oxford Companion to Fairy Tales* (2000), 467, 476 and E.S.Hartland, *The Science of Fairy Tales; an Inquiry into Fairy Mythology* (1891), 247. Examples include the fourteenth-century Catalan version, 'Frayre de Joy e Sor de Placer' and Charles Perrault, 'La Belle au Bois Dormant', Histoires on Contes du Temps Passe, 1697.

[13] See Hartland,op.cit., 205-212.

[14] C.E.Robinson, 'Mary Shelley and the Roger Dodsworth Hoax', *Keats-Shelley Journal*, 24 (1975), n. 10, 26-27.

[15] See Fraiices Sheridan, *The History of Nourjahad* (1767) and Michael Kelly's dramatic adaptation, *Illusion; or the Trances of Nourjahad, an Oriental Romance* (1813).

[16] See MSCT, 44. She indicates in *Frankenstein*, published in 1818, that the idea had already occurred to her. She prefaces her 1831 edition with a description of Erasmus Darwin 's work on galvanising which had inspired the story: "perhaps a corpse would be re-animated" (p9). The creator's description of his monster reads: "A mummy again endowed with animation could not be as hideous as that wretch" (p.58).

[17] See Robinson, 1975, 26 n. 9 who cites evidence for composition sometime during the spring of 1819, although Mary Shelley does not discuss the tale in her letters. The edition used is MSCT, 332-344.

biographers.[18] It recounts the experiences of an ancient Roman who claims "1 died at the age of forty five defending my country against Cataline" (MSCT 333). He awakens from the dead - by means which are not explained - to see the changes time has wrought on his beloved capital. Deeply shocked by the ugliness of the modern city, and the superimposition of Christian edifices on what he remembers as a once noble skyline, he deplores the lack of heroism of modern Romans, and feels an irrevocable alienation from a city that seems strange and overlaid by barbarous architecture. As he wanders around the city the landscape which so beguiled other Romantic writers seems to him only evidence of ruin and decay. Modern Romans are not, he claims, the true descendants of his own race, manifest none of their nobility and pride and the architecture has been desecrated, with much its original sacred purpose lost forever. Only in the Colosseum - even though it was built after his "death" - does he find some solace.

From its height, I beheld Rome, sleeping under the cold rays of the moon: the dome of St Peter's and the various other domes and spires which make a second city, the habitations of gods above the habitations of men; ... The Coliseum was to me henceforth the world, my eternal habitation.... if Rome be dead, I fly from her remains, loathsome as those of human life. It is in the Coliseum alone that I recognise the grandeur of my country - that is the only worthy asylum for an ancient Roman (MSCT 336).

Modern travellers to Rome might share some of Valerius's annoyance at the changes time has wrought, even since his own day, though perhaps not his dislike for any evidence of the "catholic superstition" (MSCT 337). He responds though as a true citizen of a Rome that antedates Nero: he exhorts the gods by the Tiber, his concern is for the affairs which governed his state rather than the domestic, and he speaks with the authority of a Roman who "died" before the worst excesses of Roman imperialism: "I need not trouble you with the history of my life - in modern times, domestic circumstances appear to be that part of a man's history most worth enquiring into. In Rome, the history of an individual was that of his country. We lived in the Forum and the Senate house" (MSCT 333). The fact that he retains a countenance that is "placid and commanding" (MSCT 332), despite his vicissitudes, is a tribute to the stoic values of his upbringing, and he represents a sympathetic attempt at recreating the speech, manners and beliefs of the ancient man. This certainly impresses his one close friend, an English lady, Isabell Harley, whose acccount concludes the story as she describes her almost hostess-like delight in showing the Roman round the galleries, reading the Georgics with him in a modern setting and enjoying the "exquisite statues and paintings" (MSCT 343).

Some biographical and background information is helpful here, for we may see in the depiction of this strange figure transplanted from his age something of a chemical reaction between the events of Mary Shelley's own life, her own fictional preoccupations and the place Rome still held as a source of learning for intellectual and literary circles at a time when a classical education was still the mainstay of intellectual life. At the time of composition Mary Shelley was now three years into her controversial marriage to Percy Shelley, whose first wife had commited suicide after he left her, and two years after the completion of her most famous work, *Frankenstein*, she was now a well-known literary figure in her own right. She was only twenty two, and in her tumultous short period with Shelley she had already outraged English society, dismayed her father, William Godwin, written copious letters and stories, travelled widely in Italy and produced three children. Two of these, girls, had already died shortly after birth: the third, William, was to contract malarial fever and die in June of that year. At the time of writing she was probably already pregnant with her fourth child, a boy, the only product of the union who was to survive both parents.

In the midst of this extraordinarily harrowing sense of loss and chaotically organised personal life her visit to Rome lent her, as it did other figures such as Keats and Byron, a sense of reassurance through the past and, for a while, a chance for tranquil reflection. Both Shelleys, like other early nineteenth-century writers and artists, were captivated. Her husband Percy wrote: "Rome is the capital of the world. It is a city of palaces and temples, more glorious than those which any other city contains, and of ruins more glorious than they."[19] On Dec 18th to Maria Gisbourne Mary Shelley reports that she is "enchanted" by her first visit to Rome, a love which she retained for the rest of her life. After a visit to the Colosseum and Forum in March 1819 she enthuses "but my letter would never be at an end if I were to try (to) tell a millionth part of the delights of Rome - it has an effect on me that my past life before I saw it appears a blank & now I begin to live - in the churches you hear the music of heaven and the singing of Angels."[20] In April 19th 1819 she writes to Maria Gisbourne again, this time revealing some anti-Christian sentiment, fuelled by the recent visit of the Holy Roman Emperor from Austria: "We saw the illuminated cross in St Peters last night, which is very beautiful; but how much more beautiful is the Pantheon by Moonlight! As superior, in my opinion, as is the ancient temple to the modern church! I don't think much of St Peters after all – I cannot - it is so cut up - it is large - and not simple."[21] Even after the death of her son William, she still felt the pull of the ancient city, and in 1820 wrote "I own that during all this time my heart is still at Rome".[22]

---

[19] Perey Bysshe Shelley to Thomas Love Peacock; Rome, March 23rd, 1819 in Roger Ingpen and Walter E. Peck ed., *The Complete Works of Percy Bysshe Shelley*, 10 vols (1926), X,41.
[20] Betty T. Bennett ed, *The Letters of Mary Wollstonecraft Shelley*, 3 vols, (Baltimore 1988),1, 83.
[21] *Letters*, 1, 93
[22] *Letters*, 1, Jan 19th 1820 to Amelia Curran, 127.

---

[18] For some recent discussion of the tale though see MSCT notes, 397-8 and John Williams, *Mary Shelley : A Literary Life* (2000), 66-7.

In a later novel, *The Last Man*, published in 1826, the civilisation of Ancient Rome provides a kind of touchstone for ancient values. In this work it is seen not just as a respository for ancient monuments and artefacts, but as the place of last refuge for the only surviving member of the human species. This bleak depiction of the future provides us with another hero irrevocably dislocated from any communication with those of his own time. Lionel Verney, the sole survivor of plague, travels to Rome, the "majestic and eternal survivor of millions of extinct men", after desperate attempts to find and establish communication with any other survivors have failed: the road from Ravenna to Rome is littered with his graffiti.[23] Verney struggles to find solace in the ruins of many layers of civilisation, but the shadows appear as ghosts that cannot reach him: here he decides to write his biography, dedicated to the dead.[24]

The authority Mary Shelley assigned to this city and its ancient culture may also be seen in her choice of location for the frame narrative, which is set in the recesses of the Sybilline cave, stumbled upon by chance. Here the narrator finds leaves inscribed with prophecies in many languages, past and future: these scribbled bits of flotsam and jetsam are written in Babylonian, Egyptian, English, Italian and languages not recognisable to her or her companion. Mary Shelley's willingness to adapt the classical to her own purposes is indicated by the fact that this chronicle about the future extinction of the species arrives by a modern dislocation in the laws of time, for these leaves appear to have blown to the cave in piles, manuscripts posted from the despairing and the hopeful of all times. That its final resting place however is in the cool rocks that sheltered the Sybil herself is a testimony to Mary Shelley's sense of the enduring powers of Roman mythology and the culture that shaped it.[25]

This I think is the key to her earlier tale, for despite the problems of Valerius's alienation from his fellows, Rome and Roman culture itself does merge victorious, as a kind of yardstick for the measure of civilised life. Valerius seems to be speaking with a voice that would represent for Mary Shelley all the classical values of stoicism and public responsibility she admired. The story ends with her account of Isabell's delight at reading Latin in the Roman sunshine with a genuine if reluctant ambassador from the past, a pleasure overshadowed by her ambivalent awareness of "the earthly barrier placed between us" (MSCT, 344).

In 1818, Henry Hallam had written in *A View of the State of Europe during the Middle Ages*:

We cannot expect to feel in respect of ages at best imperfectly civilised and slowly progressive, that interest which attends a more perfect development of human capacities., and more brilliant advances in improvement.[26]

This rationalist and progressivist attitude towards the past - which persisted throughout the nineteenth century with the work of figures such as Macaulay - was constantly challenged by a new appreciation of historical difference.[27] Mary Shelley anticipates a sentiment found also in Carlyle, that may seem patronising to us now, but does at least accord the ancient world respect. "The Great antique heart: how like a Child's in its simplicity, like a man's in it earnest solemnity and depth.[28] Mary Shelley, like the ancient Roman's one friend, Isabell Harley, seems to be seeking reassurance in this tale, through a living survivor, from the ancestral roots of her own culture. The tale is unsatisfactory however, and we feel she cannot quite find a way of bringing her companion and, it seems, the spirit of an older Rome, to life.

'Roger Dodsworth, the reanimated Englishman'

The next story is unashamedly comic and is based upon a hoax which, in 1826, seems to have been perpetrated with some success. It certainly gives us some historical evidence for the long tradition of the silly season, for it is based upon a newspaper story published in Paris in the June of that year that excited comment, satire and debate throughout the summer months. It purports to describe the "find" in Swiss mountain snow of the body of an apparently dead seventeenth-century Englishman whose faculties, it transpires, have been kept in frozen abeyance for the past one hundred and sixty six years.[29]

Dr Jas. HOTHAM, of Morpeth, Northumberland, returning from Switzerland, is stated to have reported that a most extraordinary event had lately passed at the foot of Mount St Cothard, a league from Aizoli, in the valley of Levantina. At the bottom of a kind of cavern, the body of a man, about 30 years of age, was perceived under a heap of ice, proceeding from an avalanche. As the body seemed to be fresh as if it had been stifled only half an hour before, Dr HOTHAM caused it to be taken out, and having had the clothes pulled off, ordered it to be plunged into cold water. It was then so frozen that it was covered with a crust of ice. It was then placed in lukewarm water. Afterwards it was put in a warm bed, and treated as usual in cases of suffocation, by which means animation was restored. What was the astonishment of every body, when the individual having recovered the use of his faculties. Declared that he was ROGER DODSWORTH, son of the Antiquary of the same name, born in

---

[23] H.J.Luke ed., with notes and critical introduction, *The Last Man: Mary Shelley* (Lincoln, Nebraski 1965), 335.

[24] See *ibid* 339.

[25] See *ibid*, 3.

[26] Quoted with discussion in J.R.Hale, ed., *The Evolution of British Historiography: From Bacon to Namier* (Cleveland and New York 1964), 198.

[27] Macaulay writes that science "has lighted up the night with the splendour of day. Its law is progress" *Edinburgh Reivew*, 65 (1837), 82-3. But for the emergence of the new historicist understanding see J.S.Mill, *The Spirit of the Age* (1831), 1, who notes that the very idea of comparing our own age to another is for the first time "the dominant idea". For discussion see H.E. Barnes, *A History of Historical Writing*, revised ed., (New York, Toronto, Londoii 1963), 178-206.

[28] Thomas Carlyle, *Past and Present* (1843), 116.

[29] For a comprehensive account of the incident and its treatment in the contemporary press see C.E.Robinson, art.cit., 20-28.

1629, who returning from a Italy in 1660, a year after the death of his father, was buried under an avalanche.[30]

The story "broke" in France, but was widely circulated in newspapers such as *Morning Chronicle*, (July 5th), the *Sun*, (July 5th) the *Manchester Guardian* (July 8th) and the *Scotsman* (July 8th).[31] Theodore Hook, the editor of the Tory *John Bull*, announced, presumably in jest, "We have since been informed that Mr DODSWORTH has actually arrived in London, and is residing in St James's Place, where he may be seen at a bow window looking into the Green Park every morning after breakfast - he still looks very dead, and pretty miserable; but he is worth looking at."[32] Speculation about his clothes and "the frill, which until it was thawed, stood stiff under the mingled influence of starch and frost" also extended to the way that the Englishman would react to modern Europe (MSCT 44). Newspaper interest culminated in letters purporting to be from Roger Dodsworth himself, in which he comments with the enthusiasm of a convert on nineteenth-century life. He reveals however a highly developed polemical tone in his bemusement at modern intellectual and literary self-esteem, and his questions display a Gulliver-like probity.[33] He asks for instance to be told "when and where a sect or nation flourished, remarkable for every vice under the sun, called 'modern philosophers'?"[34] The fact that the hoax itself could exercise such a hold, with articles on the subject appearing in all the major newspapers, itself gives us an extraordinary glimpse into the dawning historicist interest of the early nineteenth century: his clothes, possessions and manners all come under scrutiny.[35] The wit and liveliness of the debate certainly acted as a stimulus to Mary Shelley's imaginative speculations. As she notes she had "often made conjectures how such and such heroes of antiquity would act, if they were reborn in these times"(MSCT 48).

Her story, although written in 1826, was not published until 1863 in the reminiscences of Cyrus Redding, editor of the new Monthly Magazine.[36] It also has been largely forgotten and I have not found it discussed in any accounts of Mary Shelley's life and works. The tale begins with Mary Shelley's delighted questions about the implications of the incident: how does he speak? Can he reclaim his own estate? She then imagines the conversation between the doctor who revives the body and the Roger Dodsworth himself, which unfolds as a comedy of misunderstanding. Both speak at cross-purposes about the parlous state of affairs in England. The Tory doctor mistakes Dodsworth's reference to his "poor distracted country" for the

comments of a radical and Dodsworth, who fell into his curious sleep in 1654, reacts with wary, if secretly delighted, astonishment at the mention of the king (MSCT 45).

Many features of modern existence alarm this ambivalent republican, from government, to clothes and even to the pronunciation of his native tongue. The tone is more jaunty than the earlier tale, as Roger Dodsworth's old manners, Mary Shelley imagines, thaw away too, and he is soon espousing nineteenth-century speech and dress, though not a neck-cloth and hardboarded hat (MSCT 47). The tale concludes with Mary Shelley's speculations about other possible voyages through time: reincarnation, metempsychosis, and Virgil's *Aeneid* book 6 are all discussed. If, as suggested by Virgil, we come back in a thousand years time, what would happen if we could remember our earlier lives, and the judge find out that he had once condemned Christians, the freethinkers that they had been persecuted before under Domitian? She writes:

If philosophical novels were in fashion, we conceive an excellent one might be written on the development of the same mind in various stations, in different periods of the world's history. (MSCT 48)

The story is significant for Mary Shelley's own playful enjoyment in creating a confrontation between what is in effect a sophisticated tourist from the past set amidst modern manners, and it reveals a humour not often uppermost in her work. It also creates a new twist to the motif of the "sleeper" in that archaeology, science and the popular imagination together produce a new possibility, or at any rate a new variation, on an ancient story type. In this, and in the other reports of the hoax, the process is one which can and should be explained by means of scientific jargon: it starts with a description of how the body has been "hermetically" sealed by frost, the "corporeal atoma" thereby protected, so that effective "animation" can be suspended (MSCT 44). This is no longer the old kind of folktale, reliant on some kind of enchantment, but a piece of science fiction: given the right physical conditions a man from the past, could, it suggests, be reawakened and be brought to comment upon the present.

Other examples of the sleeper or corpse revived

Throughout the nineteenth century variations on the idea of the extended sleep or the reanimated body continued to trouble and sometimes amuse the popular imagination, and I am afraid I can give them only the most superficial treatment here: Washington Irving's 'Rip van Winkle' appeared in 1819, taking the theme of the fairy or enchanted sleep from *volkssagen* and employing it as a means to present an American fairy tale of modern man's dislocation from his roots and past. This justly renowned tale is about a simple henpecked man who walks in the Catskill mountains with his dog, meets the fairies, falls asleep after drinking their ale and reawakens to find his old

---

[30] London *New Times*, July 4th, p.3, quoted in Robinson, 1975, 21.
[31] See Robinson, art.cit,, 22.
[32] *John Bull*, July 9th, 223.
[33] In *John Bull*, September 3rd, 285, September 10th, 292 and September 17th, 300. For Dodsworth's argumentative comment on the contemporary literary, political and fashionable scene see *New Monthly Magazine*, 17, 453-8.
[34] In *New Monthly Magazine*, 17, 458.
[35] *Ibid.*
[36] See C. Redding *Yesterday and Today*, 2 vols. (1863) 11, 150-65. Reprinted with notes MSCT,43-50.

village inn now the bustling and modern American Union Hotel, life in his old village changed beyond recognition, and his allegiance to the King regarded with suspicion. At the time Irving was accused of plagiarism from an earlier German folk tale, a charge he freely admitted, though there is something decidedly fresh and "New World" about the way the uprooted hero adapts.[37] Unlike some other sleepers, he comes to like modernity, and while mortified that his longlived dog does not recognise him, he is decidedly relieved to be free of his nagging wife. The continued public interest in archaeological excavations ensure that a number of unwrapped and revived mummies also satisfy the Victorian appetite for evidence of the mystery represented by the past of Ancient Egypt, from W.B.Bayle's *The Mummy! A farce in one act* to E.Lee's *Pharoah's daughter; a story of the Ages*, in 1889.[38] Cryogenic bodies are less common, but I would also like to mention a now forgotten gem: W. Clarke Russell's *The Frozen Pirate*, which describes the unfreezing of an eighteenth-century pirate found encased in ice.[39] The pirate's immoderate behaviour bursts into the well-regulated life of a lone Arctic sailor who is made very uncomfortable by random swashbuckling violence. Here the idea that the bravado of a more freespirited age might be defrosted in the present, along with a body, gives us a decidely breezy perspective on the often earnest historical comparison that is sometimes associated with the idea of the suspended sleep. Mention should also be made of Mark Twain's *A Yankee in the Court of King Arthur* (1889), one of the few major works of fiction to hinge upon the idea of the sleeper from another time. Hank Morgan, propelled back to the sixth-century court of King Arthur by a blow on the head, learns to adjust to the Britain; he is a very unwilling victim of suspended sleep, an enchantment imposed by Merlin himself. The story is a flawed but effective account of the rift between two times that seem to create a faultline in the character of Hank himself, divided between nostalgia and Yankee distaste for injustice. The sixth-century Britain he describes is riddled with superstition, fear and poverty. It is though where he has found domestic happiness, and where he feels his progressivist desire for social reform constantly tugged by his own enchantment under the spell of Arthurian manners. The comic incongruity of his encouragement of mediaeval knights to carry billboards advertising toothbrushes, his wife's adoration of all things from the future, along with Hank's impassioned social comment make this one of the most ambivalent, intensely realised and, occasionally,

funny of all stories of contact between the present and an age that has gone.[40]

We may never have the means of bringing back the dead, or of finding a body that can be revived to tell us about another age, but the idea that out of the ice of modern manners the spirit of another age might be thawed out and brought to life in the present gives us a convincing metaphor for the aspirations we hold for historical, archaeological and literary research. Nowadays we can feel like the inhabitants of a lost age, and fictions of the cinema and the novel continue to produce, with other forms of time travel, ways in which we can meet and invite comment from those whose values were shaped in the past. It seems to me that the appeal of stories of this kind is that they represent a fictional means of questioning our ancestors and common heritage: we hope these ambassadors from our past might lend us some sort of clue as to how to decipher the way we live now. Indeed like Valerius, Roger Dodsworth and Rip van Winkle, in the twenty-first century those of us who participate in a present where cities seem to change overnight and customs, clothes and language metamorphose with ever-increasing rapidity, sometimes feel a little like time travellers ourselves, waking up to a culture that can be fun, but also decidedly new and strange.

---

[37] See H.A. Pochmann, 'Irving's German Sources in The Sketch Book', Studies in Philology, 27 (1930), 477-80 and 494-7.

[38] W.B.Bayle's *The Mummy! A farce in one act.* Lacy's Acting editions of Plays, Dramas, Farces, Extravaganzas etc.vol 53, 1836 and E.Lee's *Pharoah's daughter; a story of the Ages*, Bristol and London 1889. This interest joined forces with the future tale with the reanimation of a mummy in the future in Jane Webb, *The Mummy: a Tale of the Twenty Second Century*, 1827. For study of Egyptian archaeology in this period see Cleator, *op.cit.*,117ff and Daniel, *op.cit.*, 135-6,162-4,174-8 and 195-9.

[39] Published in two volumes in 1887.

[40] See for instance G.C Bellamy, *Mark Twain as a Literary Artist* (Norman, Oklahoma 1950), 309; E.Wagenknacht, *Mark Twain: the Man and his Work* (Norman, Oklahoma 1971), 44 and S.Bremner, op. cit., 234ff.

On a Cornelian heart which was broken

Martin Henig

Ill-fated heart! and can it be,
That thou should'st thus be rent in twain?
Have years of care for thine and thee
Alike been all employ'd in vain?

Yet precious seems each shatter'd part,
And every fragment dearer grown,
Since he who wears thee feels thou art
A fitter emblem of his own.

These stanzas, written by George Gordon, Lord Byron in March 1812, related the breakage of a valued object, in fact an example of a fairly common type of contemporary artefact though in this case with an added high personal value, with his own response to the mishap. The verse reveals a personal, emotional archaeology which is quite independent of the exterior world. As an excavator, or student of glyptics, finding and cataloguing a broken gem would we archaeologists ever guess at this secret history?

To some degree a conference session entitled 'Outside Archaeology' is, inevitably, bound to be a misnomer; it is no more possible to be beyond archaeology than it is possible for Mephistopheles to live outside his fate: 'I am in Hell; nor am I out of it'. What is true, however, is that individual 'job descriptions', how others see us, undoubtedly vary. I recall that when I was an undergraduate at Cambridge, reading for the History Tripos I was accused by an Archaeology student, a former schoolfellow of mine, of 'not being an archaeologist' and thus, somehow not having a right to express opinions on the subject. The title of Professor Kermode's delightful autobiography, 'Not Entitled' comes to mind. Viewed against our human ignorance of the past of our own species, let alone its future, is any of us truly competent to discourse on anything?

What is an archaeologist? The definition has changed with time and, even today, is perceived differently from person to person. For most of those who work in the Institute of Archaeology, Oxford, as I suspect in other University Departments of Archaeology, it seems to be mainly concerned with excavation in the ground, with pottery analysis, radio-carbon dating and other techniques. On this definition my friend was right: I am not an archaeologist. However, for 19th-century scholars, 'archaeological' was a term having to do with the correct representation of the Gothic orders while Classical Archaeologists since Winkelmann at any rate have tended to use archaeology (or did until until recently) as a study connected with the taxonomy of Greek architecture, sculpture, painted pottery and gems. So there are many archaeologies. I feel happiest with the way 'archaeology' seems to be used by most of the contributors to the British Archaeological Association, which is rather different or has a different nuance from all

the above though it draws on each of them. This concept of archaeology sees the study as a sort of conduit into the appreciation of a past culture, both in its material manifestations and in its inner life. If this makes me an 'outsider' to those in archaeological laboratories, that is merely a symptom of a growing dislocation in the academic community in general. The only equable answer to these clashing definitions is that we should each use the term 'archaeology' in her or his own way, provided it deals with the study of the past but it may help to begin at the beginning.

Ancient archaeologies

How did our forebears view the past? Archaeology is nothing if it is not a journey through the mind, employing an imagination replete with monuments and images. Amongst the earliest strictly archaeological inferences I know are those of Thucydides in the introduction to his great history of the Peloponnesian War. In the 5th century B.C., Mycenae was a small and rather insignificant place, but he does not find that a good reason for doubting its past importance. Suppose Sparta was abandoned and only known from its ruins? Future generations would surely find it hard to credit its power; if the same disaster overtook Athens, people would imagine it was twice as powerful as in fact it was (see Thucydides 1,10).

We care about these places, about Mycenae, and its Asian adversary Troy, as we do about historical Athens and Sparta, primarily because they have entered our own emotional landscapes by way of literature. The Classical Greeks knew the Homeric epics and associated stories. The sack of Troy and its aftermath, including the punishment of the Greek heroes for impiety, amongst them Odysseus condemned to wander the earth for ten years as a result of sacrilege and Agamemnon who had slain his own daughter Iphigeneia and was destined to meet a terrible end at the hands of his own wife Clytemnestra. Such tales formed the basis for plays by Thucydides' contemporaries. By the 2nd century A.D. visitors to Mycenae were shown the Lion Gate and the tombs of Agamemnon, Electra, Clytemnestra and Aigisthus (Pausanias ii.16,4-5). Troy too was a literary landscape : Arrian tells us that Alexander the Great, upon landing in Asia, first visited Troy, sacrificing to Athena, the patron goddess of the city and also to Priam to avert his anger against the family of Neoptolemus from whom he was descended. Above all he honoured Achilles, who was lucky enough to have Homer to preserve a record of his deeds (Arrian, *Alexander* i.11-12).

Even in Archaic times Athens was renowned, at least by her own citizens, for a heroic past centred around the person of king Theseus who, as a youth, had vanquished the man-eating Minotaur. He is the type of the good king and so, in Sophocles' poetic masterpiece, *Oedipus at Colonus*, he gives succour and an eternal resting place to the blind outcast, Oedipus. Sparta, with its peculiarly philistine organisation might have seemed, by contrast, hardly the place in which to create the same sort of literary landscape, but it could be visited by pilgrims as the home of Menelaus, cuckolded brother of Agamemnon and of his wife Helen, carried off to Troy by Paris - except in the version which we know from Euripides' witty burlesque *Helen*, in which she is abducted to Egypt by the gods, who wishing to burden mankind with a useless war, let Paris abduct a wraith to Troy. In Pausanias' time there was a sanctuary of Helen at Sparta where she was venerated as a goddess (iii,15,3) and across the Eurotas at Therapne, the sites of the tombs of Menelaos and Helen were shown (iii,19,9). When I came to visit Sparta in 1965 two mounds were pointed out to me by a proud local resident as the tombs of the pair. Perhaps he was right.

Epic status of a truly different order was given to Sparta and above all to Athens through their resistance to Persia at the beginning of the 5th century. The account given by Herodotus of Halicarnassus is near enough contemporary, and it has something of the resonance of Churchill's great speeches of the 1940s, which endowed Great Britain and her Empire with heroic status in their battle against the Axis powers. Certainly the tone of phrase in which the overwhelming might of evil tyrannies are humbled by the forces of democracy are similar. Indeed, 'the Greek spirit', epitomised by the Athenian victory at Marathon in 490 B.C., and Spartan attempt to hold the pass of Thermopylae as well as the decisive Athenian naval victory at Salamis in 480 B.C., played a significant part, at least amongst the Public and Grammar school educated, in bolstering British resolution in the early 1940s!

One other famous ancient city deserves particular consideration here and that is, of course, Rome. Its physical remains have been examined and excavated since at least the Renaissance but in Antiquity physical traces of its legendary past such as Romulus' hut were nurtured and as late as the Civil War of 69-70, 6th-century Etruscan style terracottas were still to be seen embellishing buildings. Apart from physical remains a whole system of memory propounded in the *Auctor ad Herennium*, attributed to Cicero, produces a sort of abstract archaeology, a Pompeii of the mind, which is equally deserted in Tacitus' account of Vitellius, deserted by all his followers, wandering terrified through his abandoned and shuttered palace, knowing that every move he made was the wrong one, before being dragged out and butchered by the mob on 20th December A.D.69 (*Hist* iii,84). Another, very much later, snapshot of Rome lists buildings, all of which recall events in Rome's past; but in A.D.357 Constantius II is unable to equal the achievements of Trajan even if he thinks himself equal to commissioning an Equestrian statue like that of Rome's great warrior Emperor (Ammianus Marcellinus xvi,13-18). More domestic settings are provided by Petronius in his essentially comic account of Trimalchio's preposterously vulgar banquet in his over-decorated, over-furnished house and more seriously by the younger Pliny's description of his own far more refined seaside residence. Thirty years ago when I was excavating with Barry Cunliffe at Fishbourne I realised that this sumptuous *domus* in Sussex, the palace, as I think we both still believe, of the client king, Tiberius Claudius Togidubnus, was very similar to the seaside home of his Roman contemporary, the younger Pliny. One can therefore explore the site simply through its ruins or at one remove through Latin literature, in Pliny's account of his Laurentine villa (*Epistulae* II,17).

The archaeology of power

In any case mention of England recalls us to the major theme of this paper. I realise now that my introduction to archaeology as something vital and living in the contemporary world goes back to early childhood when I was fortunate enough to be taken to *Julius Caesar* by my parents. I was gripped; here was an introduction to two cultures, Rome and Renaissance England in about equal measure. Shakespeare's major source was Plutarch but he invested the story of the end of the Republic with picaresque detail, the Dictator's deafness in one ear, symbolic of his failing physical powers for example, or Brutus' gentle consideration for his servant Lucius. The central argument was: is it ever right to kill your friend, even if he is undermining the constitution? Dante had had no doubts and in the *Inferno* had placed Brutus and Cassius within the inmost circle of Hell. For Shakespeare, here is the theme for a debate. It is addressed by Brutus and then Antony before the Roman people...but the winner here is the one (Antony) with the best oratorical tricks and in the event he and Octavius are *even more* cynical and bloody in their proscriptions than their adversaries. This was gripping stuff for me then, and is so still; but there is more.... In his History plays Shakespeare had asked whether it was right to kill an anointed king who had abused his powers. *Richard II*, another of my first Shakespeare plays, had showed that it was not permissible. England, unlike Rome, was a monarchy, and in some ways the person who came to challenge the king, Bolingbroke, has something in common with Caesar. As Richard prophecies:

> Yet know --my master, God omnipotent,
> Is mustering in his clouds on our behalf
> Armies of pestilence; and they shall strike
> Your children yet unborn and unbegot,
> That lift your *vassal hands against my head*
> And threat the glory of my precious crown.
> (*Richard II* Act 3,iii,85-90)

By contrast, in the Roman Republic, Brutus can muse, that:

> Th' abuse of greatness is, when it disjoins
> Remorse from power. (*Julius Caesar* Act 2,i,18-19)

The theme of regicide (even the overthrow of Caesar) was one very dangerous to voice at the time. If Queen Elizabeth, on the day of the Earl of the Earl of Essex's Rebellion had thought darkly of the deposition of Richard II, some half a century later in 1849 King Charles I would perish theatrically on the scaffold erected at Whitehall outside Inigo Jones's great Renaissance-style Banqueting Hall.

He nothing common did or mean
  Upon that memorable Scene:
    But with his keener Eye
    The Axes edge did try:
Nor call'd the Gods with vulgar spight
To vindicate his helpless Right,
    But bow'd his comely Head.
    Down as upon a Bed.
  (Andrew Marvell, *An Horatian Ode upon Cromwel's Return from Ireland* 57-64).

Marvell, like Shakespeare, could see both sides of the arguement. Veering at the time to favour the short lived British Republic of the Commonwealth, he could nevertheless empathise with the chief victim of the Revolution. But behind these simple lines lay a wealth of knowledge of history, ancient as well as modern. Revolutions have a tendancy to devour their children; there was no satisfactory end to the Roman Revolution as the late Sir Ronald Syme showed our parents' or grandparents generation, before 'the War'- or, realising my advancing years, the Second World War! Shakespeare lived at a time when the Wars of the Roses still had some resonance to an audience. In *Henry IV*, *Henry V* and *Henry VI*, Bolingbroke (as Henry IV), his son and grandson and their Yorkist adversaries are haunted by the consequences of that primal regicide. If a late Elizabethan dramatist had to applaud Henry VII, the historical consequences of the Tudor age, which in the next reign would sweep away the monasteries and usher in even more radical Reformation, brought graver ills to the country.

Another example of how Shakespeare was able to remould history for his own contemporaries, but leaving a strong sense of recognition for us, is to be seen in *Macbeth*. It apparently deals with the usurpation of an 11th-century king in Scotland but the factual element is at best tenuous. Indeed the historical Macbeth (as Peter Berresford Ellis shows in *MacBeth- High King of Scotland*, 1980) was a far better ruler and better man too than his predecessor and successor. With his Classical education (and the teaching resources of the Grammar School at Stratford are not to be underestimated) and the general style of life of reasonably well-to-do Elizabethans, ancient Rome was evidently more approachable than the early Middle Ages. However political murder, atrocities against the innocent and the effect of their actions on the perpetrators of such crimes have universal resonance, and there is a truthfulness in the play beyond history. Macbeth's sleeplessness is in part echoed in the night-time wakefulness of that other more recent usurper, Henry IV.

Canst thou, O partial sleep, give thy repose
To the wet sea-boy in an hour so rude;
And in the calmest and most stillest night,
With all appliances and means to boot,
Deny it to a king? Then,happy low, lie down!
Uneasy lies the head that wears a crown.
(*King Henry IV*,part ii,Act 3,i,27-31).

In the end the fates juggle with Henry's hopes of absolution through a pilgrimage to Jerusalem : He dies at Westminster in the Jerusalem Chamber:

It hath been prophesied to me many years,
I should not die but in Jerusalem;
Which vainly I suppos'd the Holy Land.
But bear me to that chamber; there I'll lie;
In that Jerusalem shall Harry die.
(King Henry IV,part ii,Act 4,237-41)

The mental anguish of Macbeth and of his equally ruthless, and vulnerable, wife in sleepwalking, nightmare and apparent hallucination is evidently worse. The riddling gods make a mockery of his apparent invulnerability when Birnam Woods appears to move against Dunsinane and he is slain by MacDuff, a man not 'born of woman'. One thinks back to the utter despair of Cleon after his orders had led to the death of his son and his niece in Sophocles, *Antigone* and to the brief Tacitean vignette of Vitellius wandering from room to room through his empty palace, but I will never forget a moment captured on television when in Romania Nicola Ceaucescu suddenly found himself facing his countrymen who had moved against him and waved his hand over his eyes in total disbelief at the sudden ending of his power...and his life; thus was the fall of the Macbeth of our own time. In *Macbeth* right triumphs; but in real life, or rather in the lives of many men including kings and queens, there can be no such simple fairytale ending.

Archaeology, as the knowledge of ancient things, is far too important to be left to the mere technician; the excavator without imagination betrays his calling. The truth about a potsherd is very unlikely to provide anything of value to us as human beings. However skilled, the enormities of the mind of a Macbeth or of Henry IV defy the skill of the man wielding the trowel. Henry lies in Canterbury cathedral, within a fine monument ...but did he ever find peace? did he ever find absolution for his sins? Contemplating his effigy, I thought of the ambiguous, but evidently despairing words Shakespeare puts into his mouth.

The archaeology of love

A recent exhibition at the British Museum was concerned with the life and reign of Cleopatra VII, her influence on her country (Egypt) and on Rome and the Ancient World in general. Central to her story are her relations with Julius Caesar and especially with Mark Antony. The most beautiful objects, statuary, coins, gems, silver plate evoked the power and exotic luxury of her court. My especial response, which I did not find sufficiently reflected in Susan Walker's and Peter Higgs's otherwise excellent catalogue, was to the relation of these things to another text, to me Shakespeare's greatest play *Antony and Cleopatra*. It was because of Shakespeare that as a youth I felt a quickening of the blood when a bought and held in my hand a denarius struck by Antony before the fateful battle of Actium in 31 B.C....It was because of Shakespeare that I was excited to find a cameo, probably showing Cleopatra herself, in the great Jacobean jewellery treasure from London, the Cheapside Hoard. Politics is here, but also the strongest of human passions, love, investing the mundane with radiance:

> Let Rome in Tiber melt, and the wide arch
> Of the rang'd empire fall! Here is my space.
> Kingdoms are clay; our dungy earth alike
> Feeds beast as man. The nobleness of life
> Is to do thus... (Act 1,i,33-37)

Antony, the most noble general of the Roman world, renowned for prowess in the field, statesmanship, generosity, joie de vivre, is utterly subdued by her. Enobarbus describes the captivating arrival of the queen on the river Cydnus:

> ...She did lie
> In her pavilion, cloth-of-gold, of tissue,
> O'erpicturing that Venus where we see
> The fancy out-work nature... (Act 2,ii,202-205).

He paraphrases Plutarch but any beholder, any reader must think of Queen Elizabeth seated in her State Barge and of the ceremony of Tudor and Jacobean England. Maecenas is impressed and, as it were, questions Enobarbus about it.

Maecenas: Now Antony must leave her utterly.

Enobarbus: Never! He will not.
> Age cannot wither her, nor custom stale
> Her infinite variety. Other women cloy
> The appetites they feed, but she makes hungary
> Where most she satisfies...(Act 2,ii,237-242)

The music in the play is really Shakespeare's more than his source ...right down to the dying fall of her handmaid Charmian's last sentence; a line with not a word out of place:

> It is well done, and fitting for a princess
> Descended of so many royal kings. (Act 5,ii,324-325).

One of these kings was her own father,Ptolemy XII Auletes--'the lyre-player', hence the thrill of recognising and publishing a gem of that less than admirable despot, discovered in Graham Webster's excavations at Wroxeter.

Antony is the loser but it is he, not Octavius, who is the hero of the play. Death is, after all, not the worst thing that can happen to a man; that worst thing is dishonour. Unlike false Macbeth or false Bolingbroke, unlike even Brutus, troubled by Caesar's ghost, Antony can leave the world without reproach,

> The miserable change now at my end
> Lament nor sorrow at; but please your thoughts
> In feeding them with those my former fortunes
> Wherein I liv'd the greatest prince o' th' world.
> The noblest; and do now not basely die,
> Not cowardly put off my helmet to
> My countryman--a Roman by a Roman
> Valiantly vanquish'd... (Act 4, xv, 51-58)

We are made to feel this is a sort of victory; not as the world prizes victory but in cosmic terms. After Cleopatra's death Caesar order that:

> She shall be buried by her Antony;
> No grave upon the earth shall clip in it
> A pair so famous... (Act 5,ii, 356-357)

Not for nothing was Dryden's elegant Restoration version, 'All for Love', subtitled 'The World Well Lost'. The familiar world of Roman *realpolitik* seems shrunk, and Augustus Caesar strangely diminished. If I were producing the play I would make Octavius, a drab, prosaic figure, stoop in order to leave the vast Egyptian monument where Antony and Cleopatra lie in the sleep of death. In this play the Roman world is re-created; we seem to know more about Rome and find a truth about Rome and about human nature that we could never find by scratching in the ground.

The 'excavation' of such a text, like all those with which we have been concerned, may play a crucial part in our understanding of our place in history. This is because texts are essentially concerned with self- discovery and relating what we find in them to the ground of our moral being, the eternal Logos. The actual excavation of an ancient city whether Troy, Pompeii or Bath (think of the Anglo-Saxon poem,'the Ruin'), is only worthwhile when it is conducted with the same poetic imagination. It should remind us, in Hector's words, that:

> The end crowns all;
> And that old common arbitrator, Time,
> will one day end it. (*Troilus and Cressida* Act 4,v,224-6)

Shakespeare is not alone in his assessment of past time, that the life of man is short and soon passes away. It is there in *Ecclesiastes*.   In the St James's (Authorised) version:

Vanity of vanities; all is vanity...One generation passeth away, and another generation cometh: but the earth abideth for ever. (I,2 and 4)

Later in the 17th century, the lyric poet, Robert Herrick, with Horatian elegance, enjoins us to make the most of it while we can:

Gather ye Rose-buds while ye may
  Old Time is stll a flying
And this same flower that smiles to day,
  To morrow will be dying.

The same elegiac mood informs the writing of the Norwich doctor and antiquary , Sir Thomas Browne, best known for his *Religio Medici*, also wrote an objective excavation report, *Brampton urns* and philosophical musings on this discovery of the burials in *Hydriotaphia or Urn Burial*. Here he applies some of these same thoughts culled from the scripture and the classics to a consideration of what we have no difficulty in regarding as archaeology:

What Song the Syrens sang, or what name Achilles assumed when he hid himself among women, though puzzling questions, are not beyond all conjecture. What time the persons of these Ossuaries entered the famous Nations of the dead, and slept with Princes and Counsellors, might admit a wide solution. But who were the proprietors of these bones, or what bodies these ashes made up, were a question above Antiquarism.

If we cannot ourselves engage with the thoughts of a long dead skeleton or cremation, we can, as I have shown, excavate a text and find the life still there, whether this is fictional (as for instance in Browning's dramatic monologues) or in an imaginative biography like Boswell's life of Dr Johnson. Ultimately what gives life to this sort of enquiry is its ability to analyse thought, what people in the past thought and cared about and what we can care about, too. Emotional involvement is the one essential necessary here.

Certainly such commitment plays a key role in many of Lord Byron's works. Cornelian, the colour of blood, was certainly a fitting symbol for the poet's inner life. The poem with which this paper began is echoed by another, earlier, work simply called 'The Cornelian':

Some, who can sneer at friendship's ties,
Have,for my weakness,oft reproved me;
Yet still the simple gift I prize,
For I am sure the giver loved me.

He offer'd it with downcast look,
As fearful that I might refuse it;
I told him, when the gift I took,
My only fear should be to lose it.
(*Hours of Idleness*, published 1807)

The earlier poem is *sentimental* in the true sense of the word; the later one is expressive of a sadder, more resigned mood. But Byron was never a cynic; he understood, for instance, that Greece was more than the ruined buildings of Antiquity and in his great poem, 'The Isles of Greece', which is to be found in canto III of *Don Juan* he recalls the defeat of Persian tyranny:

The mountains look on Marathon--
And Marathon looks on the sea;
And musing there an hour alone,
I dream'd that Greece might still be free;
For standing on the Persians' grave,
I could not deem myself a slave.

On 19 April 1824 Byron died of fever at Missolonghi; he had come to Greece, equipped with helmet and armour modelled on those of Achilles, though he died before charging into battle with either sword or gun; he expired without ever having fired a shot, his reputation intact, in what inevitably developed into a very dirty war indeed. Yet his commitment to the cause of the Greeks did much for the cause of the Philhellenes and the re-establishment of the Greek nation. In this way love of archaeology came to affect the political destiny of a people. An outsider, a virtual exile from England, the achievement was ironically greater than those of many of the kings and politicians who have been considered here, who diced with time and found no real reward. Every Greek town has a street or a square named after him. Though not many of us can expect to do as much, we can try.

Blake in his best-known poem asks the rhetorical question:

And was Jerusalem builded here,
Amongst the dark Satanic mills?

As Percival Turnbull, a learned and widely read authority, has pointed out to me, this is nothing to do with the factories of the Industrial Revolution let alone schools; the 'mills' illustrated as a frontispiece to *Jerusalem* are the great stones of Stonehenge; a pagan pre-Christian antiquity whose meaning has to be equated with the supposed presence of Christ, brought hither by Joseph of Aramatheia to this land. It is not only professional archaeologists who would benefit from pondering such questions and I am not certain that the excavators of the recent past have done us much of a service with regard to this particular monument. Maybe all they can show us are their own limitations. But the jumbled 'finds boxes' of our minds are full of fragments from our intellectual past, quotations and half-remembered episodes which are just as much part of the recovery of old, lost things as the excavation of a crop mark. These may be more fruitful hunting grounds. At any rate I firmly believe that students of English and History have always had every bit as much right to call themselves archaeologists as those whose job description is archaeologist, as I trust other contributors to this volume will have shown.

This paper began with an artefact, transformed by poetry into raw emotion, which was ultimately a small part of what made one of Europe's very greatest heroes. I have chosen to end my selection of extracts in the natural world of plants, often regarded as the province of the environmental archaeologist, but here given human (and humane) contours by the pen of Andrew Marvell, who could praise an orchard as well as a king. This he did in faultless Latin in his poem *Hortus* in which the Roman gods, the muses and figures from mythology are ever present and more famously in passionate English which evokes a world before the Fall, still available for us now. Archaeologists, 'Theoretical Archaeologists' especially, are prone to disparage the scholarship and the understanding of past times. It is my contention that much that is most important to our understanding of the science of man lies buried in the words as well as the bones and pots of our forbears. The lovely artifice of the language is in tension with the naturalness of the subject. A report on seeds in an environmental report on a 17th-century garden might read: 'seeds or pollen of apple, grape, nectarine/peach, melons, various cultivated and wild flowers etc.' Contrast Marvell's poem wherein is true wisdom, peace -- and love. I think I would prefer to excavate that!

> How vainly men themselves amaze
> To win the Palm, the Oke, or Bayes;
> And their uncessant Labours see
> Crown'd from some single Herb or Tree,
> Whose short and narrow verged Shade
> Does prudently their Toyles upbraid;
> While all Flow'rs and all Trees do close
> To weave the Garlands of repose.
>
> What wond'rous Life in this I lead!
> Ripe Apples drop about my head;
> The Luscious Clusters of the Vine
> Upon my Mouth do crush their Wine;
> The Nectaren, and curious Peach,
> Into my hands themselves do reach;
> Stumbling on Melons, as I pass,
> Insnar'd with Flow'rs, I fall on Grass.
> (Marvell, *The Garden* stanzas 1 and 5).

There is something here of contemporary Dutch still-lifes of fruit, painted by the likes of Jan Soreau, Willem Frederick van Royen and Harmen van Steenwijck. These, as it were, turn the abstract idea of fruitfulness enshrined in the poem back once more into a material object, paint on canvas, and thus an artifact, the theme of most archaeologies.

Past as contemporary: a note on sources

It did not seem appropriate to reference this paper; essentially we should seek out the past in the works themselves, visually (as I have done in my other contribution) or here in literary quotation. Four books deserve to be singled out amongst those which have informed my archaeological speculations. Michael Foot's *The Politics of Paradise* (1988) is a superb exploration of Byron's life, and his passion for Freedom against all the odds. God will not always be a Tory even though, now as then, and despite a nominally left-wing government it seems so. Charles and Michelle Martindale, *Shakespeare and the Uses of Antiquity* (1990) is a splendid essay in the blending of two historical worlds, those of Rome and the

English Renaissance. The recent excavation of the Rose and Globe theatres and the re-creation of the latter on another site have further bound together these two ages with us. The Elizabethan theatre in which Cassius imagines:

> ....How many ages hence
> Shall this our lofty scene be acted over
> In states unborn and accents yet unknown!
> (*Julius Caesar* Act 3,i, 112-114).

was essentially a Graeco-Roman theatre, recreated first in Italy and now transfered to England. The audience would surely have read the 'states unborn' as England and the 'accents yet unknown' as Elizabethan English.

Cleopatra is terrified that she will be led in triumph through Rome and see:
> Some squeaking Cleopatra boy my greatness
> I' th' posture of a whore.
> (*Antony and Cleopatra* 5,ii,218-219),

again a reference to the Elizabethan-Jacobean stage with its boy actors.

The other two books are especially important, both being written by personal friends, and published in 2001. Elizabeth Cook's searingly beautiful prose poem *Achilles* is composed with a respect for and love of the Greek epics, and a sensibility to the English literary tradition which is ingrained. When I first encountered it in a dramatic reading and later when I read it at a single sitting I thought of all the little gems I had studied showing, for example, Achilles with the armour of Thetis (the subject of my first full-length paper), Achilles with Penthiseleia, the dead Achilles carried by Ajax (this last on an intaglio from Waddon Hill, Dorset)...I also thought of that wonderful painting from the Herculaneum basilica of wise Chiron teaching the child Achilles the lyre, but I had not considered Chiron's pain from an unhealing wound when I taught Roman Art last year; now I always will. Alexander the Great and Byron who, as we have seen, both wore Achilles armour, are part of this story, this web which enmeshes all sentient beings from the very origins of life and which embraces death too. The figure with which the work begins, the two seperate rivers of life and death, which at one point intertwine in a single cable is an image of wise and sad and tranquil beauty, bringing to the archaeologist instant recognition. For in his work in the field and in his writings he too must confront the dead; his death; his mortality; his immortality. This most lovely work brings together the life of a hero with the joys and pains of power; the joys and pains of love. Here is, indeed, a true excavator, 'burrowing like a mole', the phrase is Keats, of which Dr Cook is a foremost authority, but in place of the destructiveness of 'curious Conscience' here is a passion to understand, and a wisdom which can transmute historical character into as present reality. The truth of what I read here, takes my breath away. My spine tingles, as though I am possessed by a spirit, by Lorca's

Duende!

Finally, what seems at first a radically different treatment of archaeology....or is it so very different? I have been very privileged indeed to read my co-editor's *Artifacts. An Archaeologist's Year in Silicon Valley* ahead of publication. In a world of frightening technological advance, the replacement of a gentle fruit-growing culture in the Santa Clara Valley in California by high tech industry and innovation is a climactic event, even though there are rumbles of disaster as the market rocks in the end, just as the god Apollo wills the death of Achilles and Poseidon and Athene stir up tempest against the returning Greeks. My own acquaintance with computers is minimal...this paper is being written on an AMSTRAD which proves it! But my own knowledge of how to use spears and swords and long shields, the theme of Dr Cook's book, is likewise non existent. Like Byron, I would have perished with pristine armour. Dr Finn, too, remains true to human nature; she too has the magic power to bring the past, the past of lost cities covered in sand, and of people long dead into our early 21st-century present and so to transform and heal. Literary and historical perspectives give life and dignity to the often rather ordinary 'artifacts' central to this book. Here too I have found the poetic muse and come to understand, perhaps for the very first time, what archaeology challenges us to become.

The true archaeologist is, and has to be, inevitably and always, gloriously and without shame, the wanderer, the outsider...He is Odysseus, the Roman Ulysses and for an Anglo-Irish audience brought up on Joyce what sudden Bloomsday recognition this identificatian brings. He is Wotan, truly the Wanderer of Wagner's Ring; he is Aeneas, exile from Troy, and progenitor of the Romans who is swept from Dido's arms to the cruel chances of a war he would so much rather avoid; and with Arthur's knights he seeks the Holy Grail, the most beautiful of all vessels (but is it of silver or crystal or merely of earthenware) in Glastonbury or Tintagel ...or in some other place. ALL archaeologists have to seek the Grail. And may be one of them WILL find it? Assuredly our discipline is not, and never has been, concerned with wealth, nor is it concerned with appointments in Universities or Archaeological Units, the first increasingly enslaved to government directives and the latter to business; it is assuredly not about University assessment exercises of any kind or scribbling unreadable reports. All manner of so-called archaeological techniques are taught at University from radio-carbon dating to Classical Art. None of these preserve the essence of archaeology.

Rather archaeology should be more fully related to the unextinguishable flame of the mystic's search for ultimate reality. It flies through the air with the winged beasts of the Apocalypse, it descends from Olympus with the primal gods. I like to think of the tympanum of the church at Charney Basset, Oxfordshire, where Alexander the Great is taken up into the air by griffins, flying upward to the meat the king holds above their heads and which they can, of course, never reach. The student of the Ancient Wisdom, but finding herself confronted with a manufactured (thus artificial) discipline may, with my full approbation, decide to walk off in the diametrically opposite direction, away from paths or artificial aids. Like Oedipus she needs no human guide. Diogenes, close to the earth, knew what the life of the past, the life of the future was really about. He alone could not envy Alexander save for that brief moment when the thoughtless king stood in front of the philosopher's barrel, blocking out his sun. Whether the ideas sketched out in this paper are so heterodox that they leave the writer of them as a genuine archaeologist, however much he is outside the general limits of the discipline, or whether they condemn him to live forever 'outside archaeology', in company with what Glyn Daniel used to call the 'lunatic fringe', it is up to the reader to decide!

Urania's Mirror: Archaeology as an inspiration for Astronomy

Nigel Henbest

The starry skies have undoubtedly inspired cultures throughout prehistory. But it's less well known that archaeology has provided inspiration for astronomical researchers, the followers of the Muse Urania. Here, I discuss the reflections in both sides of Urania's Mirror. On the one hand, I assess the case for precision megalithic astronomy, in sites like Stonehenge; and tentative evidence that a celestial impact influenced the collapse of the Akkad civilisation. On the other, I investigate the role of archaeological artefacts in inspiring astronomers to a deeper understanding of celestial phenomena as diverse as supernovae, the Earth's rotation and comets.

Our general perception of astronomy today is exemplified by the stunning images returned by the Hubble Space Telescope. Such cutting-edge astrophysics can reveal objects throughout almost the whole visible Universe. But these views lack one crucial dimension: time. For only a few decades have astronomers been able to use powerful telescopes, so our views of the Universe are very much snapshots of the cosmos.*

Historical sources lengthen the time base to a couple of millennia in certain circumstances - where complete astronomical records were kept. Through archaeology, we may hope to complement historical observations and to extend the time base farther into the past.

Archaeology thus becomes an inspiration for astronomy. In addition, it is able to provide unique data for astronomical research. In broad terms, archaeology can inform astronomy in two areas: events that are rare; and events that are slow.

The category of 'rare' includes the appearance of comets, novae and supernovae (both types of exploding star). Examples of 'slow' events are the motion of stars across the sky and changes in the rotation of the Earth.

The background

The application of archaeology to astronomy was a twentieth century phenomenon. But it builds on a long tradition of 'applied historical astronomy.' Since the Renaissance, astronomers have occasionally looked back to classical writings of astronomical events - in particular, eclipses - for information on the workings of the Universe.

The first scientist to attempt this task systematically was Edmond Halley[1], contemporary of Isaac Newton and England's second Astronomer Royal. Halley is of course best known for 'his' comet. Halley observed the comet in 1682, though he did not discover it. Instead, his claim to fame was using Newton's newly formulated law of gravity to conclude that the comet was in a closed orbit around the Sun, and so it must reappear at more or less regular intervals. Searching through the astronomical literature, Halley found previous appearances of the comet in 1607 and 1531. He predicted it would return in 1758, which it duly did, long after Halley's demise.

Halley also checked out the Almagest, which catalogued the positions of stars in the sky. It was compiled by the Alexandrian astronomer Ptolemy in 150 BC, and based on observations by his near contemporary Hipparchus and by Timocharis who observed in 300 BC. Halley discovered that three bright stars - Sirius, Arcturus and Aldebaran - had shifted their positions by about the apparent width of the Moon (half a degree). Through this early example of applied historical astronomy, Halley showed that the stars have their own individual motions across the sky ('proper motion').

Finally, in his later years, Halley turned to measuring the motion of the Moon with high precision. Again, he checked back on classical references to eclipses and discovered that - over the millennia - the Moon seemed to be gradually accelerating in its motion across the sky. (The full explanation is rather more complex, as I shall discuss later.)

Archaeoastronomy

Around the year 1900, the interaction of archaeology and astronomy led to a new interdisciplinary area: known at various times as megalithic astronomy and astroarchaeology, it is now universally known as archaeo-astronomy. In its 'classical' form, archaeoastronomy is the study of astronomical influences on archaeological sites[2]. Since the purpose of this paper is the converse, I shall undertake only a brief discussion here, concentrating on some of the more controversial claims. The pioneer of archaeoastronomy was the British polymath Sir Norman Lockyer. Founder of the journal Nature and a solar astronomer, Lockyer also co-authored The Rules of Golf! Impressed by the accurate and intentional alignments of Egyptian monuments, Lockyer turned his attention to the great British megalithic monument, Stonehenge.

---

* This is not to dispute the fact that all astronomical observations take us back in time. Because light takes a finite period to travel any distance, we see every astronomical object as it was in the past: the Sun as it was 8 minutes ago, the Andromeda Galaxy as it was two million years ago. But we do not see the evolution of any individual object: these are snapshots of different objects taken at different points in time.

[1] Alan Cook, 1997, Edmond Halley, Clarendon Press (Oxford)
[2] For an overview, see Anthony F. Aveni 1989, World Archaeoastronomy, Cambridge University Press (Cambridge). Current archaeoastronomical research is published principally in Archaeoastronomy (supplement to Journal for the History of Astronomy) and Archaeoastronomy (Journal of the Center for Archaeoastronomy, College Park, Maryland)

The axis of Stonehenge was already known to point towards sunrise at midsummer. The Sun's rising point changes very gradually over the centuries, and so Lockyer hoped that an accurate survey would lead to an astronomical dating for the monument.

According to popular belief, the Sun rises behind a prominent outlier, the Heel Stone, on Midsummer's Day. In fact, as seen from the centre of Stonehenge, the Sun rises well to the left, and is just clear of the horizon as it passes above the Heel Stone. In earlier times, the Sun would have sailed even higher above this outlier at the solstice.

Lockyer was well aware of this problem, and proposed instead that the crucial direction of Midsummer sunrise was marked by the Avenue that stretches away from Stonehenge. Lockyer's 1901 survey established that an observer at the centre of Stonehenge would see the Sun first twinkle above the horizon along the axis of the Avenue on Midsummer's Day around the year 1680 BC[3].

Since then, the idea of Stonehenge as a solar observatory has become part of folklore, with more recent claims it was also a lunar observatory and even an eclipse-calculator[4]. But even the basic sunrise claims are difficult to substantiate. In the 1970s, Richard Atkinson resurveyed the Avenue, and ascertained that Lockyer's measurement was out by 0.3 degree - about two-thirds the Sun's diameter! At no time in prehistory did the Midsummer Sun rise along the newly ascertained axis of the Avenue.

As an astronomical observatory, Stonehenge is anyway appallingly designed. An observer within the monument cannot readily discern the direction of Avenue's centre line. Even worse, there's nothing to indicate the exact centre of Stonehenge, for example a megalith that might define the observer's position. And this position is critical. If the observer's left eye was used instead of the right, the calculated date of the solstice changes by 500 years![5]

Stonehenge, in conclusion, was almost certainly not an observatory: its solar connections were presumably symbolic, ritualistic and/or ceremonial. The astronomical Stonehenge of the 1960s reflected public interest in space, the Moon Race, newly discovered quasars and pulsars, and the supposed power of the computer to solve ancient enigmas. As Jacquetta Hawkes elegantly observed[6]: "every age has the Stonehenge it deserves - or desires."

Before this episode closed, however, archaeologists and astronomers saw the emergence of the era of 'Megalithic Astronomy.' The instigator was Alexander Thom, a Scottish engineer who surveyed in intricate detail the megalithic monuments of his native country. Thom claimed that many were designed as precision observatories, for studying the motions of the Sun and Moon.

Thom was well aware that a major argument against the use of Stonehenge as an observatory lay in the fact that the difference in sunrise position from the day before the solstice to Midsummer's Day itself is almost imperceptibly small - about 2% of the Sun's diameter. The only way to make such a fine discrimination with the naked eye is use a distant foresight, such as a mountain slope where the Sun just twinkles through a notch at its most extreme position, on solstice day itself.

After surveying hundreds of megalithic sites in Britain and Brittany, Thom concluded that many of them indicated foresights for making precise observations of the rising and setting of the Sun and Moon[7]. Thom's research was persuasive at the time: it led even Richard Atkinson to write[8]: "I am prepared... to believe that my model of European prehistory is wrong, rather than that the results presented by Thom are due to nothing but chance."

Subsequent field investigation and statistical analysis, particularly by Clive Ruggles, have however have led to increasing scepticism[9]. Ruggles' negative conclusions are highlighted by his astronomical background, and by his own initial enthusiasm for Thom's ideas. After re-surveying 189 megalithic sites in western Scotland, Ruggles finds, for example, that there are no precise alignments on the direction of the Midsummer sunrise - the very date apparently picked out so dramatically at Stonehenge. Overall, Ruggles concludes[10] "we are forced to conclude that the idea of prehistoric orthostatic monuments in Britain incorporating astronomical alignments precise to anything greater than about a degree is completely unproven by the sort of approach taken by Thom."

Investigations of how the Earth's atmosphere refracts light have put the final nail in the coffin of Megalithic Astronomy as a precise science. Refraction raises the apparent position of the Sun or Moon in the sky: when we see the Sun 'on' the horizon, in reality it has just set. Now it turns out that refraction is highly variable[11]. It can

[3] Norman Lockyer and F. C. Penrose, 1901, 'An Attempt to Ascertain the Date of the Original Construction of Stonehenge from Its Construction', Proceedings of the Royal Society of London, vol 69, pp 137-47. See also Norman Lockyer, 1906, Stonehenge and Other British Stone Monuments Astronomically Considered, Macmillan (London)

[4] For an overview, see Nigel Henbest, 1979, 'Astronomy and Stonehenge', in Michael Balfour, 1979, Stonehenge and its Mysteries, Macdonald and Jane's (London) pp 37-49

[5] Richard Atkinson, 1978, 'Some New Measurements on Stonehenge,' Nature, vol 275 pp 50-52

[6] Jacquetta Hawkes, 1967, 'God in the Machine,' Antiquity, vol 41, pp 174-80.

[7] Alexander Thom, 1967, Megalithic Sites in Britain, Oxford University Press (Oxford); Alexander Thom, 1971, Megalithic Lunar Observatories, Oxford University Press (Oxford)

[8] Richard Atkinson, 1975, 'Megalithic Astronomy: A Prehistorian's Comments', Journal for the History of Astronomy, vol 6, pp 42-52

[9] Clive Ruggles, 1999, Astronomy in Prehistoric Britain and Ireland, Yale University Press (New Haven)

[10] Ruggles, op.cit., p 75

[11] Bradley E. Schaefer and William Liller, 1990, 'Refraction near the horizon,' Publications of the Astronomical Society of the Pacific, vol 102, pp 796-805

change the Sun's apparent position more than a tenth of its diameter in the sky - far more than its daily creep along the horizon. As a result, an observer could well see the Sun or Moon twinkle along one of Thom's 'precision foresights' on a very different date from the one he originally calculated.

On the positive side, the lasting legacy of this era may prove to be the acceptance in archaeological circles of a general cosmological perspective in megalithic cultures[12].

Applied Historical/Archaeological Astronomy

Returning to the main topic of this review, the inspiration of archaeology on astronomy has passed a new milestone in recent decades. It has led to quantitative measurements of the Universe that would be impossible to achieve in any other way.

The interdisciplinary study that Halley pioneered in the historical arena is now beginning to include archaeological source material. Spurred largely by the pioneering work of British astronomer Richard Stephenson over the past 25 years, the International Astronomical Union recognized the value of historical records to contemporary astronomy with its first symposium on 'Applied Historical Astronomy' at its General Assembly held in Manchester in August 2000. In view of the subject matter, a more appropriate - though admittedly more cumbersome! - title would be 'Applied Historical/Archaeological Astronomy.'

Here I'll describe three particular areas of research that pick up the theme of 'rare' or 'slow' events being illuminated by past human experience. These are not exclusive: many other areas of astronomy - e.g. the study of sunspots, aurorae and meteors - also benefit from the historical dimension.

First, supernovae. These brilliant exploding stars appear very rarely: in the past 2000 years, only nine or ten have been recorded that became visible to the naked eye[13],[14]. Although supernova from 1572 onwards are well reported in the western astronomical literature, the main source for earlier supernovae - back to 720 BC - comprises Chinese records[15].

According to Stephenson, the earliest supernova that can be definitely identified occurred on 7 December AD 185. In the contemporary astronomical treatise the Hou-han-shu, we find the following[16]: "A guest star appeared within Nan-mên. It was as large as half a mat; it showed the five colours and it scintillated." Chinese observers were interested in astrology rather than astronomy, so the account continues with an interpretative gloss. "According to the standard prognostication, this means insurrection... Wu-kwang attacked and killed Ho-miao, the general of chariots and cavalry, and several thousand people were killed."

Nan-Mên is an asterism (small constellation) comprising a pair of bright stars that western astronomy now calls Alpha and Beta Centauri. Between these two stars, Stephenson and his colleague David Clark have identified a source of radio waves that is almost certainly the remains of the AD 185 supernova. For astronomers studying this supernova remnant, the Chinese observations provide a critical piece of information - the time elapsed since the original explosion occurred[17].

My second example - the study of comets - inevitably brings us back to Halley, and in particular the comet named after him. Prior to its 1986 re-appearance, historical records had revealed Halley's Comet in previous appearances back to 87 BC, with a Chinese reference to an appearance in 240 BC that contains little precise information.

In between, there should have been an appearance of Halley's Comet in 164 BC. With Chinese records silent - presumably incomplete - Richard Stephenson turned to Babylonian cuneiform tablets in the British Museum's collection. He located an astronomical diary from that year with an unambiguous sighting[18]. "The comet which previously had appeared in the east in the path of Anu in the area of the Pleiades and Taurus passed along in the path of Ea..."

Combined with more recent historical texts, this precise archaeological account has led to a better understanding of the nature of comets. The Giotto spacecraft in 1986 revealed that the core of Halley's Comet comprises an icy nucleus, 16 kilometres long, which ejects jets of gas and steam as it approaches the Sun's heat. The historical and archaeological accounts of the comet's continuing visibility provide strong evidence that the outgassing from the nucleus has remained constant over at least two millennia[19].

The long timeline of the historical and archaeological records also reveals that Halley's Comet does not return exactly on the schedule imposed by the gravity of the Sun

---

[12] For example, in Colin Renfrew and Paul. G. Bahn, 1996, Archaeology: Theory, Methods and Practice (2nd edition), Thames and Hudson (London)

[13] David H. Clark and F. Richard Stephenson, 1977, The Historical Supernovae, Pergamon (Oxford)

[14] As well as the eight supernovae listed in ref. 13, a further 'historical supernova' is believed to have been sighted in 1680 by the first Astronomer Royal, John Flamsteed; and a recent naked eye supernova (Supernova 1987A) appeared in 1987.

[15] Richard Stephenson, 2000, 'East Asian observations,' oral presentation at the International Astronomical Union symposium 'Applied Historical Astronomy' (August 2000)

[16] Clark and Stephenson, op. cit., p 83.

[17] Clark and Stephenson, op cit., p 211.

[18] F. Richard Stephenson, Kevin K. C. Yau and Hermann Hunger, 1985, 'Records of Halley's Comet on Babylonian Tablets,' Nature, vol 314, pp 587-592

[19] Donald K. Yeomans, 1995, 'Ancient Chinese Observations and Modern Cometary Models,' oral presentation at the American Astronomical Society meeting (December 1995)

and - to a lesser extent - the planets. Each return is four days late. According to Donald Yeomans, of NASA's Jet Propulsion Laboratory, the delay is caused by the outflowing gas pushing on the nucleus itself [20].

In contrast, observations of another comet, Swift-Tuttle, back to 69 BC show that it runs precisely on schedule. Swift-Tuttle's outflowing gas jets evidently cause little perturbation to the comet's motion. The simplest interpretation is that the nucleus of Swift-Tuttle feels less effect from its jets because it is some ten times more massive than the nucleus of Halley's Comet[21]. Here, the historical and archaeological record is allowing astronomers to "weigh" comets.

Earth's inconstant rotation

My third example represents the most scientifically important contribution of archaeology to current astronomy. Here we pick up on the role of the archaeological dimension in illuminating rare events, and then develop its potential to define slow events - in this case, the changing rotation rate of planet Earth.

We start with ancient records of eclipses. Eclipses of the Sun, in particular, are so spectacular that they are noted in many general historical records, as well as in specifically astronomical diaries. Amongst the earliest is an inscription on a Chinese oracle bone, stating "three flames ate the Sun and there were big stars." The "three flames" are undoubtedly the Sun's glowing corona, visible only during a total eclipse, when the brighter stars ("big stars") would also be visible. The oracle bones, unfortunately, give only the day number in a 60-day cycle, so the year of the eclipse is ambiguous: in the case quoted[22], it was probably 1176 BC.

Chinese records from around 700 BC provide more definitive data. Babylonian tablets provide another unique archaeological resource, for the period from 700 to 50 BC. Later periods are covered by medieval European and Arabic records. From these, Stephenson has compiled a comprehensive listing of eclipses over more than two and half millennia[23].

Immediately we try to compare these observations with dates and places calculated for past eclipses, we run into a major problem (as Halley was the first to note). Take, for example, the unambiguous record of a total solar eclipse

recorded on a Babylonian tablet on 15 April 136 BC[24]. "It became entirely total... Venus, Mercury and the 'normal stars' were visible; Jupiter and Mars, which were in their period of disappearance, became visible in the eclipse."

If we 'rewind' the rotation of the Earth and the orbital motion of the Moon, we find there should indeed have been a total eclipse on that date. But it would not have been visible in Babylon. Instead, the total eclipse should have been seen only in western Europe.

How do we reconcile the observation and the theory? It's inconceivable that the Babylonians fabricated their observations, so let us look more closely at the theory. The calculation I've described assumes that the Earth always rotates at a constant rate, exactly 24 hours long. In fact, precise chronological measurements now reveal that the Earth is gradually slowing down, and as a result days are gradually growing longer. (That's why we must insert 'leap seconds' every year or so, to keep clock time in line with the Earth's natural period of rotation.)

This slowing down is caused by the tides. The Moon raises tidal bulges in the Earth's oceans, and these act like brake shoes as the planet rotates. Friction between the water and the sea beds slows down the Earth's rotation rate. At the same time, the Moon is forced to move slowly away from the Earth. (These are the effects that Halley first noticed, though they were inexplicable in his day.) Calculations show that these tidal effects should be increasing the length of the day by 0.0023 seconds per century[25].

To a first approximation, tidal slowing explains the discrepancies in the locations where ancient eclipses were recorded. If we run backwards the Earth's rotation to 136 BC, allowing for this slowdown, we find that the track of the eclipse does not pass through the western Europe, but through the Near East.

This is more consistent with the archaeological record, but the path of the eclipse would now run slightly to the east of Babylon. With Leslie Morrison of the Royal Greenwich Observatory, Stephenson has undertaken a thorough analysis of ancient eclipse records like this. To satisfy all the observations, they find that tidal slowing cannot be the only influence on the Earth's rotation: there must be one or two extra effects at work[26]. Unlike the tidal slowing, which also shows up in precise modern astronomical observations, these very slow changes are discernable only with long timebase of the historical and archaeological records.

The first of these non-tidal influences on the Earth's rotation is related to the end of the last Ice Age. During the Ice Age, the massive ice sheets at the pole squashed the

---

[20] Donald Yeomans, 2000, ''Creating Cometary Models using Ancient Chinese Data,' oral presentation at the International Astronomical Union symposium 'Applied Historical Astronomy' (August 2000)

[21] Kevin Yau, Donald Yeomans and Paul Weissman, 1994, 'The Past and Future Motion of Comet P/Swift-Tuttle', Monthly Notices of the Royal Astronomical Society, vol. 266, pp 305-316

[22] Xu Zhen-tao, F. Richard Stephenson and Jiang Yao-tiao, 1995, 'Astronomy on Oracle Bone Inscriptions,' Quarterly Journal of the Royal Astronomical Society, vol. 36, pp 397-406.

[23] Richard Stephenson, 1997, Historical Eclipses and the Earth's Rotation, Cambridge University Press (Cambridge)

[24] Leslie Morrison and Richard Stephenson, 1998, 'The Sands of Time and the Earth's Rotation,' Astronomy and Geophysics, vol. 39, pp 5.9-5.10

[25] Morrison and Stephenson, op.cit., pp 5.8-5.9

[26] Morrison and Stephenson, op. cit., pp 5.12-5.13

Earth into a slight tangerine shape; with the melting of the ice, the Earth is now more spherical. This slight change in shape is sufficient to affect the Earth's rotation rate measurably during the past 2000 years. Over that period, it has counteracted the tidal slowing to some extent. It has reduced the rate at which the day-length is increasing from the expected 0.0023 seconds per century to 0.0018 seconds per century[27].

The ancient eclipse observations also suggest that the rate of the Earth's rotation is varying cyclically over a period of some 1500 years. The most likely reason is a change in the friction between the Earth's mantle - its main body - and the liquid metal core at the planet's centre[28]. Here, archaeology is taking us downwards not just the few metres of a conventional dig but to a region thousands of kilometres beneath our feet!

Impacts and Armageddon

Finally, a look to the future - to one arena where archaeology and astronomy may come to work more directly together, and where archaeology provides a bridge between history and geology.

Astronomers have recently become aware of the danger of impacts from space. For example, a small asteroid exploded over the Stony Tunguska valley in Siberia in 1908, with an energy of 12 megatons - roughly 1000 times that of the Hiroshima atom bomb. A far more severe impact in the Yucatan region of Mexico 65 million years ago coincided with the Cretaceous-Tertiary mass extinction event which killed the dinosaurs and two-thirds of all species on Earth[29].

Between these two timescales (roughly 100 years and 100 million years) we expect impacts of an intermediate energy - not sufficient to wipe out species, but severe enough to disrupt cultural evolution at a level that may be discernable in the archaeological record. During the past 5000 years, the Earth should have been subjected to over a hundred impacts as severe as Tunguska, with a few at the 1000 megaton level[30].

While there is no incontrovertible field evidence for such an impact, Marie-Agnes Courty has recently discovered tantalizing hints in northern Syria. Excavating in four separate regions, she has found an unusual dust layer at a level corresponding to 4000 BP (2350 cal BC), coincident with an abrupt climate change and the collapse of the

Akkad Empire. Initially, Courty and her coworkers attributed the dust to a volcanic eruption[31].

Further investigations, however, are inconsistent with this hypothesis. In particular, Courty finds that the dust layer contains particles of carbon created by extensive high-temperature combustion in a dense forest. This soot could not have originated in the local region, of cultivated fields and open scrubby steppes. Instead, it must have been blown in from an intense conflagration in a dense savannah or tropical forest region possibly thousands of kilometers away[32]. The high-temperature combustion is atypical of normal forest fires, but is characteristic of extraterrestrial impacts: the 1994 impact of Comet Shoemaker-Levy-9 with Jupiter, for example, created fireballs with temperatures up to 5000°C[33].

Although the putative impact site for the 4000 BP event has yet to be identified, a major cosmic impact at that time could account for severe climatic changes, ecological disasters and the collapse of the Indus and other civilizations, in addition to the Akkadian[34].

There is also astronomical evidence for the break-up of a giant comet around this time. Disintegration fragments would have abounded in the inner Solar System, leading to a high possibility of impacts on the Earth[35].

This possible convergence of archaeology and astronomy could provide a unique new synergy. Impacts in the archaeological record can inform astronomers of the Solar System environment over past millennia; while the well-developed theory of astronomical impacts may lead to an understanding of whether human civilizations - like the dinosaurs - have been exterminated by cosmic forces.

[27] Leslie Morrison, 2000, 'Ancient Eclipses and the Earth's Rotation,' oral presentation at the International Astronomical Union symposium 'Applied Historical Astronomy' (August 2000)

[28] *Ibid.*

[29] For an overview of cosmic impacts and their effects, see Duncan Steel, 2000, Target Earth, Time-Life (London)

[30] William M. Napier, 1998, 'Cometary Catastrophes, Cosmic Dust and Ecological Disasters in Historical Times: the Astronomical Framework,' British Archaeological Reports International Series 728, pp 21-32

[31] H. Weiss, M-A. Courty, W. Wetterstrom, R. Meadow, R. Guichard, L. Senior and A. Curnow, 1993, 'The Origin and Collapse of Third Millennium North Mesopotamian Civilisation,' Science, vol. 261, pp 995-1004

[32] Marie-Agnes Courty, 1998, 'The Soil Record of an Exceptional Event at 4000 BP in the Middle East,' British Archaeological Reports International Series 728, pp 93-108

[33] S.J. Kim, M. Ruiz, G.H. Rieke, M.J. Rieke, K. Zahnle and M. Mac Low, 1995, oral presentation at the American Astronomical Society meeting (December 1995)

[34] Benny J. Peiser, 'Comparative Analysis of Late Holocene Environmental and Social Upheaval: Evidence for a Global Disaster in the Late 3rd Millennium BC,' British Archaeological Reports International Series 728, pp 117-39

[35] Mark E. Bailey, 'Historical Variability of the Interplanetary Complex,' oral presentation at the International Astronomical Union symposium 'Applied Historical Astronomy' (August 2000)

The Empire Strikes Back: Imperial motifs in Edwardian jewellery*

Helen Molesworth

'We have such wealth as Rome at her most pride,
Had not (or having) scattered not so wide...
Lo! Diamond that cost some half their days
To find and t'other half to bring to blaze.'
(Rudyard Kipling, *The Birthright*, 1899)

We see here a contemporary comparison between the British Empire and that of Imperial Rome, and a focus upon the power of diamond and jewels as symbols of the wealth and durability of empires. These lines encapsulate the potential of jewels to express the social messages of wealth and power, in addition to the political undertones of dominance and leadership. In this paper I would like to explore the power of jewels as propaganda, and offer some further thoughts regarding the possible usage of classical imagery and motifs within jewellery during the late-nineteenth and early-twentieth centuries, that is the apogee of the British Empire.

The jewellery of this period has a very characteristic appearance, known today as 'Garland Style'. It is typified by a lightness, delicacy and pure whiteness, fluid lines, and stylised floral motifs. These include garlands and swags, ribbon bows, tassels, and most specifically scrolling acanthus, and laurel wreaths with their laurel berries. This was very much in opposition to the previous Victorian style of jewellery which was heavy and chunky, awkward (today one might say unwearable), and typified by its realistic, rather than stylistic, portrayal of flowers. Technically Victorian jewellery would have been made either from yellow gold or from a laminate of gold backing with silver setting for the gemstones: a technique developed to achieve not only a white setting for the white diamonds while structurally strengthening the silver with gold, but also to prevent the silver from tarnishing both dresses and skin.

However with the turn of the century came the introduction of the use of platinum, and with it a revolution in jewellery design. The element platinum had been used within jewellery for millennia ever since Egyptian craftsmen had used it unknowingly as an alloy with other metals. It had been known about as an element since the Spanish mathematician, Don Antonio de Ulloa, had reported a new metal *platina* ('little silver') found in 1748 in Columbia, and only with difficulty distinguishable from gold. Yet it was not until the second half of the nineteenth century that platinum began to be frequently worked for jewellery purposes. It was only after the invention of the oxyhydrogen torch that a flame hot enough to reach the exceedingly high melting point of platinum (1755°C or 3190°F) could be produced. (Nadelhoffer, 1984, p. 58; GIA, 1989, 9 p.14)

The stylistic importance of the effect of the use of platinum upon jewellery design was twofold. The new diamonds, discovered in South African mines in the latter half of the nineteenth century, soon became the dominant gemstone and they needed to be set in a white, untarnishable metal to display them at their very best. Being relatively inert, platinum fulfilled this role; being very strong and rigid the amount of metal used in a jewel could be reduced producing a far more light and delicate setting.

This new technique and style within jewellery design was complemented perfectly, and indeed partly encouraged, by contemporary fashion and clothing design. A certain delicacy and femininity was being encouraged in ladies' fashions, characterised by sinuous lines, delicate fabrics (perfect for off-setting the whiteness of the diamonds and the lightness of the platinum) and an overall feminine form. (See Figure 1) A leading exponent of this style and couturier of this period was the House of Worth whose main premises were located on the exclusive *Rue de la Paix* in Paris. It was no coincidence, however, that such fashion and jewellery designs were so complementary; in fact the two leading proponents of each in Paris were inextricably linked. The couturier Worth was situated next door to the pre-eminent jeweller of the period, Louis Cartier, with the fashion house of Worth situated at Number 7 Rue de la Paix and Cartier at Number 13 in 1899 and then also Number 11 by 1912. They shared the same rich and prestigious clientele from both aristocratic and royal European families and the new American entrepreneurs. In addition the families of Worth and Cartier were also allied by marriage (Nadelhoffer, 1984, pp.37-41). It is well recognised that Louis Cartier was the prominent proponent of the new jewellery fashion that we refer to as the 'Garland Style' which was followed and adopted by other jewellers worldwide. (See Figures 2 and 3) Figures 2 and 3 are two Cartier corsage brooches, designed to be worn at the base of the neckline on a low-cut dress, which display the characteristic stylistic elements of the jewellery of this period. In figure 2 we can see the centralised wreath of laurel, identifiable by the shape of leaves and the berries, framed by the two scrolls of acanthus and the suspended floral swags and tassels. Figure 3 again portrays the acanthus scrolls, swags and tassels in a slightly more architectural form.

----

* I am very grateful to Mr Giles Gasper for his kind help and enlightening discussion, to Mr William Thomas for his informative criticism and historical insights, and above all to Dr Martin Henig for the invitation to deliver a paper at the Theoretical Archaeology Conference and his continual support, enthusiasm and inspiring ideas.

Not least amongst Cartier's impressive and loyal clientele were the Prince and Princess of Wales, who later became Edward VII and Queen Alexandra in 1901[1]. It was in 1904 that Cartier was to create this magnificent 'Garland Style' *collier resille* (literally 'hairnet') for the Queen (See Figure 4). In fact Alexandra was herself a mighty influence upon the fashions and styles of the day, promoting the pastel colours in her dress (often to be seen in lavender and grey) and the delicate diamond jewellery in which she was frequently draped. She popularised *colliers de chien* or dog-collars, a jewellery form intrinsic to the 'Garland Style', allegedly to cover a neck-scar which she received in her childhood.

It is generally accepted that the sole inspiration for the Garland Style, particularly through Louis Cartier, was the splendour of the eighteenth century court of Versailles and Louis XVI rococo decoration. Records show that Louis Cartier personally consulted several eighteenth-century pattern books (dating to the reigns of Louis XV and XVI) which were re-circulated in the 1850s showing designs of flowers, wreaths, garlands and vases. He also encouraged his draftsmen to go out into the streets of Paris and study seventeenth and eighteenth century architecture for inspiration. Their drawings of, for example, structural details from patrician houses in the Faubourg St Germain, or fruit garlands from the Petit Trianon, were reproduced in the jewellery sketch books for the House of Cartier (Nadelhoffer, 1984, pp. 45-48).

This is the extent of the modern argument for the creation of, and inspiration for, the Garland Style: that is the introduction of the use of platinum, the new clothes fashions and their exponents and the designs of the jewellery house of Cartier. In this sense the use of classical iconography within early twentieth century jewellery is, to a great degree, second-hand: while the court of Versailles was directly using classical motifs within its art and architecture, the early-twentieth century jewellers merely copied the court of Versailles[2]. It may be well documented that Louis Cartier encouraged his draftsmen to take inspiration from eighteenth century French pattern books and architecture, but that, I believe, is only one dimension. Another, is that the implications of the original Roman Imperial motifs would have been understood and publicised, especially by the clients who wore and popularised these jewels: the aristocracy and royalty of the major Empires in Europe. Contemporary Imperial aspiration could draw on ancient Imperial motifs.

These motifs were originally employed and disseminated as a form of propaganda by Augustus in the first century BC. Following the defeat of Mark Antony and Cleopatra at the Battle of Actium in 31 BC, Octavian effectively attained sole power and control of the existing Roman Republic. In 27 BC he was officially recognised as saviour of the State and for his 'restoration of the republic' was awarded the title of Augustus together with the highest honours the State and Senate could bestow. As he himself recorded in his *Res Gestae*, his political autobiography: 'For this service [the restoration] I was named *Augustus* by the resolution of the Senate. The doorposts of my house were officially decked out with young laurel trees, the *corona civica* [an oak wreath] was placed over the door, and in the Curia Iulia was displayed the *clipeus virtutis* [the golden shield].'(*Res Gestae*, 34; Brunt, 1970)

The symbolism of these honours is best explained by Paul Zanker: 'The laurel trees, the *corona civica*, and the *clipeus virtutis* were modest and simple honours in the old Roman tradition….Laurel wreaths and branches had always crowned victors and were the attribute of Victory herself….The *corona civica* was rooted rather in the military sphere. The oak wreath had traditionally been awarded for rescuing a comrade in battle….for Augustus's successors the oak wreath [and the laurel] became an insigne of power, completely removed from its original meaning.' (Zanker, 1988, pp. 92-94)

These motifs became part of what Zanker calls a 'new Imperial style' used by Augustus to promote and strengthen his political position. The oak and laurel became symbols of Augustan victory. Both were used as wreaths to represent victory (as the victor's crown) and restitution (as the *corona civica*). According to Zanker 'laurel and oak leaves became widely understood as synonyms for 'Augustus' and gradually lost their original meaning' (Zanker, 1988, pp. 79-100). On the Temple of Apollo in Rome dedicated by C. Sosius in 25 BC laurel branches stand out on the frieze above the ornate acanthus capitals (see Figure 5a).

As part of this 'new Imperial style' Zanker also refers to an Augustan 'program of cultural renewal' (Zanker pp 101 – 166). The new emperor made use of the visual, and particularly sculptural arts, to demonstrate the restoration and rebirth of the republic under his guidance. He characterised the new 'Golden Age' as a time of abundance and fertility, symbolised by foliate swags and garlands, and peace and piety, symbolised by fillets or ribbons. These images, together with representations of oak and laurel leaves, can be seen on some of the most famous monuments of Augustus's rule, including C. Sosius' Temple of Apollo and the *Ara Pacis* (see Figures 5a and 6). It is these very motifs (oak and laurel, wreaths, acanthus, garlands, swags and fillets or ribbons) that we see re-used in late-nineteenth and early-twentieth century decorative arts.

---

[1] It was upon the suggestion of the Prince that the first London branch was opened in 1902, on New Burlington Street as a joint premise with Worth. According to Nadelhoffer 'a branch in London had been a strong possibility ever since the English high nobility had begun crowding in to the rooms in the rue de la Paix and, back in London, been forced to wait impatiently for their orders to be delivered from Paris' (p.42). Before then, Pierre Cartier had used the Hotel Cecil as his base in London for the many orders placed for the coronation and had subsequently visited the new Queen in Buckingham Palace to take her orders.

[2] For the fullest accounts of the development of the 'Garland Style' within the House of Cartier, see Nadelhoffer, 1984, pp. 45-66, Cologni and Nussbaum, 1996, pp. 9-20 and Rudoe, 1997, pp. 65-101

The extent to which not only classical learning but also a very wide classical awareness permeated Edwardian society is well recognised. A familiarity with the Classics was not only found amongst the higher-educated and administrative classes, but all the way throughout society, to the degree that classical parallels and influences could be recognised by the majority. Numerous authors in children's and adult fiction of the period could draw upon classical allusions, reference and even languages, expecting their audiences to provide the obvious connections (for further reference see Stray, 1998). Rudyard Kipling makes consistent reference to classical literature and history for instance in *Puck of Pook's Hill*, 1906, especially in the stories 'A Centurion of the Thirtieth', 'On the Great Wall' and 'The Winged Hats'.[3] Rider Haggard in his novel *She* puts in several pages of Greek and Latin in the introductory sections of the story.[4] Edwardian familiarity with the classical world was not confined to the literary, but extended equally to the visual arts. Classical, and particularly Roman, images were everywhere for all to see, and as we already know, for all to appreciate and understand. One of the many wonderful architectural examples in London is the Foreign and Commonwealth Office in King Charles Street designed by George Gilbert Scott as 'a kind of national palace or drawing room for the nation' and completed in 1868.[5] Original artefacts were also readily accessible to the public in the museum collections in Great Britain as for the rest of Europe. The Campana Collection had been on view in the Louvre since its acquisition by Napoleon III in 1861.

Also of paramount importance to the Edwardian mindset was the concept of Empire and Great Britain's dominance. The traditional jewel in the British Crown was the Imperial dominion over India initiated by, and formally manifested with, Victoria's accession as Empress of India on 1st May 1876, and the Prince of Wales's six-month tour in 1875-1876. In addition, after 1874 and Lord Carnavon's attempts to secure a white confederation, events in South Africa also contributed to an upsurge in popular enthusiasm for the imperialist ideal.[6]

As Richard Hingley sets out so thoroughly in his new book *Roman Officers and English Gentlemen*, the comparisons to be made between the Empires of Rome and Great Britain were inescapable. One of the earliest parallels to be drawn was made by John Collingwood Bruce in 1851 in his book *The Roman Wall*: "Her [Britain's] Empire is threefold that of Rome in the hour of its prime…The

sceptre which Rome relinquished we have taken up. Great is our Honour - great our Responsibility" (Bruce, 1851, pp. 449-500). A significant number of writers, particularly in the period 1880 to 1914 also drew upon Rome in considering Britain and her Empire from such administrators and politicians as Lord Curzon and Lord Cromer, to such Youth Workers as R.S.S.B. Baden-Powell, and academics as F. Haverfield. Such comparison was not only made but also needed, to the extent that, as Hingley puts it, "images derived from classical Rome were used to help inform British imperial policy during the late nineteenth and early twentieth centuries" and to clarify Imperial and national identity. Nor was it, he argues, simply literary or academic, but a form of "State-sponsored Imperial propaganda" that had commercial repercussions: "Writers, publishers and manufacturers took their own commercial decisions based on the positive image that the Empire instilled in the minds of the public and which helped to sell their products." (Hingley, 2000, pp. 1-27). I would like to take Hingley's argument in a new direction and apply the possibility of this Edwardian 'Imperial Discourse' to the area of jewellery.

Jewellery has been used as a display of wealth and a form of propaganda throughout history. The most obvious type of jewellery to have such connotations is the diadem or the tiara.[7] In its simplest form the diadem signifies victory: in Ancient Greece it was given to Olympic and musical victors.[8] Two and a half thousand years later a hellenistically-inspired victor's laurel wreath, dated November 6th 1917, was given to Vera Boarman Whitehouse by the women of New York State in recognition of her efforts as the leader of the women's suffrage movement. Its inscription, which reads 'To Vera Boarman Whitehouse from the women of New York State whom she led to victory November 6 1917' demonstrates a clear contemporary recognition of the laurel as a symbol of leadership and victory (Wartski 1997, p. 13; Scarisbrick, 2000, pp. 162-163). The more widely acknowledged associations of the diadem, tiara, or crown, are as proof of nobility, position and royal power. A golden fillet (diadem with loose fabric ties at the back of the head) was discovered upon the head of the mummy of Tutankhamun (1371-1352 BC); in 325 AD the diadem re-appeared again as a fillet and only the Emperor Constantine the Great had the right to wear it; in Byzantine art the diadem was worn as a symbol of any high office; and as Diana Scarisbrick puts it in her book *Tiara*, "In France the Tiara was used by Napoleon as a means of asserting the authority of absolute power. His precedent was Imperial Rome and just as Augustus, his empress, and their successors wore tiaras as

---

[3] The theme also emerges in the school stories *Stalky and Co.*, 1899, where one story is explicitly constructed around the parable of Regulus.

[4] Another book which would have been well known to public school men of the period would have been Macaulay's *Lays of Ancient Rome*. Although written in 1847, it was reprinted again and again and presented as a prize at school speech days.

[5] Dr Martin Henig has kindly drawn my attention also to the clocktower in Redcar, Cleveland, decorated with carved swags, erected in 1913 in memory of Edward VII who is described as *Rex et Imperator*.

[6] For further reference to what is a vast area of research see Bernard Porter *The Lion's Share, A Short History of British Imperialism 1850-1995*, Third Edition, London, 1996.

---

[7] In his *Treatise on Diamond and Precious Stones*, 1823, John Moore wrote of diamonds set in tiaras:
'Blazing on the crown of state, in courts and feasts and high solemnities, wreathing itself with the hair…proclaims to the surrounding crowd the person of the monarch, of the night, and of the beauty.'

[8] The Greek lyric poet Pindar (518-438BC) refers to στεφανοι (victory crowns or garlands) throughout his Olympian and Pythian victory Odes; such as the 'lofty deeds and crowns won at Olympia' (Olympian 5 lines 1-2).

symbols of their sovereignty, so did Napoleon and the women of his court." (Scarisbrick, 2000, p.11)[9]. A more contemporary example would be the crown made for George IV, and still worn today by Queen Elizabeth II for the opening of Parliament and on postage stamps, decorated with the symbolic rose, shamrock and thistle to advertise the monarch's royal power as Head of State and ruler of England, Ireland, and Scotland.

Of course this use of jewellery as a form of propaganda applies not only to the diadem, tiara, or crown, but also to gemstones and all forms of jewels. Moreover there is the additional importance of the power instilled in a jewel in the context of Empire and Imperial dominion. During his tour of India in 1875-1876, the Prince of Wales had been presented with three trunks of jewels as tribute from the Indian Maharajahs. Included in this tribute was a magnificent Indian necklace set with emeralds, rubies and diamonds. It was this piece of jewellery which was dismantled by Cartier in 1904 to be re-set as Alexandra's famous diamond *collier resille* (see Figure 4), the *collier* termed by Suzie Menkes in her book *The Royal Jewels*, "the ripe fruit of Empire" (Menkes, 1988 pp. 36-37). So this necklace was not only produced in the style propounded by the Edwardian Queen, but it was also created using the very materials directly procured through British Imperial power.

Two of the most magnificent diamonds ever procured by the Crown, from opposite ends of the empire -India and South Africa - serve to highlight the symbolism of jewels within the Imperial message of dominance and submission, power and deference. In 1849 the *Koh-i-Noor* diamond, meaning 'Mountain of Light', obscurely known from the sixteenth century through Moghul tradition, was presented to Queen Victoria by the 10 year old Maharajah Duleep Singh following the annexation of the Punjab[10]. This magnificent stone, originally weighing 186 1/10th carats was shown at the Great Exhibition of 1851 before being re-cut from its original Indian shape into a more modern European style. Both its presentation in India from the Maharajah and its exhibition to the British public in London were indications of the power of Victoria and her country. Its Imperial symbolism and imagery were again put on display in 1902 and 1911 when the diamond was set in Queen Alexandra's and Queen Mary's respective coronation crowns.

The Cullinan diamond, discovered in 1905 at the Premier Mine in South Africa, is the largest ever to have been found, weighing in at an enormous 3025 carats. In 1907 it was purchased by the Transvaal government and cut in 1908 by I.J. Asscher into nine major stones (known as Cullinan I-IX). The government formally presented Cullinan I and II to Edward VII on the 21st November 1908

as a birthday present at the end of the Boer War. The motion introduced by General Louis Botha, the Prime minister of the Transvaal, had authorized the Government to present the Cullinan to the King 'in token of the loyalty of the Transvaal people and in commemoration of the grant of responsible Government' (Balfour, 1987, p. 166). The message of deference and tribute to the Imperial power was clear.[11] Edward himself bought Cullinan IV to give to his wife Alexandra while the remaining major stones were bought and given to Queen Mary in 1911. The symbolism of the two Cullinan stones was also dominantly displayed by their setting in the Crown Jewels: Cullinan I (530.2 carats) was set in the Sovereign's Sceptre and Cullinan II (307.4 carats) in the Imperial State Crown (Field, 1987, pp. 27-29, 72-74, Balfour, 1987, pp. 15-29, 161-174). The Imperial State Crown itself further displayed the major motif of classical empire. Originally designed for Victoria by Rundell, Bridge and Rundell in 1838, and worn subsequently by Edward VII and George V, it incorporated the acorn and oak motif, or more explicitly, the *corona civica* of ancient Rome; a symbolism strengthened by the addition of Cullinan II in 1910.

We can apply the argument of Imperial Discourse within jewellery of the period more directly and specifically to the jewels already discussed. Comparing figures 2, 3 and 4 with figures 5a, 5b and 6 we can see the architectural and foliate motifs of the Roman monuments transposed into stylistic representations in the jewels, still heralding the same visual messages: the laurel wreath as symbolic of Augustan victory and power; the scrolling acanthus and floral swags as representative of abundance and fertility; and the flowing tassels as possible interpretations of the ribbons or the fillets of peace and piety. It is almost as if these jewels, the creations of a modern Empire, are recreating the message of the Augustan 'Golden Age' of the Roman Empire, and so translating the Pax Romana into a Pax Britannica. They are not so without meaning and intention as to be simply termed 'Garland Style', but contain such subtle undertones and implications as to be read as 'Augustan Style'.

It is a legitimate suggestion that the classical imagery of the late-nineteenth and early-twentieth century jewellery produced for well-educated royal and aristocratic clients would have been recognised. Jewels have been employed as forms of propaganda ever since their very production, and during a period so aware of its own image and identity they were still designed for maximum effect. The Garland Style may have originated amongst Cartiers' draftsmen with a resurrection of the eighteenth century, but as part of an Edwardian 'Imperial discourse' it developed specific social and political intentions and messages. And such messages, just as during the Augustan Empire, were displayed in order to be read and understood.

---

[9] For further discussion on this theme see Huet, 1999.
[10] The specific clause from the Treaty of Lahore of 1849 read 'The gem called Koh-I-Noor …shall be surrendered by the Maharajah of Lahore to the Queen of England' (Balfour, 1987, p. 23).

[11] One might compare the gift of the Cullinan diamond to Edward VII by the Transvaal government after the end of the Boer War with the presentation of the *corona civica* to Augustus by the Senate after the battle of Actium.

References

Balfour, I., 1987 *Famous Diamonds*, London

Betts, R.F., 1971 'The Allusion to Rome in British Imperial Thought of the Late Nineteenth and Early Twentieth Centuries', *Victorian Studies*, 15, 1971, pp. 149-159

Brunt, P.A., 1970 *Res gestae divi Augusti*, Oxford

Field, L., 1987 *The Queen's Jewels,* New York

Gemological Institute of America, 1989 *Coloured Stones 9,* New York

Hingley, R., 1999 *Roman Officers and English Gentlemen*, London and New York

Huet, V., 1999 'Napoleon I: a new Augustus?', in Edwards, C., ed., *Roman Presences: perceptions of Rome in European culture, 1789-1945*, Cambridge,

Kipling, R., *Stalky and Co.,* London, 1899, numerous editions
Puck of Pook's Hill, London, 1906, numerous editions
Rewards and Fairies, London, 1910, numerous editions

Koebner, R., and Schmidt, H. Dan, 1964, *Imperialism: the story and significance of a political word, 1840-1960*, Cambridge

Mears, K., 1996 *The Crown Jewels, Crowns and Diamonds: the Making of the Crown Jewels*, revised edition, Thurley, S., Murphy, C., Keay, A., Crown Copyright, 1984, Historic Palaces Agency

Menkes, S., 1988 *The Royal Jewels*, 3rd Edition, London

Moore, J., 1823 *Treatise on Diamond and Precious Stones*, London

Nadelhoffer, H., 1984 *Cartier Jewelers Extraordinary*, London

Nussbaum, E., and Cologni, F., 1995 *Platinum by Cartier*, Milan

Rider Haggard, H., *She,* London, 1887, numerous editions

Rudhoe, J., 1997 *Cartier 1900-1939*, London

Scarisbrick, D., 2000 *Tiara*, Boston

Stray, C., 1998 *Classics Transformed: Schools, Universities and Society in England, 1830-1960*, Oxford

Wartski, 1997 *One Hundred Tiaras An Evolution of Style 1800-1990*

Zanker, P., 1988 *The Power of Images in the Age of Augustus*, trans., Shapiro, A., Ann Arbor

Figure 1: A black sequinned ball or court gown, French, circa 1909, worn at the Imperial court balls in Berlin between 1909 and 1912 by Countess Mary Joy van Limburg Stirum, the wife of a captain in the Emperor's elite regiment. Sold Sotheby's 19th December 2000, Lot 316. Catalogue, *Passion for Fashion*.

Figure 2: *Devant de corsage*: diamonds in open-back millegrain platinum setting, oval laurel wreath superimposed on acanthus scroll motifs with laurel wreath swags and drops. The central oval wreath is detachable for wear as a brooch. Made for Cartier Paris, 1910. See Rudhoe, 1997, pp. 78-79 for other examples of this design.[12]
Photo: M. Feinberg, copyright Cartier.

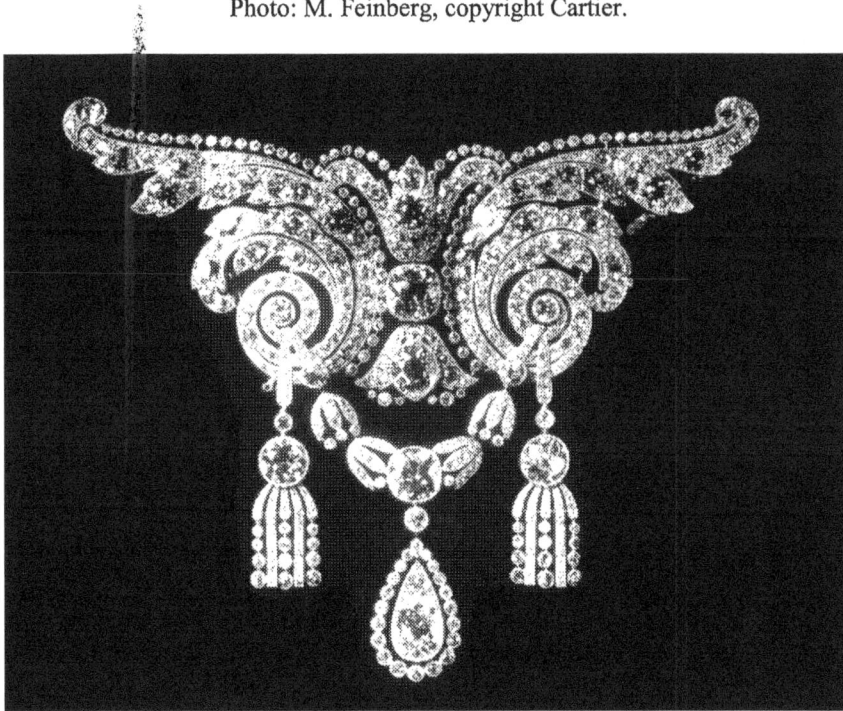

Figure 3: Corsage brooch in platinum and diamonds, 1910, designed as acanthus scroll motifs suspending swags and drops. Photo: Cartier Paris Archives, copyright Cartier.

---

[12] For a tiara stylistically comparable to this corsage see Scarisbrick, 2000, pp. 126-127 showing the magnificent tiara made for the Queen of the Belgians by Cartier in 1910. Both scrolling acanthus and trails of laurel are again used.

Figure 4: Diamond *résille* necklace of laurel leaf and garland design in circular and pear-shaped diamonds weighing 141 carats. Commissioned by Queen Alexandra in 1904.
Photo: Cartier Paris Archives, copyright Cartier.

a

b

Figure 5: Temple of Apollo dedicated in Rome by C. Sosius in 25BC
A. Capital and entablature (detail). Photo: Institute of Archaeology, Oxford.
B. Capital, after R. Falconi, BSR 30 (1962), pl. 10.2.

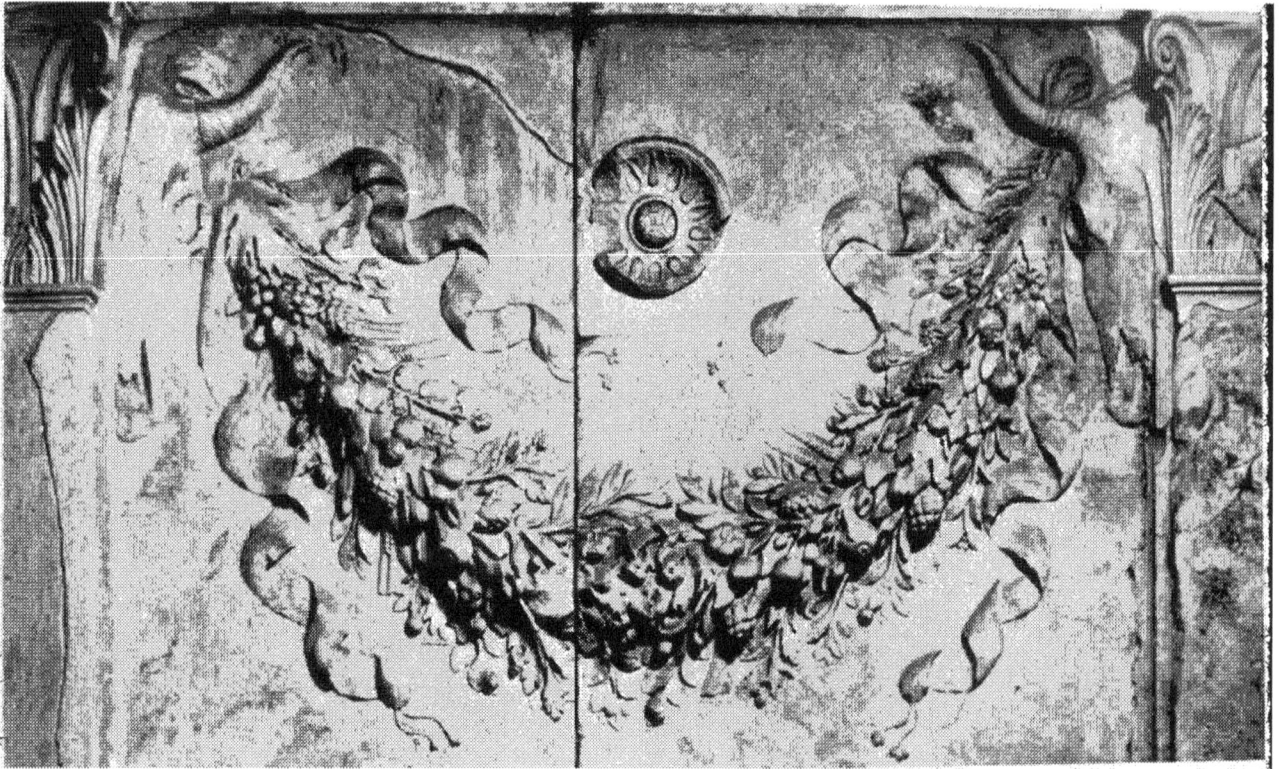

Figure 6: Garland from Interior Screen Wall of the Ara Pacis, 13-9 BC.
Photo: Institute of Archaeology, Oxford, photoarchive.

The Great Circle: Stonehenge, the Sacred and the Problem of Authority

Kate Prendergast

It is perhaps something of a luxury, given the usual strictures of archaeological publication, to base the starting point for this article on my own personal experience of a prehistoric sacred site. Yet, it is also perhaps appropriate, given the theme of this volume of papers, to write from such a perspective. Prehistoric sacred sites – whether natural or constructed, whatever their age and wherever they are found - are locations that are pre-eminently defined as sacred by humans. They are thus also subject to different interpretations: over time, sites have been reused, remade and reinterpreted; and within any one living community there will be different experiences, interpretations and claims to such sites – and their sacredness or power. Thus the issue of personal experience of a sacred site is of direct relevance to archaeology, not only because archaeology as an academic discipline may not exhaust claims to or ways of interpreting a sacred site, but perhaps more importantly because archaeology itself can and should be informed by the wider web of personal and collective experiences, interpretations and claims that such sites inhabit, and may even construct.

This paper will explore the ways in which our own contemporary personal and collective experiences – and the relations between them - create and recreate a sense of a sacred place: in this case, Stonehenge. Stonehenge is a place that inhabits an important and contested position in the web of our personal and collective experience, and defining both its original and its contemporary meaning and purpose is of real significance in our culture. I will argue in this paper that if the meanings *we* give to Stonehenge are both significant and contested, this may reflect the ways in which the site is both inherently meaningful and that the meanings it generates – for us as for its original users – are inherently ambiguous.

The contested status of Stonehenge in recent history has already been extensively explored (e.g. Bender 1993; 1998; Chippendale et. al. 1990). This article will not therefore retrace this ground in detail (although it will offer a brief update of this history where relevant). Instead, it aims to expand a point explored in the existing literature on Neolithic uses and interpretations of such sacred sites to our contemporary uses and interpretations of Stonehenge. In discussing the way in which we construct Stonehenge as a significant place in our lives – and the way in which as a place Stonehenge constructs significance for us – I want to briefly explore how certain themes around the issue of authority, around Stonehenge in particular, and Neolithic sacred sites in general, appear to be reiterated in both ancient and contemporary use and interpretation, and in particular the ways in which authority – or control – over the site is invoked in relation to notions of the personal, the collective and the sacred.

It is perhaps appropriate, therefore, to begin with a discussion of my own personal relationship to Stonehenge. My own relationship to Stonehenge is complex, and as such, a useful starting point from which to discuss the wider claims to its significance in our collective biographies, as well as in my own. Stonehenge is, of course, a place with which, to some degree, we are all familiar, because of the ubiquitous presence of its image. Although I am not sure exactly when I first saw Stonehenge for real, perhaps my most abiding first impression was the incongruous juxtaposition of the heavy traffic of modernity and the truly ethereal ancient monument appearing simultaneously over the horizon (a contradiction, like many that arise over Stonehenge, that has informed, not only my impressions, but a lengthy debate on the future management of the monument (English Heritage 2000)).

Since that first encounter, I have visited Stonehenge several times. I visited Stonehenge with my mother on my birthday in 1994. I took part in a sunrise ceremony with friends inside the stones in the summer of 1998. I visited the site with my partner and family in 1999. I planned - and failed - to go for the first sanctioned celebrations for 14 years at summer solstice in 2000, and did manage to get there for the solstice celebrations in 2001 (although that is another story!). I have also studied it in the context of my own archaeological research. Thus, over the years, Stonehenge has become a place that features in my own intellectual and emotional biography. It has become a venue at which I have experienced personal moments: of intimacy, beauty, disappointment. These times had and have significance for me and those who were with me, yet, the details and significance of such experiences remain inconsequential, if recognizable, for others, precisely because of their personal nature. Exploring the significance of Stonehenge is also, as this article is testimony to, important in terms of my own intellectual interests.

But my own personal encounters at and with Stonehenge are not isolated from collective encounters at and with Stonehenge. From the collective – and contested - nature of archaeological knowledge about Stonehenge in the public domain, to the ways in which people close to me came together to share experiences of mutual personal significance, and the genuinely collective gathering of different life pathways, and the raising of issues of inclusion and exclusion that something like the summer solstice celebration entails and represents, my own experience of Stonehenge and those of others are not isolated. They are woven into the same cultural fabric of expectations, experiences and interpretations we in our contemporary culture have of the site.

There are moments, then, when events and discourses of significance in our personal and collective lives come together, and a place like Stonehenge encourages and even creates such 'meetings' because of its own status as a prominent prehistoric sacred site. Our small ceremony, for example, not only involved women coming together from across the country, but also those English Heritage workers administrating visitors at Stonehenge. The summer solstice festivals, meanwhile, are the result of a much longer and wider set of negotiations between the authorities and revellers, involving English Heritage, the National Trust, Wiltshire police and numerous groups. And at the same time, such gatherings have significance for and are reported and interpreted by a far wider range of critics than any private gathering at the stones (e.g. Denison 2000). The collection, advancement and discussion of archaeological knowledge, meanwhile, is also the result of extensive collaborative effort involving a wide range of institutions and individuals. It has generated a large corpus of work, but also a series of ongoing debates, both about the original meanings and uses of the monument, and of its status in contemporary culture (see for example, Bender 1998; Cunliffe and Renfrew 1997; Parker Pearson and Ramilisonia 1998).

Stonehenge thus occupies an important place in our collective lives, at a variety of levels. But it also a place that is subject to contestation and control. The relationship between free festival goers and the authorities perhaps represents the most hotly contested dispute about who has access to use and interpret Stonehenge. The recent negotiations about access at summer solstice are the culmination of a long and difficult history between free festival goers and the authorities at Stonehenge. As is well documented, free festivals began at Stonehenge in the early 1970s, but became increasingly contentious over time, culminating in the now notorious Battle of the Beanfield in 1985 (Bender 1993:266; 275; 1998:4). As a result, Stonehenge was subject to a four-mile exclusion order at summer solstice, banning any celebration at the site. Bender has demonstrated how the roots of this struggle over access to Stonehenge lie in developing English notions of private property in the eighteenth and nineteenth centuries, and the more recent appropriation of such a notion by the state in its control of ancient monuments (1993: 265). It is perhaps no surprise that the clash between a state intent on enforcing exclusive rights over 'privately' owned 'heritage' and alternative communities seeking to reclaim unlimited rights of access to an ancient monument culminated under Thatcher; one of a series of clashes that lead to the Public Order Act of 1986 (amended in 1994) – arguably the most oppressive of recent years.

Ironically, however, it may also have been the stridency of the Thatcherite administration that revealed the ultimate unsustainability of a draconian state position in these areas. In 1999, for example, a landmark legal ruling against the use of the 1986 Public Order Act to ban assemblies on the public highway by Stonehenge was won by two demonstrators: Dr Margaret Jones and Richard Lloyd. Jones and Lloyd were arrested for 'trespassory assembly' after taking part in a peaceful roadside demonstration in June 1995, marking the 10th anniversary of the 'Battle of the Beanfield'. But on appeal, the Law Lords, stating that this was an issue of fundamental constitutional importance, ruled that that there was a right of peaceful assembly on the public highway – whether that highway passes through publicly or privately owned land. Not only was this right implicit in a careful interpretation of common law precedent, the Law Lords argued, to have ruled otherwise would clash with Article 11 of the European Convention on Human Rights (1999).

There have been other victories in the struggle to make Stonehenge more accessible to 'outsiders'. Successful free festivals held at recent years at Stonehenge included the party on VE day in 1995 – a celebration of the end of Nazism and a huge feather in the cap of those campaigning to get access to the stones again. English Heritage and the National Trust have also been concerned to widen public access to Stonehenge more recently, perhaps recognising that facilitation and containment is a more effective policy than exclusion and conflict. In 1999, the National Trust allowed revellers onto land surrounding Stonehenge at summer solstice and, despite some skirmishes, by 2000 the full array of Druids, neo-pagans and ravers were officially allowed to celebrate within the stones; a significant rapprochement between such intensely different claims to access Stonehenge and interpret its significance.

If there has been some limited resolution of the contested status of Stonehenge as a site for free festivals, other – related - aspects of recent plans for Stonehenge remain problematic. English Heritage have embarked on ambitious plans to completely redesign the visitor facilities at the site, intended to transform the current 'Stonehenge experience' available to visitors and tourists (English Heritage 2000). These are particularly contentious because the whole relationship between tourists and Stonehenge is clearly highly problematic. As Bender has shown, the state has envisaged Stonehenge as a money maker in accordance with the general trend of the 1970s and 80s to package and sell 'heritage' (1993:268). Tourism at Stonehenge does indeed generate an enormous amount of money for English Heritage, but little of this money filters through to the local economy. In 1998, there were over 800,000 visitors to the site, over half of whom were foreign tourists, and many of these visitors were bussed in for an average stay of 45 minutes (English Heritage 2000: 26; 82). Moreover, the current facilities, as English Heritage acknowledge, provide little in the way of a satisfactory experience of Stonehenge; an assessment recently reiterated by the *Which Guide to Tourist Attractions* (2000). The *Which* report not only discusses the inadequacy of the facilities at Stonehenge in particular, but also the iniquitous pricing at many English tourist attractions, which can often include parking fees, expensive guidebooks and food and drink on top of the entrance fee, frequently making a huge outlay for a family day out. The costs of visiting Stonehenge are compounded by the lack of any direct access to the stones given to the public, and the soul destroying experience of hundreds of people walking uncomprehendingly around the outside of the monument like excluded automatons, with little attempt made to involve such visitors in actively experiencing Stonehenge. As the leader of our ceremony put it, 'they don't even walk around the monument sun wise' – perhaps, given the clear role of astronomy in structuring Neolithic ritual uses of the site (North 1996; Burl 1999), one minimal way in which enormous numbers of people could be herded around the monument with some mutual respect.

Perhaps more significantly, using Stonehenge to generate profits for a state body rather than for the local area, from tourists who are then denied access on the grounds of numbers and protection of the monument appears highly questionable. While the state has a clear responsibility to protect Stonehenge and its environs, current policy gives Stonehenge a profit-making role that seems at odds with a sacred prehistoric site, while simultaneously providing a perfect excuse for maintaining a policy of exclusion and control. Such a policy completely fails to address the more fundamental questions of who Stonehenge is for and what its purpose is for those people who wish to interpret, use and benefit from it. In contrast to our private ceremony, which allowed us to experience the beauty of the stones in a highly spacious and intimate way, the tourist 'experience' at Stonehenge remains essentially dislocated. The larger festivities at the site, while always subject to the danger of vandalism, disruption or 'profanity' also have a quality of aliveness, joy and participation. People are within the stones, enjoying them and actively celebrating them. These forms of celebration, in and of the stones, seem to me to be in many ways far closer to their original use and purpose than the herding mentality of the tourist industry, the exclusionary attitude of property owners or even the academic austerity that can result from studying them as archaeologists.

The English Heritage management plan for the Stonehenge site does recognise that current visitor numbers are a problem, both in terms of the issue of lack of access such visitors have to Stonehenge and in terms of their impact on the local infrastructure. It hopes to reconcile these problems by: turning the core area of the World Heritage Site into open grassland without fences and accessible by the public; by significantly reducing traffic levels in the area by burying the A303 under a tunnel where it passes the monument, and closing the A344 altogether; and by building a new visitor's centre at some distance from the stones (2000: 83; 104). They hope that in doing this, the large numbers of visitors can be dispersed across the World Heritage Site as a whole, thereby alleviating some of the pressure on Stonehenge itself, whilst simultaneously maintaining an open access policy. They also hope that by placing a visitors centre within or near a local settlement, such visitors can be encouraged far more effectively than they do at present to spend money in the local economy.

But these plans have been criticised by a variety of parties. Environmental groups have expressed concern that the scheme may in fact encourage traffic levels in the area to increase, while as Bender reports, locals have been against the proposals on the grounds that they represent 'big shots from London' telling them what is good for them (1993:269). Determining the ways in which the stones are accessed and managed, therefore, remains an ongoing source of both conflict and negotiation.

Even within archaeology itself, despite the privileged access archaeologists have to Stonehenge and the surrounding landscape (in collaboration with English Heritage) for the work of preserving such a significant prehistoric landscape, and despite recent advances in dating and resolution of chronologies (e.g. Cleal et.al. 1995; Cunliffe and Renfrew 1997), the significance and interpretation of Stonehenge within archaeology has been, and continues to be, contested. To cite one recent example: Parker Pearson and Ramilisonia, in a radical interpretation, have argued that Stonehenge was never used by living Neolithic peoples, but was an 'empty' monument reserved for exclusive use by the ancestors (1998). The fact that Parker Pearson and Ramilisonia reiterate yet another 'exclusive' claim to Stonehenge, albeit this time by unseen beings, makes their theory perhaps less original and radical than they had intended. Not suprisingly, it has received a variety of responses and reactions, and has provoked an ongoing debate within *Antiquity*[1].

In attempting to summarise these conflicts, two points can be made. The first is that in recent history, there are repeated attempts by various agencies (whether political, territorial, cultural or theoretical) to make an *exclusive* claim to Stonehenge and its role, and to keep others, with competing or divergent views out. The second is that these claims to exclusivity almost always end in failure; and while there are clear (and in many cases successful) attempts for certain discourses to dominate (leaving others, in Edward Ardener's famous phrase, 'muted' (1975)), attempts to completely silence other discourses always seem to fail. Moreover, over time even dominant discourses can lose their status. As we can see in the state's attempt to completely control access to the site, or in the ways in which exclusive interpretations of Stonehenge are contested in the literature, controlling Stonehenge is simultaneously of high cultural and political importance and impossible to completely achieve.

These points raise further ones. What is it about Stonehenge that compels particular agencies to seek to control it? And what is it about Stonehenge that generates resistance to such control and invites assertions of other claims about its significance? The fact that Stonehenge is both subject to control and to the disputation of that control suggests both that it is not a site amenable to a single

---

[1] See for example the responses from John Barrett and Alisdair Whittle to Parker Pearson's and Ramilisonia's interpretation of Stonehenge in *Antiquity* Vol. 72, December 1998.

interpretation or use, but that it is nonetheless a culturally and politically powerful site. Ironically, therefore, its power may reside precisely in the fact that it eludes a single interpretation or control by a single agency. As a result, it becomes a contested site.

Recent interpretations of later Neolithic monuments have emphasised both that sites like Stonehenge may embody and represent the increasingly public nature of ritual in later Neolithic cultures, and also the difficulties in arguing that they represent straightforward evidence for a later Neolithic 'ritual elite', controlling access to and interpretations of such sites in these societies (e.g. Barrett 1994; Bradley 1998). I will now argue that this somewhat double-edged role postulated for sites like Stonehenge in Neolithic societies may be reiterated in some form in the fact that it eludes a single interpretation, and is subject to control conflicts in our own contemporary society. Moreover, I will argue that its contested status, far from being a cause of anxiety, could in fact reveal something profound about the way in which the relationship between sacredness and authority is invoked at a prehistoric sacred site like Stonehenge.

I want now to draw on two interpretations of the ways in which monuments such as Stonehenge may have been used and understood in the later Neolithic cultures that built and used them. John Barrett (1994) has argued that any attempt to read an original single meaning into late Neolithic ceremonial centres is misguided, for two reasons. Firstly, it is to engage in a modern intellectual attempt to 'read' the archaeological record for particular 'objective' meanings, rather than to attempt to situate the real – and hence multiple, opened ended and complex - contexts in which Neolithic peoples may have built, used and interpreted such sites (1994:70-2). Secondly, it is also, Barrett argues, to fundamentally misread the nature of the record itself, since the structure of such sites, their modification over time and the meanings we may read into them, also indicate the potential for a plurality in the ways they may have been originally used and understood (1994:79-81). While Barrett does not entirely reject the dominant interpretation of later Neolithic monuments – that they were 'theatres' for religious or ritual elites to enact and thus reproduce their own social and cultural power – he cautions against a simplistic interpretation of such elitism. Sites such as Stonehenge, Barrett argues, were places at which discourses may have been constrained by dominant or prevailing ideologies, but could never have been entirely controlled. Moreover, while the structure of sites like Stonehenge indicate some emphasis on the themes of display, and of inclusion and exclusion, Barrett suggests that that the locus of power of any such set of religious practitioners would have ultimately remained, not with any 'chief' or class of ritual specialists, but with the community itself (1994:164).

Barrett's arguments are supported by those recently made by Richard Bradley (1998). Bradley argues that, despite a 1500 year history, from c3000-1500BC, in which a series

of major modifications were made, the basic form of Stonehenge – a circle – remained remarkably consistent over that time (1998:91-9). While the form of the monument may have been contentious, therefore, and subject to revision and change, nonetheless its overall shape was honoured and retained – as if the invocation of its original form was crucial to the preservation of its integrity as a sacred site. However, the retention of the original basic form at Stonehenge is indicative of more than just the importance of references to the past in such ceremonial monuments. As Bradley argues, in ceremonial or cosmological terms, the retention of the shape of the monument is significant, since the circle itself is highly evocative of cosmological and ceremonial themes (1998:108-9).

Bradley explores the importance of the circle form of later Neolithic monuments primarily in two ways. He argues that it is a monumental form that develops widely across later Neolithic Britain, and may owe its genesis as an arena to incorporate and reflect the ways in which ritual moved away from private, enclosed ceremonies associated with chambered tombs, towards larger and increasingly public rituals associated with henges and stone circles (1998:110-5). Thus, echoing Barretts' ideas about the locus of authority, Bradley suggests that many later Neolithic circular monuments can be seen, not as a locale for use by a narrow elite, but as a representation or microcosm of the landscape – and by implication – of the community itself (1998:121-4; and see Bender 1998:5).

Bradley also argues that the circle may have invoked a variety of meanings, including the surrounding landscape, the sky and seasons, and ultimately the cosmos itself (1998:109). Perhaps an important point to add to this – and one also of direct relevance to the ideas developed by Barrett – is that as a sacred space, a circle is ultimately not reducible to any single meaning. It may, as Bradley suggests, have represented the community, the landscape, seasonality, the cosmos, and perhaps more intangible ideas such as the cycle of life; it may have represented any or all of these ideas, and perhaps further ones too. As a sacred Neolithic form, Stonehenge was therefore beyond single or narrow interpretations, and as such was inherently available to different sections of the community, with their different interests, to claim it for themselves.

We can see how these interpretations of the form of Stonehenge resonate, not only with possible original uses of the site, but also with the ways in which claims about authority over and access to the site are articulated today. The contested status of such authority may point to something profound about ways in which the construction of Stonehenge itself sets up and determines the ways in which communities interpret sacredness in relation to the site. As a humanly constructed place, one that 'defines' the nature of sacredness experienced there, Stonehenge draws us into a dialogue that is created by very nature of the site itself. As a simple stone circle, we define its use and impose meanings on it, but such impositions are also facilitated and constrained by the structure of the architecture and space. Thus, just as archaeologists postulate that there were no single or simple meanings or claims attributed to the site in the Neolithic, so there are no single or simple claims about its meaning and use today.

Thus the points in our life we may spend there – whether personally as visitors, partygoers or archaeologists, or the debates we get involved in about its use and significance directly reiterate Barrett's point about the relationship between individual life pathways and sacred sites in the Neolithic: that dialogues around and encounters at such sites are constrained by dominant discourses but are not made homogenous by them. They also echo Bradley's point about the meanings attached to the circle in Neolithic cosmologies, since in our culture too, Stonehenge also facilitates a series of meanings associated with the natural world, the community and the cosmos that are both contested, and relatively fluid and open ended.

Stonehenge is of course, not unique in generating meanings that are both contested and multivalent. As Coleman and Elsner have shown in their analysis of the medieval and modern Christian pilgrimage site at Walsingham in Norfolk, there is a similar constellation of features as at Stonehenge: contested archaeological excavation and interpretation, and claims by different Christian traditions to interpret and control the space (1999). But, unlike the sacred architecture of text-based religions, the architecture at Stonehenge does not refer proscriptively to texts with a specific set of symbols, but to a more fluid set of motifs. We cannot ultimately know whether Stonehenge was originally subject to the kinds of disputations and control that seems to epitomise more modern forms of religious and secular behaviour. Perhaps all sacred sites in fact attract both disputation and multivalence or fluidity in the meanings attached to them. But it may be that the coalescence of an ongoing need for different sections of the community to have access to the site, ongoing debates about its role both now and in the past, and the nature of the architecture itself are indicative of something inherent about such prehistoric sacred spaces and the way they 'set up' an experiential and discursive relationship with our articulation and understanding of the sacred. It is not suprising therefore, that Stonehenge should in some ways embody a crisis in authority around the definition of the sacred, because without the authority of a text, and with a fluidity in the textuality of the architecture, it becomes *explicit* that such crises can only be resolved through human negotiation. Stonehenge may attract such a range of claims and interpretations, and it may well occupy such a significant place in our culture because of the decline in the established textual authority represented by world religions such as Christianity and the rise in cultural and spiritual importance of prehistoric scared sites. We should, however, see the range of claims and interpretations Stonehenge attracts as a sign of health, if only because it reveals very directly the ways in which human power and definitions of the meaningful or sacred are intimately related.

Acknowledgements

I would like to thank the editors of this volume, Christine Finn and Martin Henig, for their generosity in allowing me to contribute this article to the volume of papers at a late stage of the conference proceedings; George Dice and John Kenton (www.dicenews.com/stonehenge) for their permission to reproduce the photograph of the 2001 summer solstice gathering at Stonehenge; and Anna Grear of Oxford Brookes University for her help in interpreting recent legal rulings in relation to Stonehenge.

References

Ardener, E. (1975) Belief and the Problem of Women and the "Problem" Revisited, in Ardener, S. (ed.) *Perceiving Women.* London, Dent: 1-28.

Barrett, J. (1994) *Fragments from Antiquity.* Oxford, Blackwells.

Bender, B. (1993) Stonehenge – Contested Landscapes (Medieval to Present Day), in Bender, B. (ed.) *Landscape. Politics and Perspectives.* Oxford, Berg: 245-279.

Bender, B. (1998) *Stonehenge: Making Space.* Oxford, Berg.

Bradley, R., (1998) *The Significance of Monuments.* London, Routledge.

Burl, A. (1999) *Great Stone Circles.* Yale, Yale University Press.

Chippendale, C., Devereux, P., Fowler, P., Jones, R. and Sebastian, T. (1990) *Who Owns Stonehenge?* London, Batsford.

Cleal, R., Walker, K. and Montague, R., (1995), *Stonehenge in its Landscape: Twentieth Century Excavations.* London, English Heritage Archaeological Reports, 10.

Coleman, S. and Elsner, J. (1999) Archaeology and Sacred Space at Walsingham, in Insoll, T. (ed.) *Case Studies in Archaeology and World Religion. The Proceedings of the Cambridge Conference.* BAR International Series 755.

Cunliffe, B., and Renfrew, C., (eds.) (1997), *Science and Stonehenge.* Proceedings of the British Academy 92, Oxford, Oxford University Press.

Denison, S. (2000) Archaeologists Divide on Stonehenge Solstice, *Current Archaeology* 54.

DPP v Jones and Lloyd (1999) All ER 257.

English Heritage (2000) *Stonehenge World Heritage Site Management Plan.* London, English Heritage.

North, J. (1996) *Stonehenge: Neolithic Man and the Cosmos.* London, Harper Collins.

Parker Pearson, M. and Ramilisonia, (1998) Stonehenge for the Ancestors: The Stones Pass on the Message. *Antiquity* 72: 308-326.

The Which Guide to Tourist Attractions. London (2000).

Summer solstice gathering, Stonehenge, June 21 2001
Photograph: John Kenton

Bringing Caerleon to life: archaeological reconstruction and the children's novel

Stephen Henig

The historical novelist inevitably looks at archaeology from the outside. He or she will use surviving remains and museum objects, the conclusions of archaeologists and historians as recorded in textbooks and site guides and the word-of-mouth explanations of scholars, but these are all useless without imagination. The reasons for working in this way are inevitably personal. Living as I do in Gwent/Monmouthshire, my sense of place drew me to Caerleon and the monuments of the Legio II Augusta fortress. I hope that the archaeological elements in the story are sufficiently reliable to teach readers in a memorable way about certain aspects of life in the 2nd century A.D. but that is not, in itself, a recipe for a successful novel. It must have its own dynamic, and deal with issues which link the contemporary world with the past; it must explore human nature, and the moral problems occasioned by it, as much as the purist Roman world of the academics. Most of the basic facts I need can be found in the excellent guidebooks to the site, but there is something more needed to bring the place to life.

The book on which I have been working is called *Gandalf and the Gladiators*. Briefly, Gandalf Jones is a boy living in the future at a place euphemistically called Finetown, on the site of Caerleon. It is by then a totally degraded and poisoned landscape where the minds of the rulers are also debased by greed. Gandalf (with the help of the Druid who cares for the world of nature) contrives to go back in time to a period when the landscape is still flourishing and green, around A.D.150, to bring back gladiators who will fight against the totalitarian regime in Finetown. It would have been easy to glamourise this past, and so many of the recreations put on by reconstruction societies do so, but in fact the elements in human nature which eventually create Finetown are present in the brutality of the arena and the self indulgence of the Legionary Legate and his obnoxious, greedy and bloodthirsty neice, a child-from-hell if there ever was one. In many ways she is the antithesis of Gandalf and a reminder to young readers that they have the power to shape the destiny of the planet, by being loving, generous and loyal. In the Orwellian phrase 'he who controls the past, controls the future'. It is all up to us.

Roman Holiday

The first episode in the book sets the scene at the legionary fortress of Caerleon above the fast flowing waters of the River Usk, and introduces the reader to Gandalf. The time is A.D.150 on the occasion of a festival dedicated to Jupiter.

The gladiatorial games were about to begin. Crowds of people jostled by the entrances to the great amphitheatre just outside the ramparts. The amphitheatre was almost full.

'Watch this tapestry of hope and despair!'a drunken tribune cried, 'Victory and defeat drenched in blood! This is the supreme experience!'

A centurion shook his head. The cloud above him was shaped like a chariot; Jupiter was there, awaiting the first drops of blood to be shed in his honour. The stalls were selling skins of wine and clay-fired pots brimming with beer to the legionaries surging through the entrances to that circle of death.

The sturdy bridge, spanning the Usk was crammed with civilians; amongst them jugglers, fortune-tellers, pickpockets and beggars.

'Any spare change?', asked a nearly naked beggar, in the centre of the bridge. 'Lady, I haven't eaten. I give every morsel to my little dog, Braveheart'.

'Quite right!', snapped the lady looking with gentle eyes on the flea-bitten mongrel. 'Here is an as; I expect you to feed the dog. You can go without!'

'Sir,'pleaded another beggar clutching at the tunic of a rich shopkeeper. 'Go away!' grunted the man. 'But I'm a fortune-teller!' 'I don't care'.

'Charms!', another vendor carrying a tray of amulets shouted. 'I charge only an as for a potent charm which wards off unexpected death.'

'I want an amulet!', a tall, black teenager murmured softly as he peered curiously at the tray. 'I'm the legate's gladiator.'

'The legate has dedicated these games to Jupiter', replied the vendor, eyeing the boy's torn leather tunic, ripped and torn in hand-to-hand combat. 'Here's one dedicated to Jove!'

'Not to Jove', he answered.

'Anyway, aren't you too young to fight?'. 'No!', replied the boy.

'Then you must be Gandalf, the black gladiator, the boy-wonder who hypnotises his adversary.'

'What's this one?' asked the tall youngster fingering a bright medallion on its chain.

'Let me see. That has a horse on its obverse, Celtic style. On the reverse, just here, is a magician's eye. It is already on a chain so you can wear it round your neck, now.'

'It will bring me luck: here's your money.'

'You are the black gladiator everyone is talking about', said the man, smiling. 'I didn't catch the name?'

'I'm Gandalf', said the boy, putting the medallion around his neck. Gandalf was only fourteen but looked older. He was agile; brilliant with his swordplay. He could throw knives with unerring precision and he was deadly with the sling. The legionary legate had singled him out at his gladiatorial school as the best new recruit. He was neither too young nor too weak to fight in the arena.

Much of this is universal, crowds pushing their way through the streets to a football or rugby match are still to be seen at Caerleon as elsewhere. The name of the dog, 'Braveheart' is a personal joke at the expense of a neighbour's very small but enthusiastic small dog. But the belief in the power of the gods and especially in the efficacy of amulets of all types especially those for warding off the Evil Eye was a universal feature of the Ancient World. We don't have any evidence for a local gladiatorial school or of the involvement of legionary legates in such; but although the Caerleon amphitheatre was primarily a ludus for weapon training it was doubtless also used for gladiatorial fights as a well-known curse tablet addressed to Lady Nemesis attests, as well as a probable Nemeseum, set into the arena, directly opposite where the legate's box was situated. This features later in the story. A Nemeseum, identified by an altar to the goddess was certainly present in the Twentieth Legion's amphitheatre at Chester.

But first the reader meets a couple of other gladiators on their way to the arena, still off-duty and contriving to be cheerful.

The booths that sold food and drink were very busy. Gandalf bought himself a bowl of soup and a thick hunk of bread and joined a group of other gladiators by the river.

'Isca warrior', announced Marcus a cheerful gladiator who had somehow survived to middle age, 'Our legate has pitted you against the tallest and strongest man in the world'.

'I know!', replied Gandalf, as he continued to munch his bread.

'You will lose, Gandalf', sighed a young gladiator. They will give you a fisherman's net but no trident. He is from Germany and because he is very valuable he'll have a sharp sword'.

'We are all slaves of the arena, Julius', Gandalf pointed out.

'You can choose because you are a freeman', cried a sickly-looking young gladiator called Eros. 'I have to fight because I am only a slave! Surely the German can show mercy?'

'He murdered two trainees yesterday', Julius snapped. 'The troops realised it was the boys' first combat and held their thumbs up.'

'Weren't they spared?', asked Eros in horror.

'The German was dazzled. He didn't see five thousand troopers with their thumbs up, or so he says. He killed both boys; he cut their throats. Does he sound like a merciful man?'

'Let's throw the dice!' suggested Gandalf. 'You will only have to face him if I lose'.

'If?', screamed Eros. 'Don't you mean when?'.

Here we meet free and slave gladiators and learn a little about gladiatorial combat. There is one example of deliberate inaccuracy here; it is probable that the action of putting one's thumbs up meant 'finish him off!' while thumbs down signified 'sheath your weapon', but English usage has become so general that it would sound odd to reverse it.

At the games

The amphitheatre at Caerleon, excavated by Sir Mortimer Wheeler is well conserved and consolidated, and is, indeed, one of the most impressive surviving relics of Roman Britain. It does, however, require some effort for the visitor to replace the legate's box and the baying crowds and see it as a symbol of Imperial might. I have tried to suggest what it might have been like with the aid of what we know about Roman food and furniture. It is impossible to ignore the cultural references ubiquitous in Roman society where, for example, even the games could be given a mythic dimension by equating what happened with the Labours of Hercules or (in this case) the exploits of Theseus.

Inside his box, the legate sat on a bronze throne inlaid with ivory, as one young slave in a plain, white tunic carried a chair for Lavinia, his fourteen-year-old niece. Another slave fairly groaned under the weight of a heavy tray of food.

'Light refreshments my dear', said the legate, smiling at the slave. 'We have oysters, mussels and snails fattened on milk; pastries filled with honey, raisins and nuts; also roast suckling pig, roast peacock stuffed with small birds and herbs, fruits and salads. If you need anything else, just ask!'

The legate sipped his wine, imported from Spain and cooled in the Usk, from a silver goblet. He could hear the already boozy troopers making bets with one another from around the arena. The afternoon sun was hot.

'You look lovely this afternoon, Lavinia', he murmered sleepily.

Lavinia agreed with him. Her slaves had set her golden hair in the style of the empress, Faustina as she was shown on her coins. Her clothes were dazzling. Some people looked ugly in beautiful things; she simply looked lovelier.

'Uncle', asked Lavinia, 'can I lay a wager on who will win in the combats?'

'It certainly makes them more interesting,' agreed her uncle. 'Back Gandalf, if you fancy mysterious, dark, handsome Numidian princes'.

'I want to back him.'

The Legate stood up and raised his right hand. The arena was hushed.

'Second Augusta' he cried, proudly.

'Second Augusta, always victorious' answered the legionaries.

'We begin with a combat to the death', proclaimed the legate. 'We send a young Theseus into the labyrinth to confront the Minotaur.'

'I know that story', said Lavinia. 'The boy kills the Minotaur with the aid of Princess Ariadne'.

In the events which follow Gandalf tames a wild bull and takes on and kills or disarms his human opponents. At one point he is chosen by Nemesis to fight his sickly friend Eros, although in the event this disaster which would naturally have ended in Eros' death (or the execution of them both) is averted, evidently by a divine prodigy.

The steward marched over to the legate's box, carrying a large and beautifully fashioned silver bowl ornamented in relief with figures including on one side a scantily clad lady who seemed to Lavinia to be searching on the ground for a fig.

'Is that full of some local delicacy....or figs?', Lavinia asked hopefully.

'No!', snapped the legate. 'It just contains coloured marbles'.

'Very well, Uncle' said Lavinia. 'I can see this is a custom I know nothing about. Please explain it to me.'

'Do you see the statue of Nemesis, goddess of fate, recessed into the wall over there?' asked the legate. 'The arena is a fitting home for Nemesis. The next bout is certain death for somebody'.

'I see the goddess', answered Lavinia.'She looks angry!'

'She is! She is shown scowling and spitting in to her bosom. The next bout is dedicated to her.' The legate spoke with irritation. 'It's a lottery, and I don't approve, Lavinia'.

'Why not?' Lavinia sounded puzzled.

The legate sighed.

'Of course, I will explain', he said. 'I select my gladiators to provide an afternoon of high-quality fencing. The last bout showed that. Now I have to stand aside and let Nemesis preside in my place. She selects two gladiators. Very often the men are mismatched and one kills the other directly. Where's the sport in that? It's barbaric!'

'What a pity!'Lavinia agreed, tucking in to a bunch of juicy red grapes.

'The gladiators each pick a coloured marble from the bowl', explained the legate, 'You Lavinia will choose a colour, green, red, blue or yellow. The lads open their hands and the two who hold the balls of the colour designated by you will fight to the death. There is no reprieve. That is our custom! There it is.'

Lavinia watched legionaries, centurions, tribunes, sailors, merchants and bakers calculating odds, and betting one with the other at the tops of their voices. Coins clinked as if an emperor were driving by in his chariot at a triumph in Rome, and his slave was hurling handfuls of money to the humble citizens.

'What do they bet on?', asked Lavinia.

'Everything!' replied the legate, sourly. 'They are gambling on which gladiators will be chosen and who will win. They hazard how long the bout will take...I declare the amphitheatre has become a money exchange'.

'They are shameless'. Lavinia agreed.

'Hear me!', the legate cried in a commanding voice. 'Gladiators approach!'

'Nemesis will decide your fates', he cried. 'If she selects you to fight a superior swordsman and you are overcome at once, you must not die nursing a grievance against any of us. You will die, knowing it to be the will of Nemesis. There can be no clemency for the defeated gladiator. The fallen man is to be beheaded and his head placed on a shield to lie beneath the statue of the goddess.' He turned to Lavinia,'Colour, lady?'

'Blood red!' shouted Lavinia.

'Open your hands boys', ordered the steward. 'Who has chosen red. Gandalf and...huh! Eros!'

The troopers groaned as well. Eros would be snuffed out and most of them would lose money.

'Not Eros!' exclaimed the legate, 'He is utterly useless.'

'I'm not sure', said Lavinia, agonising as to whether nuts with honey or stuffed dormice would make her sick... perhaps, if she had a little of both...

'Not sure?', the legate's voice rose. Despite himself he proposed a bet to his ward. 'I'll show you how sure I am...I'll bet my denarius against your as that Eros will be dead in minutes. Do you still think you made the right decision?'

'Yes, uncle!' said Lavinia reaching for a stuffed dormice, with a few nuts, all coated in honey...'

Betting was ubiquitous in the Roman world, and was surely practiced at Caerleon. I chose blood red not only as an obvious colour for Nemesis but because Collingwood and Wright's translation of the Lydney curse (RIB 323) reads: 'Lady Nemesis, I give thee a cloak and a pair of boots; let him who wore them not redeem them except with the life of his Blood-red charger'. Roger Tomlin, reasonably corrects the last to 'except with his life and blood'...but the idea is the same. The passage allows me to explore the morality of the legate, selective as is the morality of our own leaders. On the whole liking fair play, disliking indulgence in gambling but of course not questioning the ethics of the arena. Lavinia continues to be the greedy, sensation-loving child.

The climax of the day is a naval battle; while in some amphitheatres in the Mediterranean world such a naumachia was achieved by flooding the arena, this would have been impossible at Caerleon. The transformation is achieved using essentially theatrical machinery, as must generally have been the case. The Germans intended by the Legate for the Imperial Guard have outlandish-sounding names which I have in fact borrowed from epigraphic sources concerned with Roman Britain, to be found in RIB or more conveniently in Anthony Birley's *The people of Roman Britain* (London 1979).

A dozen slaves quickly covered the sand with blue material to represent the sea, white pegs being scattered over the cloth to represent the waves.

'Masters!', shouted the steward.'See, our arena has been transformed into Neptune's ocean'.

A number of legionaries entered the amphitheatre carrying tools, boarding nets and prefabricated wooden panels. Within a few minutes, they had created the bows of two warships, one large vessel and a smaller one. The large ship was a patrol boat with a golden eagle painted on the sail which now billowed in the breeze.

An impressively tall German stood in the centre of thye arena, trident in hand and kicking away the wooden waves.

'Neptune will kill with his trident any young gladiator who falls overboard', cautioned the steward staring hard at Gandalf. 'Each of you take a dagger and climb aboard the small vessel. The Germans, destned for the Imperial guard, sail in the patrol boat. From Germania's endless forests let us welcome Alimahus, Dailus, Rautio, Unsenis, Fersomeris, Burcanius, Arcavius, Crotilo, Hnaudifridus and Vagdvarcustus. No, centurion, I shall not repeat the names because you heard the first time'.

Unequal as the contest seems to be the young gladiators win, killing or neutralising their opponents. Gandalf and the gladiators achieve the applause and approbation of the legate and the legion and Gandalf has presented to him 'a fine sword, made for a guardsman who should have gone to Rome'. This will play a part in the story later on. Perhaps one should think of the early 1st century Fulham Sword, its scabbard embellished with acanthus and a representation of the Roman wolf and twins, but it seemed best at this point not to tangle with the expertise (sometimes rather a myopic expertise) of the students of Roman weaponry.

The Roman Baths

My final extract is a contrast with the bloodthirstiness of the arena and introduces Gandalf to the Fortress Baths in Caerleon, whose remains are now in the guardianship of CADW. Here, as we can read in Tacitus *Agricola* 21 for example, or the encomium of Aelius Aristides on Rome, are some of the blessings of the Pax Romana, as they might have appeared to someone (Gandalf) not quite used to them. Gandalf's companion is his friend Julius, a common enough name in the Roman world, but with some special resonance at Caerleon where Julius and Aaron are the names of early Christian martyrs. However my Julius is not the same Julius, but a slave of the legate and presumably a pagan.

'Would you like to cool off?', asked Julius.

'Yes,I would!', gasped Gandalf.

'We could take a dip in the famous baths and drink from the fountain. The baths are much more fun than the amphitheatre'.

'Rubbish'.

'Not everyone fights...'

'What else do the Romans do?'

'The build aqueducts, construct temples, schools, libraries, bridges and roads. Look up there at the roof of the basilica of the baths!'

Gandalf was impressed. Just ahead stood a substantial building. The baths-basilica seemed to dominate the fortress. It was enclosed by a wall. There was no one about to stop them so the boys crept through the gate into the spacious courtyard.

'A mirage?', Gandalf was puzzled.

'It's real', answered Julius, as they looked at the great swimming bath parallel with the basilica.

'Is it for delousing oneself?', asked Gandalf loudly.

'Keep your voice down', hissed Julius, 'of course it isn't!'

Gandalf spotted the fountain-house at one end of the pool. The water cascaded from the open mouth of a dolphin. Gandalf ran to quench his thirst.

'Why hasn't the water gone green, Julius?', he asked.

'It is fresh water you are drinking; the dirty water drains away at the far end', said Julius in reply.

'She has nothing on!' Gandalf pointed at the statue of a young, slim, naked lady beside the dolphin.

'That is Lady Venus, Goddess of love and...get your hands off her! Lets go into the bath-house.'

Gandalf was impressed by the interior. It was by far the largest building he had ever been in. He gaped nervously at the vaulting decorated with abstract squares in red paint, worried that such a large unsupported ceiling might fall and crush them.

'You can enjoy a massage, and eat and drink most days', Julius continued. 'Furnaces are stoked to heat the floor beneath your sandals and, of course, the water...'

'Do you have an echo?', shouted Gandalf and the vaulted roof resonated.

'Do you want to exercise?'

Gandalf shook his head.

'Bathers leave their clothes in that room', explained Julius. 'You go through an entire suite of rooms, each hotter than the last ...Are you listening Gandalf?'

'I'm not familiar with baths!' said Gandalf politely.

'You go into a room with dry heat', said Julius. 'The next chamber is humid to make you sweat. You cover your body with olive oil which you have brought with you in a little jar and scrape it off with a blunt knife like object with a curved blade called a strigil. Then you jump into a cold bath'...

'It is all too complicated for me', sighed Gandalf. 'I will take a dip outside today'.

'At least try to imagine the exercise hall where we are standing filled with men of the Second Augusta', scolded Julius.

'I can imagine it', said Gandalf, touching the Celtic charm around his neck. He closed his eyes and when he again opened them the baths were packed.

Legionaries playing dice beside the door, laughed ruefully when they lost, calling on Lady Fortune to favour them next time.

'These dice are loaded', said one.

You just don't like losing!' replied another.

Four half-naked legionaries carried a centurion towards the suite of baths. His leg was in splints.

'Isn't the gymnasium full?' he asked.

'The fifth cohort has returned, sir!' said one of his men.

'They don't have to be so noisy!', the centurion complained. 'Wait! I want to watch the wrestling. Marcellus is taking on all comers. He's arrogant but if he wins the drinks are on me!'

Marcellus, indeed, won every round in quick succession. He threw every opponent down on the polished stone floor. The bouts were very friendly and the spectators cheered and gave advice. One man was thrown too heavily. It must have hurt but Marcellus extended a hand apologetically.

'Forgive me, Caius, I was carried away!', he said disarmingly. 'All this gambling turns the head and one forgets oneself and hurts a friend.'

'I need to practice', replied Caius. 'I would enjoy another bout in here when it is less crowded and you may show me how you do that stunt. Would you like a drink?'

There were cheers echoing around the baths. The grunts of the wrestlers and shouts of the gamblers were deafening.

A group of young soldiers threw a ball to one another. Sometimes they tossed the ball hard at the wall so that it bounced back; they scrimmaged to catch it and ended up on the gymnasium floor, laughing and shouting.

Two aristocratic tribunes walked sedately to the bath house. They gave the ball players a cold stare, and at once turned their conversation to the ill discipline of the lower orders.

'They are absolute sewers!' complained one. 'We are tribunes, we both have senatorial rank...but where is their respect! That ball could have cost me an eye. Half our troop don't take the full ritual bath...and as for the local auxiliaries, they simply have a quick dip in the hot one and, as soon as possible, run back half naked to the basilica hall for doughnuts, dicing and daredevil stunts.'

'Dirty Welsh savages', agreed Brutus. 'I actually heard one who thought a strigil was a kind of honey you put on porridge. That's what happens with native levies.'

'The barbarians are already within the gates'. Cassius continued.'The Welsh auxiliaries are barbarians. I cannot bear it. Let's find a bath uncontaminated by these louts.'

'Arrogant pigs!', snarled Gandalf. 'I hope they boil in the hot bath or freeze in the cold one'.

Most of the fifth cohort, back from the long march from the Colonia of Glevum were now wolfing down sausages and coarse wine from the Legionary tuck shop.

'Gandalf!' shouted Julius, 'Wake up; its time for our swim'.

I will take mine outside replied Gandalf, quietly'.

Archaeology has provided a great deal of evidence about bathing practices; oil bottles made of glass have been found at Caerleon - and so have bronze strigils, one superb example inlaid in silver, gold and brass with the Labours of Hercules and carrying the sentiment in Greek,' it washed you nicely'. Although the dolphin fountain-spout survives, the Venus which surely went with it was not recovered. However a statue of Venus from a fountain has been found in the destruction levels of the pre-Hadrianic fortress at Wroxeter. Incidentally, Gandalf's lustful attitude to the statue even if playful, mirrors the 'abuse' its prototype, the Aphrodite of Knidos is said by the Elder Pliny (N.H. xxxvi,20) to have endured, though I would not, of course, expect my readers to pick up this reference.

The attitudes of 'my' Romans off duty range from the easy bonhomie of the legionaries who are just the types to help each other out when in tight corners to the snobbery of the tribunes, young, aristocratic and arrogant. Local recruitment to the legions and even more to auxiliary regiments sometimes brigaded with them would no doubt have been resented by such men.

Essentially what I have presented above are drafts from the early part of my book which may change in detail in the finished novel. Just as archaeological exploration is never finished and a new hole may find fresh evidence any day, so does the imaginative writer let his characters grow and develop over time. In both instances new information allows for a measure of reinterpretation. Both have a lot to learn from each other, and it is in that belief that I, as somebody 'outside archaeology' but frequently looking in with interest, have offered this contribution to the volume.

Fig. 1. Caerleon, amphitheatre (Photo: M. Henig)

Fig. 2. Caerleon, entrance to amphitheatre (Photo: M. Henig)

Fig. 3. Caerleon, Nemesis shrine (Photo: M. Henig)

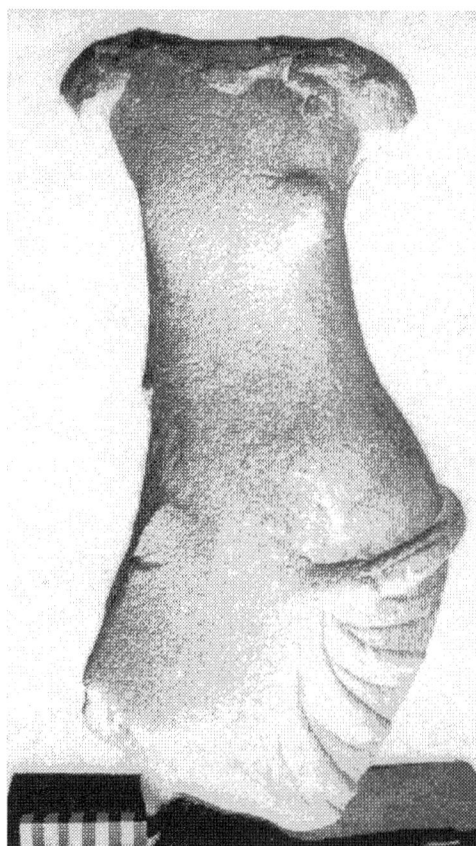

Fig. 4. Figure of Venus (Wroxeter) (Photo: R.S.O.Tomlin)

Afterthought : Mnemonic by Théâtre de Complicité

Christine Finn

Theatre-going could be described as a kind of excavation. As an audience, we pass through an opening into the dark where the stage is a kind of inner sanctum. In this suspension from the outside world, we are moved, our perceptions are heightened but in the end, the lights come up and we walk out to where things have moved on, perhaps just two hours or so. We will have journeyed to another place and time, but returned to the present, as an archaeologist who has touched prehistory back-fills a trench on the last day of a dig.

Theatre and archaeology collide poetically in 'Mnemonic', a theatre-piece which explores our own relationships with the past, and how they change over time. That's a slippery enough concept to engage with on stage, but here the complex story lines weave together the celebrated prehistoric 'Iceman', Otzi, the discovery of his body in the Alps 5000 years later, a woman's search for her father across Europe, and the trail she leaves her lover in a series of fragmentary phone calls. The essence of each story engages with the other, tendrils of personal time wrapping around objects, places, people, appearing and disappearing as memories are wont to do.

The London-based Théâtre de Complicité premiered 'Mnemonic' at the Salzburg Festival in 1999, not so far from the Alps where the Iceman was found eight years earlier.

Acclaimed in New York and London, where it reprised in 2001, 'Mnemonic' was directed and devised by the son of an archaeologist, the prehistorian, Charles McBurney. The past is a pre-eminent theme in the work of both generations.

Through theatre, Simon McBurney has taken up his late father's storytelling, and he reminds us of what cannot be reconstructed through artefacts, ruins or bodies - memory. Context provides an idea, but no surety. 'Extraordinary and intricate collisions' are at the core of this work, as McBurney explains how new archaeological discoveries provoke in him a feeling of recognition. 'They stimulate my sense of memory. But not merely a personal memory of my father whose stories are embedded in my childhood. Rather a sense of strange familiarity with the very ancient.'

McBurney begins gently, taking his audience on a brief tour of their own remembrances. The mnemonic, or trigger, is a small plastic packet containing an eye-mask and a leaf, found on each seat. Like a mesmeriser, McBurney leads us into our childhood. 'You are six years old...' and the veins of the leaf fan out like our hands reaching to parents, and grandparents and so on back for generations. We take off the mask and the play within a play begins, with McBurney as Virgil, centre-stage.

This production is intense and witty, ingenious in its use of multi-media, and stunningly simple - a collapsed chair is movingly tended as a broken body. It was devised by McBurney with members of Théâtre de Complicité, which he helped to found. The whole is shot-through with others' memories. 'We no longer live in the world of the single tale. So the shards of stories we have put together, some longer some shorter, collide here in the theatre, reflecting, repeating and revolving like the act of memory itself.' Among the works which inspired was Konrad Spindler's archaeological account, 'The Man in the Ice'.

McBurney's fascination with 'the immensity of the past', is an acknowledgment of the loss of continuity in the modern world, a sense of rupture. In the play we see a young woman trying to make sense of disparate things in a box. They are her father's belongings, but she cannot understand them, they have lost the context, the thread, that his memories would provide.

The Paleolithic inspired Simon McBurney's previous collaboration, with the writer and critic John Berger. In 'The Vertical Line', cave paintings were projected onto the wall of a disused London underground station, and the audience taken back to when the ochres and clays were not yet dry. In 'Mnemonic' it is the Iceman who engages us. Berger notes: 'Seeing the naked body of another, we make an inventory of our own. Shoulder blade, ribs, clavicle...but not in medical terms, and not only bones.'

McBurney's life and work is shaped by his close family. 'I grew up around the residue of my father,' he told me once. Charles was a leading prehistorian at Cambridge University who took his young children on excavations - 'every year, from when I was two to 17'- and encouraged them to dig. In the 1960s, the McBurneys would pitch camp near the beach at La Cotte de St.Brelade, on the island of Jersey, off the French coast. There Charles McBurney's major work was at a spectacular prehistoric kill site, where hundreds of animals were herded off cliffs in an effective, if audacious, variation on the hunter-gatherer theme. Nested with the bones, some of them of mammoth, were thousands of stone tools.

For Théâtre de Complicité, the audience is part of the final collision. The morning after seeing 'Mnemonic', I interviewed McBurney in London. I became aware that I was first taught archaeology by one of Charles McBurney's Cambridge students, the now Oxford Professor Derek Roe. And I remembered his tutorials included the story of La Cotte, the mammoth bones and the flints.

But there was something else within reach, another memory bound for collision. It was this: I was born and raised in Jersey, and each summer, I would be taken to the beach at St.Brelade's. That's where I had been in the theatre of my memory the night before, aged six. And while I was playing in rock-pools that sunny day, chances are that Simon McBurney, the same age as me, was finding prehistoric flints at the same spot, hearing the same sea.

The author would like to thank Simon McBurney for his interest in this afterthought.

www.ingramcontent.com/pod-product-compliance
Lightning Source LLC
Chambersburg PA
CBHW061005030426
42334CB00033B/3368